Matt W. Ransom,
Confederate General from North Carolina

Matt W. Ransom

*Confederate General from
North Carolina*

by
CLAYTON CHARLES MARLOW

McFarland & Company, Inc., Publishers
Jefferson, North Carolina, and London

Maps drawn by Donna Martin

Publisher's note: Clayton C. Marlow died on July 24, 1996, after completing nearly all his authorial duties but before his book was printed and bound.

British Library Cataloguing-in-Publication data are available

Library of Congress Cataloguing-in-Publication Data

Marlow, Clayton Charles.
    Matt W. Ranson, Confederate general from North Carolina / by Clayton Charles Marlow.
      p.   cm.
    Includes bibliographical references (p.) and index.
    ISBN 0-7864-0273-3 (library binding : 50# alk. paper) ∞
    1. Ransom, Matt W. (Matthew Whitaker), 1826–1904.
    2. Generals — Confederate States of America — Biography.
    3. Confederate States of America. Army — Biography.
    4. North Carolina — History — Civil War, 1861–1865. I. Title.
E467.1.R237M37   1996
973.7'42'092 — dc20
   [B]   96-26521
                                         CIP

Manufactured in the United States of America

McFarland & Company, Inc., Publishers
  Box 611, Jefferson, North Carolina 28640

To the memory of my brother,
Clovis Ray Marlow
UNITED STATES MARINE CORPS

Table of Contents

Preface

Over the years, my interest in Matt W. Ransom has afforded many pleasurable hours of travel, with opportunities of conducting personal interviews and research involving privately held documents as well as depositories including libraries and archives. Records of local and national governmental agencies have been very fertile sources of historical content. Selected published secondary works have also been utilized to great advantage in carrying out this undertaking.

This work makes no pretense of offering an exhaustive biographical account of the central figure, but I hope that sufficient and appropriate personal details have been included to provide an acceptably constructed and interesting portrait. Although the setting is primarily confined to North Carolina, important national events, personalities, and scenes outside the state have been included to give this portrait the necessary scope. Briefly illustrated is the Old North State's slide into the secessionist column of states despite the pleas and warnings of local Unionists, including Ransom. The war which followed, imposing hardships and penalties upon those forced to survive under it, comprises the major substance of the pages which follow. Particular attention has been reserved for those eastern counties of the state which, during the war, experienced untold and unwarranted suffering from Union military personnel.

During completion of degree work in the Graduate School of Georgetown University, I enjoyed many opportunities of extending my knowledge of antebellum history. A faculty member to whom I am particularly indebted is the late eminent historian Dr. Charles Callen Tansill. His scholastic competence and professional character have no equal. (As a sidelight, it is worth mentioning that Georgetown University down through the years became a favorite education center of Southern planters wishing to send their sons on to higher educational opportunities. As a matter of fact, one of General Ransom's sons, Thomas, was a graduate of this distinguished Jesuit institution.)

Any expression of gratitude on my part to individuals who offered assistance and encouragement for this project must include my wife, Grace. Any good result has come about only through an exercise of team efforts.

1

Since this narrative frequently dwells upon the subject of war, I should like to dedicate this written offering to my brother, Clovis Ray Marlow, who gave his life in the heroic United States Marine defense of Wake Island during World War II. Although I later joined the Second Marine Division on Saipan, and we both served in the same great national fraternity, I was never able, my dear brother, to ascend to your heights.

Clayton "Carolum" Marlow
Township of Jackson
The Old North State
Spring 1996

Chapter I

You Can Get No Troops from North Carolina

To many North Carolinians the election of a Republican president in 1860 "was like a sudden blow in the face"; however, it was equally evident the general public was in no mood for hasty decisions such as abandoning the Union.[1] Since Lincoln's name did not appear on any ballot, voting for the three principal candidates was as follows: 48,539 for Breckinridge, 44,990 for John Bell, and 2,701 for Stephen A. Douglas. Thus John C. Breckinridge won the state's entire electoral vote. Many citizens voted for Breckinridge after being assured he was opposed to secession. His victory, together with ballots cast for the anti-secessionists Bell and Douglas, clearly indicates Union sentiments dominated North Carolina. There was, however, some margin of contention within the state which took a far different view of Lincoln's election, insisting that secession was the only course under the new circumstances. Members of this group were principally slaveholding counties, which constituted only a small fraction of the state's population. Despite their numbers, however, they were in a position to deliver powerful political influence.[2] It was generally known that Governor John W. Ellis was sympathetic with secessionist thinking.[3]

Appealing to his northern constituents on a platform which included a protective tariff, internal improvements, free homesteads to free-soilers, and limiting slavery to its current borders, Abraham Lincoln won the presidency by pulling in the electoral votes of all the northern states with the exception of New Jersey.[4] In ten southern states he pulled no votes at all and consequently had no electors from that section.[5] The national voting performance indicated Lincoln drew considerably fewer votes than the total number of ballots cast for his three rivals, Douglas, Breckinridge, and Bell.

In searching for solutions to the troubling problems following the national elections, alert citizens wanted to know more about the kind of program the new president intended to implement during his administration. If any cleansing of his image in the South were to take place, statements of clarification were absolutely necessary. To effectively counter secessionist arguments, southern Unionists needed answers to vital questions — answers only the president-elect could give. Reflecting the anxiety of many was North Carolina congressman John A. Gilmer's letter of December 10, 1860, to Lincoln. Following all rules of courtesy in formal letter writing, the North Carolinian quickly proceeded to his stated request that Lincoln, before assuming his high office, should "give the people of the United States the views and opinions you now entertain on certain public questions now so seriously distract[ing] the country." Lincoln, in his return letter to the congressman, chose to continue his policy of silence relative to his pending administration.[6] Giving assurances he did not intend to interfere with slavery in the District of Columbia, Lincoln in his letter seemed to imply flexibility "on everything except the territorial question, and on this he would not yield." To those citizens both North and South who were thoroughly convinced that slavery extension existed more in theory than in fact, the president-elect's position bordered on absurdity. In truth, the plantation system was not destined to expand into any existing territories of the United States. The territory of New Mexico, for ten years open to settlement by slaveholders, recorded not one slave in the census of 1860. Colorado and Nevada were likewise without slaves. A few bondage blacks were to be found in Utah, and for the same year, census statistics indicated that two slaves resided in all of Kansas.[7]

Thoughtful observers knew it would be a tragic mistake for Lincoln to proceed without a thorough understanding of the present South, reflecting the conditions brought on by a decade of intense and often times bitter sectional rivalry with the North. Republican leaders, convinced as they were that an inevitable climax to the slavery issue was drawing near, surely could not overlook the strong likelihood that resolution was not attainable without secession and war. Also, might certain essential observations have escaped Lincoln in his firm belief that there still remained throughout the South a strong residue of Union support and loyalty? In truth, Union sentiment in the region was much weaker than it had been in years past. The loyalty that had made North Carolinians proud to send James K. Polk to the presidency had now been supplanted by new and disturbing sensations.[8]

Permeating southern white minds was the demoralizing perception that their part of the country was slipping into something of an inferior status and thereby becoming subservient to the population of the North, whose ways seemed strange, foreign, even baffling at times.[9] To those who were a part of it, the southern way of life was real; and if slavery was a component of this particular culture, then so be it! While most whites owned no slaves, they felt a strong compelling kinship to the land, which above all was their home. If given a choice, most southerners were not inclined to take up arms in defense of slavery, but they were willing to lay down their lives before accepting anything approaching racial equality. Northerners who shared this same attitude might still fail to understand the potency of this conviction until it was too late.[10]

For reasons valid or otherwise, there was furthermore a persistent suspicion that selfish and sinister forces were behind or perhaps a part of the northern anti-slavery movement. If an irrepressible national conflict lay ahead, as contended by some, how accurate was it to conclude that black people held in forced labor were the major cause of this impending crisis? Tariffs revised upward, a national government favorable to the industrialization and capital investments so essential to expanding industry and commerce — these and related matters occupied the attention of northern entrepreneurs and political leaders. Could it be that when spokesmen for these special interests lashed out critically against slavery, very often their zeal was intended not so much to liberate unfortunate black people as to obliterate the political power of the region in which they resided? Was not the South — represented by its phalanx of representatives in Congress, by its dominance of the Supreme Court and almost continuous past control of the executive branch, and by its agriculturally oriented economy and society under authority of white Anglo-Saxons — the real target of northern attacks? Until this establishment was dismantled, impatient but determined northern economic forces would continue to be held in check. So why not strike the South's Achilles' heel by mounting a convincing humanitarian campaign against its "peculiar" institution?

On February 23, 1861, Texas became the seventh state to leave the Union in response to Lincoln's election, the last of the group that would form the original Confederacy. North Carolina, however, still indicated no disposition to follow that path. As mandated by the General Assembly on January 29, qualified citizens were to vote February 28 on whether to hold a state convention to consider the question of secession. Finally, around the middle of March, votes were officially totaled, and the count showed that North Carolina had rejected a convention by the narrowest of margins.[11] The convention was defeated by a popular vote of 47,323 to 46,672. In the same referendum, voters had selected delegates in case a convention was approved; of the 120 delegates chosen, two were secessionists, twenty-eight conditional Unionists, and fifty unconditional Unionists. A review of eighty-six counties in the state indicated that thirty elected secession delegates, thirty-five elected unconditional Union delegates, seventeen elected conditional Unionists, and four decided on divided delegations. These are hardly surprising statistics if viewed with historical perspective. North Carolina was one of the original thirteen colonies, a participant in creating the Union, and had established strong emotional and commercial ties with that Union over the years. Citizens of North Carolina were sorely distressed at the prospect of abandoning this heritage, and before 1860 few of them were willing to resort to secession to settle the conflict between northern and southern regions.[12]

For southerners willing to seek wise advice and counsel, there were ample opportunities. Stephen A. Douglas was quick to point out that the Republican party and president-elect could "be held in check by a strong conservative

majority in both houses of Congress." Nor could the new leadership antici-
pate any drastic changes in the thinking of the Supreme Court.[13] These assess-
ments, unfortunately, enjoyed only a mild reception by southern leadership.

Even as a majority of North Carolinians prepared to register their disapproval of disunion in the convention vote, crucial events and constantly changing circumstances were causing that stance to suffer serious lack of public support and official confidence. More and more in the public mind, loyalty to the
Lincoln Administration carried an obligation to take up arms against southern states, and this was a price North Carolina Unionists refused to pay. During the Christmas holiday season just past, Zebulon Vance, from his vantage
point as a member of the House of Representatives, had reached the conclusion that the states could not remain united and that any terms proposed by
the North were unlikely to satisfy the slaveholding states.[14] Once the southern states removed their voting strength from Congress, impending legislation
for admission of Kansas was quickly added to the calendar, and another free
state entered the Union. With older states leaving and more new ones preparing to enter, the face and character of the United States were changing with
astonishing speed.[15]

These were trying days for North Carolina senator Thomas Bragg, and
oftentimes heartbreaking. On the morning of January 21, with the Senate's gal-
leries and cloakrooms packed with visiting spectators, senators of the seceded
states, including Jefferson Davis, were preparing to make their final adieux.
Senator Bragg, who watched this drama unfold, wrote that following "the
withdrawal, the Southern Senators and some of the Northern ones crowded
about the retiring Senators, bidding them farewell. I felt bad — the dissolution of this great Union of states is brought home to us — and the scene today
seemed to affect all. Even the stolid black Republicans seemed to feel it, though
some endeavored to appear indifferent. Will we ever come together again?
And, if not, what then?"[16]

Union supporters and conservatives were deeply disappointed in Lincoln's
inaugural address on March 4. Far from being reassured, they learned the president had no intentions of recognizing the legality of secession ordinances, or
of the government recently established in Montgomery, Alabama.[17] Further,
Lincoln's stated intention to "hold, occupy, and possess" government property was a reference to Fort Sumter that no one could miss.[18]

During early April rumors were circulating that federal authorities
intended to reinforce Fort Sumter. Lincoln had decided upon this undertaking on March 29 when he privately ordered his secretaries of war and navy to
organize a relief force for such a mission by April 4.[19] On April 6 federal plans
became clear when Lincoln's brief note, carried by a state department officer,
was delivered to the South Carolina governor. It read: "I am directed by the
President of the United States to notify you to expect an attempt to be made
to supply Fort Sumter with provisions only; and that, if such an attempt be

not resisted, no effort to throw in men, arms, or ammunition will be made without notice, or in case of an attack upon the fort."[20] In this tersely composed document South Carolina was informed that Fort Sumter remained a federal installation, and if necessary, it would be reinforced.

Federal irresolution concerning Fort Sumter was now ended, and there was also laid to rest at this time certain speculation that somebody other than the newly elected president would be the real source of power. Secretary of State William H. Seward, sincerely motivated by hopes of restoring the shattered Union, proposed in a memorandum to Lincoln a precipitous war with France and Spain, and suggested at the same time making offensive and provocative demands upon Great Britain and Russia. The possibilities of war with foreign powers would tend to reunite the country, reasoned Secretary Seward; however, for this plan he was reprimanded by his chief.[21]

Having set in motion a plan of extremely serious implications involving Fort Sumter, Lincoln wished to minimize his problems insofar as possible. The Virginia convention deliberating on the issue of possible secession had been convened in February, and was still in session; this body would surely object to any federal coercion, and this objection would likely be a prelude to the state's secession. This dilemma explains Lincoln's private conversation with Mr. John A. Baldwin on April 4. Lincoln asked Mr. Baldwin, a prominent Virginian well known in Richmond's political circles, "Why do you not adjourn your convention? It is a menace to me." The Virginian's reply included an admission of the administration's legal authority in refusing to recognize secession and continuing to hold federal forts, but he stated that the government "should make a concession of a disputed right in the interest of peace, and leave all questions to be settled by the conference of states." This statement apparently drew no response.

Lincoln confessed "the possible withdrawal of troops from Sumter as a military necessity," but noted that this was hardly a solution, since it failed to deal with the real problem.

The president then inquired about the collecting of duties. Baldwin replied, "The amount of duties would not be a drop in the bucket compared to the cost of war.... If a gun is fired at Sumter, I do not care on which side it is fired, the opportunity for settlements is lost. Virginia herself, as strong as the Union party is, will be out in forty-eight hours."

Lincoln asked, "What am I to do with those men at Montgomery?"

Baldwin answered, "Let them alone until they can be peacefully brought back."[22]

Lincoln's mind was obviously occupied with another matter he considered crucial at the moment when, during the interview, he remonstrated, "And open Charleston as a port of entry with their ten per cent tariff. What then will happen to my tariff?"[23]

Two days following this interview another Virginian, Mr. John M. Botts, a determined Union supporter, spoke with Lincoln. In this conversation, which took place on a Sunday night, Botts came to understand the president had earlier informed Baldwin that Fort Sumter could be evacuated in return for an adjournment of the Virginia convention. Botts enthusiastically asked, "Will you authorize me to make this proposition? I have no doubt the Union men will accept it."

Lincoln replied, "It is too late now; the fleet sailed on Friday morning."[24]

Now that the new administration's intentions had been officially confirmed relative to Fort Sumter, South Carolina responded by demanding the local garrison's surrender.[25]

Military honor, federal major Robert Anderson replied, prevented outright surrender, nor would his forces fire first. He confessed to shortages of provisions. Clearly, under continued conditions of siege, it would be only a matter of time before the fort's capitulation. This refusal of surrender was followed by South Carolina's heavy artillery bombardment of the fort beginning at 4:30 in the morning of April 12, 1861. After thirty hours of overwhelming attack, Major Anderson in the afternoon of April 13 complied with General P. G. T. Beauregard's terms of evacuation.

Lincoln's response to South Carolina's action came on April 15 in a national proclamation which stated that due to "combinations too powerful," he was calling upon the states for 75,000 troops to contend with the rebellion. And, in words of unmistakable clarity, the president warned, "I hereby command the persons composing the combinations aforesaid to disperse, and retire peaceably to their respective abodes within twenty days from this date."[26]

In his reply to President Lincoln's proclamation, North Carolina's Governor Ellis claimed it was extremely difficult to believe the document's authenticity in view of the "extraordinary character" of its contents. In any event, he regarded the request for troops for coercive action against southern states "as a violation of the Constitution, and a usurpation of power." The governor concluded very positively, "You can get no troops from North Carolina."[27]

Indeed, if loyalty to the Union meant taking up arms against sister southern states, North Carolina's loyalty would lie elsewhere. By order of Governor Ellis, Forts Caswell and Johnston guarding the entrance of Cape Fear were seized; the federal arsenal with 37,000 guns at Fayetteville and the United States mint at Charlotte were placed under state jurisdiction. The government also issued a call for 30,000 volunteers, and assured the Confederate Secretary of War that 10,000 armed "state troops" would be offered to him in several days. In a real sense, North Carolina was at war from around the middle of April.[28] Assuredly this was Lincoln's attitude when on April 27 he extended his southern blockade to include both the Virginia and the North Carolina coasts.

Chapter II

Unionists Make a Last Stand

While making an emotional speech in support of the Union to a large crowd, Zebulon Vance was suddenly interrupted by a loud voice announcing the telegraphed news that Fort Sumter had been fired upon, and Lincoln was calling for troops. At that moment Vance's hand, frozen at the peak of an expressive upward gesture, came down from that impassioned gesticulation; it fell slowly and sadly by the side of a Secessionist.[1]

Another distressed figure reacting to the presidential proclamation was Jonathan Worth. Brought up as a Quaker and having strong objections to slavery, Worth, like many of his neighbors in the state's central region, had been a Union supporter. But now Worth observed the president, "We are still at a loss to determine whether he is an old goose, thinking to preserve the Union by his course, or whether he became apprehensive that the Union men were about to gain strength enough in the South to stay secession and he desired to drive us all in rebellion in order to make a crusade against slavery and desolate our section."[2] If despondency, despair, and at times confusion seemed to characterize North Carolina citizens at this particular juncture, then it is no wonder they sought relief in action. Possibly exemplifying this new resolve was the conduct of Senator Thomas Bragg. Though he had earlier regarded secessionist colleagues as "rash" and "impetuous," he now welcomed the opportunity of joining the Confederacy.[3]

Events at Fort Sumter, Lincoln's response, and Virginia's secession on April 17 compelled North Carolina conservatives and Unionists to evaluate how these vital happenings related to any future official conduct of their state. One prominent figure of the state legislature who became involved in this process was Matt W. Ransom from Northampton County. Two months earlier, Ransom, Unionist David L. Swain and Secessionist John Bridgers had been officially instructed to repair to Montgomery, Alabama, "for the purpose of effecting an honorable and amicable adjustment of all the difficulties which distract the country."[4] Arriving there February 2, the North Carolina commissioners found their new environment marked with emotional tension and local pageantry featuring martial music, parading troops, officers dressed in colorful uniforms, and beautiful women. At the public slave market it was busi-

9

ness as usual, and the bars were doing a full-capacity business.[5] Insisting on attending only open sessions of the southern states' convention, the commissioners observed that body actively engaged in setting up the new government for six recently seceded states. There was a sense of determination to complete this project before March 4, when Lincoln would be installed in office. The formal body met its deadline early when, on February 9, the presidency of the new government was offered to Jefferson Davis of Mississippi, and the vice-presidency to Alexander Stephens of Georgia.

Having spent ten days conferring privately with individuals and attending open convention sessions, the North Carolina delegation concluded that very few delegates were favorably disposed toward returning to the Union.[6] Ransom reviewed this sad state of affairs in a letter to his wife, Pattie. He wrote that sentiment for war was strong, that reason and sound judgment were all but lost, and that he was receiving little support from his colleagues in his attempts to stem the tide.[7]

Ransom's vehement repudiation of secession and his determined support of the Union were matters of public record. Speaking before the Dialectic and Philanthropic Societies of the University of North Carolina, he had charged his young listeners to search annals of antiquity and modern history for another model of national union comparable to their own. A search for such a model, the speaker insisted, would be in vain since the "ancient world did not produce it — the modern world does not furnish it; Plato never dreamed it. Locke could not conceive it." For those southerners who contended secession was a practical and honorable means for resolving their region's plight, Ransom reserved his greatest scorn. He asked whether "any rational man could for a moment expect peaceable, friendly dissolution." To him it was all too clear that the Union could "be dissolved in nothing but blood." Secession, he said, "contemplates anarchy, war, civil war, havoc and night"; it could be regarded in no other way. Dedicated and proud of his country, Ransom earnestly hoped others of similar sentiments would join together into a kind of "American patriotism which fills the whole heart, knows no localities, and is as broad and comprehensive as the Union."[8]

Although a slaveowner himself, Ransom was no advocate of the practice of slavery, which he understood to be doomed by its own nature.[9] That this unfortunate institution had a limited future was a contention which could be argued very convincingly. Paralleling slavery's dismal adaptability in the territories, the success of the system seemed uncertain in a number of border states where in recent decades agriculture had lost ground to industry and commerce in local economies. Delaware was a slave state in name only; Maryland was rapidly assuming a similar image. Also the proportion of slaves to whites grew smaller every year in Virginia, Kentucky, and Missouri.[10] North Carolina was not, in fact, a large scale slave state. Only 133 planters owned 100 or more slaves. Nevertheless, state tax laws gave slaveholders a wide margin of benefits and advantages over other economic groups. Because slaves were taxed as persons and not as property, an owner paid the same tax on a two-thousand-dollar slave as one valued at five hundred. This flagrantly discriminatory tax system became a highly contentious issue around which rallied non-slaveholding parties of small farmers and laborers, who comprised over two-thirds of the white population. Some serious observers were certain that the mounting campaign for ad valorem taxation was the "beginning of a revolt against slavery as a political and economic influence."[11]

Returning to Raleigh and his legislative duties as a representative of Northampton County, Ransom continued to monitor the national scene's rapid deterioration. Neither Lincoln nor the new Confederate president displayed the slightest willingness to make concessions that might lead to a settlement of major sectional issues.

Earlier, on February 9, Lincoln in speech at Indianapolis had indicated his attitude and possible conduct toward the seceded states. He maintained that repossession of federal forts and properties and collection of revenues should not be interpreted as coercive acts. He implied that apart from those rights exclusively reserved to the states by the Constitution, the rights of a state above the country were but few. Then Lincoln strongly implied that states having resorted to secession had forfeited all rights; as for any wayward conduct of a state, he hypothetically observed that the federal government might impose its authority just as a state might enforce its will upon a county.[12]

For his part, Jefferson Davis in a formal inaugural address at Montgomery, Alabama, forcefully outlined his views on recent national events. Secession he justified as morally correct, appropriate, legal, and "a peaceful exercise by the sovereign people of an unassailable liberty." The new president, hoped there would be no conflict between his own country and the older one, but in the event the recently established Confederacy should be challenged by force, it would respond with determination and arms. If by chance other states of the Union solicited membership in the southern confederation, they would be accommodated. On the matter of a possible reconciliation with the former Union of states, this was "neither practicable nor desirable." Unlike some southerners who believed secession could be accomplished peacefully, Jefferson Davis was convinced it would lead to war, and that in such a war the odds were strongly against the South. In spite of this grave prospect, he believed no other course of conduct was possible in view of what had been by his observation a "systematic and persistent struggle to deprive the Southern States of equality in the Union." Davis was certain, and he believed many southerners would agree with him, that the hope of his people "was to escape from injury and strife in the Union, to find prosperity and peace out of it."[13]

Since the action at Fort Sumter, public opinion in North Carolina had undergone a dramatic shift on the matter of secession. While initially opposed to this alternative, May 1861 found a tremendous majority of citizens now disposed to sever ties with the federal establishment.[14] In this changed political environment staunch Union defenders were not only discouraged and disheartened, but most importantly, because of Lincoln's conduct and official policies, they no longer had convincing arguments to support their cause. Union supporters in North Carolina included a lengthy list of eminent public figures, among whom were George E. Badger, W.A. Graham, Thomas Ruffin, John Morehead, and David L. Swain. This is only to name a few; young Matt Ransom should also be included. But even some Unionists now admitted that war might be the only way to end the current crisis.[15]

For Matt Ransom there were only the questions of when and how his state would join the Confederacy. Under these circumstances, he had no recourse but to make the best of a tragic situation by offering his personal services and loyalty to his state. Nevertheless this decision likely caused him deep pain, since to him the state was normally a less compelling idea than the nation as a whole, which he loved devotedly.[16] Aside from vital and practical reasons for opposing secession, he did not believe it legally attainable under the Constitution. According to Ransom, if this mad course of disunion was to be followed, then at least such conduct should be carried out under the mantle of international law and established precedence. The break should be based upon the right of revolution with independence as an objective. Such doctrine had been proclaimed earlier on the American scene in a document penned in its first draft by Thomas Jefferson of Virginia. The Declaration of Independence refers to "certain unalienable Rights" of the people, and "among these are Life, Liberty, and the Pursuit of Happiness." But "whenever any Form of Government becomes destructive of these Ends, it is the right of the people to alter or abolish it." Ransom and his friends in the state who advanced this method of departure from the Union were referred to as "revolutionists" rather than secessionists.

Realizing full well the repercussions, including war, that would develop from his state's break with the federal system, Ransom assumed a full heavy work schedule in the legislature. To him, indecision and procrastination in this hour of crisis could easily prove fatal. He joined the important Legislative Joint Committee on Military Affairs, and became a member of a select group charged with designing a state flag. On the second day of legislative session, May 2, he introduced a successful bill granting the governor wide wartime emergency civil and military powers. On May 7, Ransom, again took to the floor, this time offering a resolution speedily passed which granted the governor authority to provide accommodations to southern troops en route to Virginia. A colleague introduced a bill giving instructions and authority to the governor for convening a convention, and then an amendment was offered requiring a citizen's referendum to pass upon any secession ordinance resulting from such a convention. This amendment was effectively blocked by Ransom, leaving the original bill to be passed.

Delegates attending the convention which met in Raleigh on May 20, 1861, differed only on technical matters as to North Carolina's withdrawal from the Union. One hundred-twenty delegates were in attendance with elderly Weldon Edwards, a renowned secessionist, elected as president. He defeated Ransom's friend, former governor William A. Graham, a revolutionist, for the position by a vote of sixty-five to forty-eight. Two ordinances providing methods for separation were offered on the first day's session. One, introduced by George E. Badger, embraced the right of revolution, implicitly denying that a right of secession existed.[17] The other, which received passage, was clearly a secessionist formula. Following its passage, on the very same day, convention members ratified the provisional Constitution of the Confederacy. The secession ordinance as adopted under formal convention proceeding reads:

> An ordinance Dissolving the Union Between the State of North Carolina and the Other States United with her under the Compact Government Entitled "The Constitution of the United States."
>
> We, the people of the State of North Carolina, in convention do declare and ordain, and it is hereby declared and ordained, That the ordinance adopted by the State of North Carolina in convention of 1789, whereby and adopted, and also all acts and parts of the General Assembly, ratifying and adopting amendments to the said Constitution, are hereby repealed, recinded [sic], and abrogated.
>
> We further declare and ordain, that the union now subsisting between the state of North Carolina and the other states, under the title "The United States of America," is hereby dissolved, and that the state of North Carolina is in full possession and exercise of all those rights of sovereignty which belong and appertain to a free and independent state.[18]

Chapter III

The Making of a
Southern Soldier

During those final days, as North Carolina completed necessary details for stepping out of the Union, Matt Ransom resigned his membership in the House of Commons, and after bidding farewell to his colleagues, he accepted a commission as lieutenant colonel on May 8, 1861.[1] Earlier he had advised his younger brother, Robert, Jr., to resign his commission in the United States Army and return home in the event that North Carolina seceded.[2] Anticipating many grave realities which lay ahead, Matt resolved early to "be equal to all the reverses of war, and superior to all of its successes."[3] Fulfillment of such resolutions rested in large part on how well he could achieve the confidence and trust of those officers and enlisted men under his command.

Traditionally, enlisted men were disposed to recognize and accept the reality that their officers varied widely in personality, talents, and demeanor. Buffoons, prima donnas, eccentrics, and tight disciplinarians were tolerated. Make no mistake, however: All parties were expected to deliver in combat situations. Like wild animals quick to perceive an intruder or impending danger, troops in the field could, as if by instinct, detect flaws in those intrusted to command. Unacceptable traits included indecision, incompetence, and above all, cowardice. About to be tested by such discerning scrutiny, Matt Ransom, a man without military training or experience, conditioned himself to meet the demands of his new role. In view of his seeming lack of qualifications for assuming military command, he would have to draw upon any compensating features or involvements of his past life that might prepare him for this upcoming venture. Family upbringing, local environment, and heredity have a way, by an ingenious amalgamation, of providing the ultimate development of a man's character, and in this process, Matt Ransom was no exception.

Named after an uncle on his mother's side, Matt Whitaker Ransom spent his boyhood years on his grandmother's plantation along Bridle Creek, four miles outside of Warrenton, Warren County, North Carolina. The county, founded in 1779, was named in honor of General Joseph Warren of Massachusetts, who fell mortally wounded in the Battle of Bunker Hill. As a boy of thirteen, Matt could remember how his father, Robert Ransom, Sr., was financially ruined in the panic of 1837, and how he was plagued by intense depression in the years that followed.[4] Robert Ransom, Jr., in discussing his father, has written, "In the business of life, he was not successful having failed before I was born and remained in comparative poverty till he died, sometimes he was very poor." On the positive side, however, "his quick perceptions made him understand his wife and children and his great heart responded warmly to every throb of theirs."[5] By 1844, the children of the Ransom family on Bridle Creek included Matt, Robert, Jr., his wife, Priscilla; and Mrs. Seymour Ransom, Matt's grandmother.[6] Helping to provide income and sustenance for the family, Matt and his brother worked on the farms.[7] There were occasions when the two brothers felt compelled to settle their personal differences by prolonged knock-down fist fights which led to the complete exhaustion of both parties. Robert, Jr., maintained that these contests were largely brought on when his older brother failed to use his extraordinary powers of persuasion, and "a fight was invariably the result."[8]

The Ransoms of Virginia and North Carolina were of English origin, representing a long and distinguished history.[9] The most renowned contemporary figure of the family tree was Nathaniel Macon, who resided on his plantation, Buck Spring, only twelve miles east to Warrenton. Matt always remembered that day when, as a boy, he accompanied his father for a visit with the old sage and kinsman. Mr. Ransom "was wearing a new elegant suit of broadcloth." After a friendly exchange of greeting, Mr. Macon inquired, "Cousin, how much did that suit of broadcloth cost you?" The question answered, Mr. Macon confided that his suit was made of wool produced on his plantation, and since it was made up at home, the only real cost involved was the price of buttons. Actually, Mr. Macon followed a simple rule as applied to wearing apparel. He insisted "no man should wear clothes that made him conspicuous." In Warren County he dressed in homemade linsey-woolsey garments as worn by other farmers, but in Washington, D.C., where he presided as Speaker of the House of Representatives and the United States Senate, his tailored suits reflected the best in style and quality.[10]

Most of the conversation of that visit had very little appeal to a young boy, but years later Matt would still recall his feelings upon taking his leave: "My chief impression was the dignity and benignity of the old man and his friendly words as he placed his hand on my head."[11]

While Robert Ransom, Sr., was constantly alert to the requirements of his son's early formal education, sometimes his plans ran afoul of circumstance. In July of 1838 he sent his two boys to a private school at the home of John D. Hawkins in Franklin County. As for the attending students, there was hardly a vice "that this small collection of boys did not practice. They drank, gambled, fought cocks, raided upon hen coops, plundered wine cellars and did all sorts of outrageous acts." Mr. Ransom, upon learning of this highly questionable social habitat, abruptly withdrew his sons.[12] A more successful experience resulted when Matt and Robert, Jr., were placed in the all-male Warrenton Academy. This institution was under the principalship of Mr. Robert A. Ezell, "who believed in hickory and high classics and instilled the last by a free application of the first."[13] The school had a very Spartan atmosphere, and each day students arose at sunrise to assemble in a large hall for prayer, after which they were dismissed for classes.[14] When Robert's turn came to attend the academy, he chose to live at home, walking a distance of three or four miles each way.[15] Leaving Mr. Ezell's learning establishment in 1846 to attend the United States Military Academy at West Point, young Robert must have found the change "a featherbed by comparison."[16]

Matt, who preceded his brother at the local academy, took a room in the home of a great aunt, Mrs. Hugh Johnson, who lived in Warrenton. A charming and gracious person she was, and at the same time, capable of demonstrating a very positive and assertive side of her character. However, at least on one occasion, she encountered another of equal attainment. During an afternoon tea in her parlor, she was entertaining a group of ladies when she noticed that a Mrs. Cheek, was pouring a generous share of cream over her fruit. Mrs. Johnson exclaimed, "Sister Cheek, that is cream." The reply was instant: "Thank you Sister Johnson, cream is good enough for me."[17]

At seventeen years of age, Matt set out for Chapel Hill to attend the university fall sessions of 1842. Quickly discovering that student expenses far exceeded his limited financial means, he withdrew from the institution without completing his freshman year.[18] Out of this disappointing experience evolved a plan guaranteeing him an opportunity to pursue a full college program by means of financial loans from the University Philanthropic Society. It was a triumphal occasion for the young man from Bridle Creek when he returned to the university in January of 1844, joining the class of James Johnston Pettigrew, who would become his chief rival for distinction among his classmates.

The University of North Carolina, officially mandated by the state constitution of 1776, was chartered in 1789 and opened its doors to students on January 15, 1795.[19] The university in the 1840's consisted of a small cluster of buildings in the midst of a densely wooded area where the land was flat, leveling off into a plateau. David L. Swain, after stepping down from the post of governor, had become president of the university in 1835, and under his able leadership, the campus began to take on a much improved appearance. Recognizing that North Carolina had relatively few wealthy citizens whose sons could pursue education as a leisure activity, he believed his state should follow a more practical approach toward higher formal education. Very significantly, he sought and found professional resources and exemplary of the finest qualities of personal character to build his university faculty during the 1840's.[20]

The student Matt Ransom was slender and stood a little over six feet in height. He had jet black hair, eyes of extremely dark color, and a well-proportioned body. A contemporary described him as possessing a handsome face, having "an aristocratic bearing," exercising courteous manners, and speaking well with "clear enunciation." All of these qualities and others designated him a "leader of men."[21] Having a grave and thoughtful countenance sustained by an imposing personal dignity probably explains why he rarely had to contend with over-reaching familiarity from associates. One did not take liberties with him in a manner that included coarse conversation or common triviality However, if any transgressions occurred, young Ransom instantly responded. He once became involved in a quarrel with William M. Howerton, and a fight resulted, with Howerton attempting the first blow. The two were separated by fellow students, but Howerton then removed his coat in a gesture to continue the contest. Ransom reacted by inviting his assailant "to go below the wall" for real combat. At that moment, President Swain and Doctor Elisha Mitchell arrived on the scene. Order was restored, and both antagonists were sworn to keep the peace.[22]

During his intense rivalry with James Johnston Pettigrew at the university, Ransom at no time indicated a sense of being overawed, and certainly not overcome, by his rival's credentials and reputation. Historian Samuel Acourt Ashe maintained that even from boyhood, Ransom experienced a great sense of pride and enjoyment by excelling in scholastic competition.[23] Pettigrew nevertheless was a formidable rival, of most striking appearance, possessed of a quick and cultured mind and sometimes credited a genius. Before the end of their college years, these two young men, sensitive as thoroughbreds, completely broke off all personal relations and "were not on speaking terms."[24]

After much deliberation, faculty members resolved the Messrs. Pettigrew and Ransom had earned the first distinction of their class "in order of their names." In essence, the honor of being first in the class was equally shared by these two superbly gifted youths.[25] Ransom believed, however, that had more time been in his favor, he would have eclipsed his rival.[26] In accordance with the faculty format, Pettigrew delivered the valedictory address. Attending the ceremony was a prominent alumnus, President James K. Polk. Ransom, for his part, delivered the salutatory address in honor of the important guest. Its delivery was received with great approval; a *New York Herald* reporter insisted it was by far the best given by the "young disciples of Cicero."[27]

Having been trained in the law by Judge William H. Battle at the university, Ransom now returned to Warren County to take up the profession. Though he was not yet twenty-one years of age, his performance was described as remarkable, even "brilliant."[28] Politics combined with his legal profession when, on December 17, 1852, the state legislature elected Matt W. Ransom Attorney General of North Carolina. This appointment was indeed a singular

tribute, for the state legislature was predominantly Democratic in party affilia-
tion; yet the newly designated office-holder was a Whig and only twenty-six
years old.

With success and good fortune dominating Matt's early career, one other
important goal remained to be fulfilled. He now entered a serious courtship
with Miss Martha Anne Exum of Northampton County. Pattie, as she was
known by friends and family, was orphaned at an early age. Now, having
reached her majority, she was heiress to many fertile acres of land on the
Roanoke River, together with slaves and other auxiliary properties. That Matt
finally won her consent to become his bride was no small achievement. Very
much in keeping with the young couple's preference for privacy and simplicity, they were married at the home of a mutual friend, Mr. F. C. Rives of
Petersburg, Virginia, on January 19, 1853, with a Reverend Stringfellow offi-
ciating.[29]

Unable to survive serious national conflicts of the 1850's, particularly the
slavery question, Whig Party in its final demise became a refuge for extreme
elements and causes. Within its ranks and official councils anti–Roman
Catholic sentiments and resentment toward foreign-born citizens became more
apparent.[30] Such attitudes Matt found unacceptable and unworthy of any serious interest. In 1856 he broke with the Whigs. His term of office as state attorney general having ended, Ransom and his wife took up their new residence
in Northampton County.[31]

Northampton County is located in a northeastern portion of the state,
extends along the Virginia boundary, and lies inland around eighty-five miles
from the Atlantic Ocean. Early settlers included Scots, and Ulster-Scots; then
came the English and French, who were attracted to the area because of its
rich soil and two navigable rivers, the Roanoke and Meherrin.[32] In 1741 the
new domain was severed from Bertie County and named after an English
nobleman, George, Earl of Hampton. Northampton Courthouse, the county
seat, was later renamed Jackson after the illustrious Tennessean. Extreme western portions of the county, encompassing approximately fifty square miles, lie
in the Piedmont province and have a rolling terrain with a maximum elevation of some 350 feet. Southeast of Jackson the land becomes very flat, with
the lowest elevations where the Meherrin and Roanoke rivers leave the county.[33]
Climate of the area can be described as temperate; the winters are cold, but
not bitter, and the summers are moderately warm. Timber, which is heavy
and plentiful, consists of loblolly pine, gum, poplar, oak, and cypress. Farm-
ing the rich soil along the Roanoke River was a risky and sometimes costly
endeavor, as the spring floods proved year after year.[34] Still, the area continued to draw those who would work the land. Northampton County census
statistics for 1851 indicate a white population of 5,994; there were 830 free
blacks and 6,611 slaves. The local economy, being predominantly agricultural,
featured such staple crops as cotton, corn and tobacco.

Awaiting the young couple in their new domicile were plush farmlands, worked by the slaves Pattie had inherited. Besides the standard cotton and corn, which these fertile acres produced in great abundance, there were generous pastures covered with grasses and clover which brood mares and their colts grazed along with Jersey cows and calves, sheep and frolicking lambs. In this environment, Matt spent many pleasurable hours astride his favorite black thoroughbred Arabian stallion, Ion.[35] The house planned by Ransom was completed in 1857; it conformed to a style then popular in Louisiana. According to a credible source the plantation's name, Verona, was chosen by Mrs. Ransom and inspired by Shakespeare's comedy, *Two Gentlemen from Verona*.[36]

Adjoining Verona, across the Jackson Weldon Road, was another grand and scenic plantation, Mowfield, owned by Mr. E. J. Peebles. Here the great stallion stud Sir Archie resided. Renowned in the world of racing, this horse lived the kind of life reserved for royalty until his passing in 1833. Other neighbors with whom Pattie and Matt maintained close social ties were Mr. and Mrs. William H. Gray, whose model plantation lay directly west of Verona. Several miles east along the river was Thornbury, plantation home of the Burgwyns, an illustrious and prominent family in state affairs. Possessing a versatile and prolific mind constantly active, Mr. Henry King Burgwyn pursued his many interests in an authoritative but unoffending way. It was he who designed the handsome courthouse at Jackson.

Never comfortable in a passive or observer's role, Ransom once again entered politics, and on November 15, 1858, he officially began his term as a delegate representing Northampton County in the House of Commons of the state legislature. During the next two years he became actively engaged in a wide range of legislative matters including banking, railroad expansion, and taxes. Ransom was now a member of the Democratic Party, and his skills and tenacity as a parliamentarian earned him a favorable reputation throughout the state. Then came the dawn of war, and Ransom terminated his legislative duties in May of 1861. Now he waited upon the next phase of his life.

Chapter IV

This Is War

Although he had known moments of loneliness brought on by absences from Pattie and the children during his state legislative tenure, Matt had developed a real fondness for Raleigh. Even today one can understand what his personal regrets may have been when departing in May of 1861. The city's wide streets, lined with huge spreading oaks and elms presented a splendid sight. In majestic homes surrounded by spacious lawns, well-tended shrubbery, and formal gardens meticulously maintained lived some of North Carolina's finest old families.[1] To reside in this hospitable community was a delightful experience that few could forget.

But his life in Raleigh lay behind him now. In compliance with his orders, Matt set out for Warrenton, where he assumed active duty. Near the town he had known since early youth, the First Regiment of state troops was being organized at the local race track. Mumford S. Stokes, whose past military experience included duty in the Mexican War, was appointed colonel of the newly formed unit, and Ransom was placed in second command. If any complications, stress, or discomforts troubled him during that transition from civilian to military life, the newly commissioned officer never allowed them to surface in his countenance or conduct. Only in letters to Pattie did he occasionally express real dissatisfaction with his new environment. "The dull routine of camp duty and the stupid drill are very irksome," he wrote. "They engage small minds very anxiously. I did not take to the field for these."[2] Such personal reflections were shared only in the strictest confidence. Ransom knew, and indeed he applied, all his energy in impressing upon those who served under his command, that only through strenuous training and discipline could any military unit expect to achieve success under battle conditions.[3]

Besides Matt, there were others, of course, whose lives were undergoing great change. For massive numbers of volunteers arriving at camps, military life held many surprises, and often the new soldiers adjusted only with great reluctance. Many of these southern volunteers wished only for a chance to fight Yankees, and the drudgery of drilling three of four times a day seemed totally unrelated to their objective. Equally distasteful were such mundane activities and tasks as marching, meal preparation, clothes washing, and contending with lice. Above all, guard duty was the most despised assignment.[4] How ridiculous it was to walk a prescribed beat on alert with rifle in hand when the closest Yankee must have been several hundred miles away! Rather than be party to such an insane enterprise, it was better to go to sleep at one's post. Some men dispensed with the formality of obtaining a pass when leaving camp; others were openly defiant of orders they found objectionable, such as drilling on wet ground.[5] How long such defiance and laxness would continue rested largely upon forthcoming leadership and future campaigns.

At the very outset of hostilities, North Carolinians began to witness a number of the sordid aspects of troop encampments. Opportunities abounded for women willing to sell their bodies and souls. The practice of prostitution in this war was not confined to towns and cities, but also active in rural areas. In his diary one sergeant, while near Weldon, North Carolina, recorded, "This section of the country seems to abound in very bad women."[6] With the increase in prostitution, venereal disease spread rapidly.[7] Another troublesome matter that arose early in the war to plague the Confederate Army was excessive drinking. One editor charged that "a large number of the officers of our Southern Army are both profane and hard drinkers where they are not drunkards."[8] Of course, there were thousands of Confederate soldiers untainted by alcohol and other vices; yet the numbers of those so addicted caused great concern among officers of high command and Richmond authorities. Gambling, often a form of diversion, was also a problem when it imposed hardships on participants. Among games of chance, the most common was card playing-poker, twenty-one, euchre and keno. Since money was scarce, cards and dice determined new ownership of pocket knives, jewelry, clothing, and sometimes rations.

Arriving in the midst of these highly irregular camp conditions in July of 1861 was West Pointer (class of 1850) Robert Ransom, Jr. One can only imagine what disdain or repugnance he may have experienced on seeing the local camp situation; however, it is certain that there were some very quick improvements. How well Colonel Ransom succeeded as commander of the Ninth North Carolina Cavalry Regiment was amply illustrated when, within a few months, the unit earned distinction as "one of the best drilled, most efficient and finest looking cavalry regiments in the Army of Northern Virginia."[9]

No latecomer to the military profession, Robert, Jr. brought to his post a record of high merit and achievement. Following graduation from the National Academy, then under the superintendency of Colonel Robert E. Lee, the young North Carolinian assumed charge of cavalry training at the institution. Subsequent duty included service in the Department of New Mexico and in Kansas, where he became a discerning witness to what developed into a bloody territorial civil war. Out of all his western duty experiences, an event occurring on July 4, 1856, stands out as perhaps the most noteworthy. On this date Robert Jr., while commanding his cavalry unit, "met closely the infamous and notorious John Brown" of Osawatomie. Brown, who was in command of his own civilian mounted followers, attempted to assemble his forces that forenoon, and was disbanded on two separate occasions by federal troops. Because of other pressing duties, the federal commander on the scene had reason to absent himself. However, before taking leave, he ordered his junior officer, the young Robert Ransom, not to allow any further formal civilian gatherings. No sooner was he given command than Ransom observed Brown shouting orders for his followers to join in formation. "I spurred my horse," Robert wrote later "and was instantly by his side with my pistol cocked and the muzzle at his head, and told him to order his men to disperse or I would kill him." The old grizzly, his eyes cold and steady in a studied countenance, stared at his challenger for a moment, and then commanded, "Scatter men."[10]

Careful and proper appearance, reserved dignity, and absolute adherence to military code were among personal traits of Robert Ransom, Jr. These qualities seem to suggest a stiff-necked individual. But in reality, he was a man of very sensitive feelings and capable of demonstrating generous affection. Unwilling to indulge in self-pity, he was equally reluctant to reveal personal pain or discomfort. These qualities were present even in his extreme youth. As a boy growing up on Bridle Creek he fell from a horse and broke his arm, and in subsequent accidents the same limb was broken on two different occasions. The last incident he did not disclose to his family until after some weeks; this brought about a permanent "weak arm" due to "malformation of one of the bones."[11]

Robert's unqualified love and devotion toward his parents may be illustrated by two incidents. The last day before leaving for West Point, he accompanied his parents to Shell Castle, the ancestral home of his mother (this beautiful Federalist-style mansion stands approximately three miles west of Enfield, North Carolina). During the day, Robert, Sr., at two different times, gave his son the option of remaining home — "I believe hoping I would decline to go," wrote the son, "but I resolved to try it." Standing at "the door of the dining room leading to the passage for the front door," Robert, Jr., kissed his mother goodbye, "and as ... Father and I drove off from Shell Castle I waved my last farewell to her while she stood on the open porch at the east front of the house. I saw her no more."[12] While this was an extremely sad moment, another incident of equal emotion occurred when Robert, Jr., opened a letter handed to him by his father as the two parted. Dated August 20, 1846, it reads:

My Dear Son,

With a heart so full for utterance let me with firmness of purpose inform and impress upon you a few cardinal principles. In a few short hours we shall be separated, and you shall be on your way to West Point for that improvement and high distinction which your intellect and virtues so justifiably entitle you. Bear in mind my Dear Boy, Truth Honesty, Virtuous Honesty and Valor. Nourish and cherish them in all your daily and hourly transactions. They will be a shield to ward off arrows of all malignant feeling of action and shine around your name and fame that nothing can or will dare to extinguish. May God in his great goodness inspire you to the fulfillment of these principles and may they be your guide, protector and defender is the dearest wish of your most devoted and unfortunate father.[13]

Robert Ransom

The passing of fifteen years brings many changes in a man's life, and Robert Ransom, Jr., was no longer the boy setting out for West Point. Now married with a growing family, he had reached a point of life generally regarded as the prime years. His aptitude and talents in his profession were obvious, and the degree to which the Confederacy would utilize these assets remained for the future to determine. For now, events continued to unfold, some encouraging, some sad.

On July 7, 1861, Governor Ellis died at Red Sulphur Springs, in Virginia while seeking relief from a prolonged illness. The governor's secessionist views Matt Ransom was unable to accept, but he had come to admire the immense courage of the stricken leader, whose final days were spent on a sick couch while transacting the business of his office in the state capitol. (Following his death, Speaker Henry T. Clark assumed responsibility of the state's highest elective office, an event which precipitated mild political efforts to displace him.[14]) Despite his illness, toward the end of his life the determined and efficient efforts of the governor were beginning to produce genuine results. When authorized by the state legislature in May, the governor had immediately undertaken the task of organizing ten regiments of state troops. By July, six had been trained in camps, armed, drilled, and equipped, and, were destined for Virginia. The Seventh and Eighth regiments required additional attention and preparation, with scheduled assignments of duty at New Bern and Roanoke Island. The Ninth, or First Cavalry, commanded by Robert Ransom, Jr., was assembled in due time at Warrenton. The Tenth Regiment consisted of artillery. All the while these units were forming, other men were enlisting in volunteer regiments. After the First North Carolina Volunteer Regiment was organized, five more regiments were created, joining the First in Virginia; the Seventh was dispatched to Hatteras. The Eighth, Tenth, Eleventh, Twelfth, Thirteenth, and Fourteenth Volunteers were formed between June 15 and July 18, 1861.

The fact that the volunteer regiments had the same numbers as the state troops created by Governor Ellis tended to create confusion, especially for Richmond authorities. Finally, it was decided that the numbers designating the ten regiments of state troops would remain the same, while the volunteer regiments would renumber. The First Volunteer Regiment became the Eleventh Regiment, with subsequent units numbered consecutively.[15]

In early July, amid much enthusiasm as well as the color and drama that sometimes surrounded regimental proceedings, James Johnston Pettigrew was chosen by officers of the Twelfth Regiment as their commanding officer. Pettigrew had formerly resided in Tyrell County, but had later moved to South Carolina, and there achieved, partly due to European studies and travel abroad, some distinction as a student of military affairs; he had also recently shared military duty at Charleston.[16]

Expediting the organization of North Carolina troops were the already existing facilities within the state, which stood ready to play important roles. Busy camps of instruction and training were located at Raleigh, Warrenton, Asheville, Garysburg, and other centers. The supply of arms stored at the Fayetteville Federal Arsenal was sufficient to arm recruits pouring into training camps. Fortunately and very importantly, the state had at its disposal a remarkable qualified officers corps which was reinforced by adding to its ranks competent civilian elements duly commissioned to carry out their military roles. As regiments were formed and transferred to Virginia they were assigned to brigades whose officers were appointed by the Confederate Command.[17] Defense planning and activities on the coast were proceeding, but only minimally so in the minds of most participants and observers. A two-gun battery was erected at a location to be called Fort Fisher, and likewise, batteries were placed in position near Forts Caswell and Macon. Two forts at Ocracoke and Hatteras inlets were under construction.

North Carolina's uneven coastline of recesses and indentations lies in proximity of Currituck, Albemarle, Pamlico, Core, and Bogue sounds. Into these sounds, where waters take on widths of one to forty miles, empty most of the rivers of the state's coastal plain. From Albemarle Sound, the Pasquotank is navigable to Elizabeth City; the Perquimans provides a water route to Hertford; Winton is accessible by way of the Chowan, as is Plymouth by way of the Roanoke River. Moving up the Pamlico River offers a route to Washington, North Carolina. From this point, one can voyage on the Tar River to Tarboro. The Neuse River offers excellent communications with New Bern, and further, up with Kinston. Leaving Pamlico Sound and going through Core Sound leads to Beaufort and Morehead City. To the north, the sounds region is connected with Virginia waters by way of the Dismal Swamp and the Albemarle and Chesapeake canals. Protecting the sounds region is a long sand bank which runs from Cape Henry, Virginia, along the North Carolina coast to Bogue Inlet below Beaufort. This phenomenal natural sand bar runs between the sounds and the Atlantic Ocean, interrupted by inlets at Oregon, Hatteras, Ocracoke, and Beaufort. If the Confederacy could hold these entrances and the mouth of the Cape Fear River, North Carolina could escape invasion by sea. On the other hand, if these were to fall, an invader would surely move on to take possession of the sounds and the strategic rivers flowing into them and one-third of the state would be in enemy hands. Such a disaster would place in great peril the Wilmington and Weldon Railroad, which was the principal transportation approach to Richmond.

The Ransom brothers' reunion at Warrenton was necessarily brief. Matt, in compliance with orders, accompanied his unit to northern Virginia during July 1861. Arriving at Richmond, his regiment was quickly assigned to the brigade of General Theophilus H. Holmes encamped at Brook's Station near the mouth of Acquia Creek, Virginia. Here Matt Ransom and his regiment for the next seven months would settle down to a rather dull routine of service on the Potomac. Ransom described his private quarters as a tent "almost furnitureless, a few books, trunks and writing material, a pair of pistols, a sword, some scattered clothing."[18] In a letter to Pattie written from Acquia Creek, he provided an almost eerie description of summer camp life in the midst of evening darkness:

> It is very late at night. I just heard the lonesome sentinel cry out, "It is twelve o'clock and all is well." The camp is very silent, scarcely a sound breaks the solemn stillness. All here is peace, and yet each minute may open on our ears the signal guns of death. There! went a musket, even while I wrote the last word. Doubtless some false alarm. Ah! there's another! I have waited five minutes and all is well again. Some nervous sentinel shot a phantom and that's all.[19]

At least on one occasion during this period, Ransom's resourcefulness was put to a test in responding to devious conduct by others. The incident involved himself and his commanding officer, Colonel Stokes. When Stokes repaired to Fredericksburg to attend to certain official duties, Matt was in command, and for reasons he considered valid, he refused all furloughs in the regiment. Upon his return, Stokes, in a move to improve his popularity at the expense of his lieutenant colonel, countermanded the recently imposed strict furlough policy; this he did in spite of Ransom's strong protests. Once again, Colonel Stokes returned to Fredericksburg on official duties, and during his absence, Ransom let word get around that he would now be more generous with furloughs. Within a short time, most of the regiment had received furlough and departed. The colonel returned to a nearly empty camp, where he had time and space to reflect upon his furlough policy.[20]

Only a brief distance from Acquia Creek near Manassas, Virginia, the war's first major engagement occurred on July 21, 1861. The Confederate line of about eight miles was behind a shallow wandering stream known as Bull Run Creek. In command of these forces during the first phase of battle was General P. G. T. Beauregard with about 24,000 troops at his disposal, of whom 11,000 would become actively engaged. In support of these forces were at least 9,000 men under Confederate General Joseph E. Johnston in the Shenandoah Valley. The Union Army stationed in the Washington area under George Irvin McDowell was around 30,000, of whom 13,000 would actually be committed in combat.[21]

These forces were supported by a smaller reserve army of 12,000 in the Shenandoah Valley under General Robert Patterson. Referred to by some as "the greatest battle ever fought in the New World — up to this time," it nevertheless proved indecisive, neither seriously harming the North nor significantly helping the South.[22] The contest has been described as "a conglomeration of small engagements, featuring individual combat, [rather] than a single co-ordinated enterprise."[23] And, for the first time in major combat, Yankee troops were introduced to the infamous chilling Rebel Yell which preceded serious charges or advances. In casualties, the Confederates suffered 376 killed and 1,489 wounded, compared to around 500 federals killed, 1,000 wounded, and 1,200 unaccounted.[24] Only three North Carolina regiments were present, the Fifth, Sixth, and Eleventh.

With the collapse of the Union right flank, a climax was reached in the battle, and what followed was almost a total federal rout with Confederate forces in pursuit. In view of limitations imposed upon them, it is doubtful whether southern troops could have captured the federal capital. However, a determined drive upon the city might have caused its evacuation, and what would have ensued during and after such a panicky event exhausts human imagination.[25] At the moment, however, conditions of weather, lack of communications, logistics, and many other uncertainties persuaded Southern commanders not to attempt to move in force upon Washington. Even so, Southerners were ecstatic about the victory, which many believed would end the war almost before it had begun.[26] However, inflated optimism of this kind was soon punctured by events in North Carolina.

During the following month, on August 28 and 29, federal forces launched an overwhelming land and naval attack upon Forts Clark and Hatteras. Under the joint command of Major General Benjamin F. Butler and Commodore S.H. Stringham, this attack was carried out with great success. Surrender followed after only slight resistance, leaving the vital inlet in Union hands. Upon this key location rested the defense of Pamlico and Albemarle sounds; its loss left Roanoke Island, Fort Macon, and the defense of New Bern open to direct naval attack as well as assault by land troops. Raleigh officials and knowledgeable citizens reacted with shock to these latest events, which prompted speculation concerning future federal moves against the state.[27]

Hardly had General Richard C. Gatlin been appointed to command the Department of North Carolina when Hatteras fell. As long as Richmond remained in peril, his repeated requests for assistance from the Confederate War Office met with only limited results. Confronted with the awesome task of defending a vast coastline with extremely limited personnel, he developed a strategy calling for a scattered defense of the more exposed vital areas, by which he hoped to check the progress of any would-be assailant. Four to six regiments were to be stationed in reserve at Goldsboro; from here they could be dispatched to any part of the coast to contend against invasion. Gatlin also planned to place obstructions in rivers (making them less navigable to an enemy) and to construct gunboats for service in the Pamlico Sound.

Clearly reflecting some of the problems plaguing the confederacy's costal defense is a letter written by Captain Dimmock, who was in charge of construction of Roanoke Island. Addressed to Governor Clark, the letter was an appeal on behalf of free black laborers on the island:

> Many of the Negro laborers engaged upon the defense works at this point— all I believe of whom are free—were secured many months since…without receiving either salary or clothing. A miserable squalid set…without a sufficient amount of dirty blankets, these hands were taken before May last and led to believe their days of occupation, upon coast defense would be but few—have come unprepared for so long a term.[28]

In a related matter, Zebulon Vance, now colonel of the Twenty-sixth Regiment, stationed at Camp Burgwyn of Bogue Banks, wrote the following letter to Governor Clark on September 18:

> I am sorry to say that a portion of my regiment are almost in a state of mutiny on account of the nonreception of their pay. … This state of things cannot be endured much longer by men who have nearly four months pay due them. If not relieved soon, I fear I shall not be able to maintain discipline.[29]

From Acquia Creek, Ransom continued to monitor the ominous implications of events in Eastern North Carolina. In hopes of reducing, at least in some measure, his anxiety over plantation operations during his absence, he had earlier intrusted to Pattie's uncle, Mr. Thomas V. Roberts, the responsibilities of overseer at Verona. Matt was reasonably sure at this moment that Verona was beyond danger of enemy activities. Yet caution seemed to rule his thoughts as he advised Pattie by letter hastily written in camp on September 4: "So let me again simply urge upon you the importance of keeping a vigilant lookout—I can't help feeling very anxious about you." He then referred to Mr. Roberts, who would keep her "advised … but then I trust all to you. … Do as you think best without reference to anyone else."[30]

In accord with General Gatlin's designs, Confederate policy planners placed Brigadier General J. R. Anderson in charge of North Carolina's coastal defense; under the command assignments that eventually evolved, he was responsible for the defense of Cape Fear. Brigadier General David Harvey Hill took command of the District of Albemarle. Unfortunately for the state, General Hill's assignment was much too brief. Recently promoted to brigadier general following the Bethel skirmish, he pushed ahead energetically under most trying circumstances in attempting to improve his district's military defenses. Fort Macon, he informed his superiors, could not be held unless supported by four additional long-range guns; and, since Roanoke Island determined the fate of one-third of North Carolina, he called for at least six more rifled cannons there. Some difficulties the general encountered were typical of wartime, while others were unique. Very often, new installations being constructed were remote and isolated. Finding and placing qualified subordinates was a persistent problem made more frustrating by shortages of workmen and implements. With only a limited number of troops available for labor, and no chance of securing additional hands from uncooperative slave owners, Hill called out the militia of neighboring counties to serve on the island. He soon learned that Governor Clark had rescinded this order. This action so angered Hill that following additional friction, he requested to be relieved of his post. This request was approved, and General Hill, on orders of November 16, reported for duty under J. E. Johnston. By winter's end of 1861, evidence clearly indicated that North Carolina was ill prepared to contend against a serious attack upon her vital coastal regions.

Even earlier in the year, before their own coastline was so greatly imperiled, North Carolinians had begun to register a number of disappointments and surprises concerning events outside their state. Apparently, from all indications, the remaining border states would not enter the Confederacy. Supported by federal troops, a Unionist government for West Virginia was installed at Wheeling. Maryland had settled down as a Union state. Kentucky and Missouri, having earlier seemed favorable to secession, were now safely in the Union column. Meanwhile, although perhaps not so carefully watched by the public, foreign governments were becoming an important factor; their relationships with the Confederacy would help to determine its success or failure. Before the hostilities, "Cotton is King" had become a popular and frequently accepted claim. The inference of the slogan was that European nations would act to protect their chief source of this commodity in the event of a military contest between the North and South. Thus far, however, King Cotton was proving to be a very weak monarch. In recognizing the belligerency of the Confederacy at the very outset of hostilities, says historian E. Merton Coutler, Britain and France merely acknowledged "that a war rather than a street fight was in progress, and that the rules of war were now in effect."[31] Under such circumstances, the Confederate flag would receive recognition on the high seas, and its sailors would not be considered pirates. Significantly, recognition of a state of war also cleared the way for the Lincoln Administration to initiate a blockade, an action that it could not otherwise have taken.[32] Certainly, if such a blockade were employed with determined efforts, it could have devastating results for the Confederacy. As for official diplomatic recognition of the southern states, and European support to regard the blockade as illegal on the grounds it was not being maintained, Confederate agents sought these aboard with no success.[33]

In those states that had joined the Confederacy, a general awareness was developing, difficult for some to accept, that in the current military struggle, success rested upon a public willingness to offer untold sacrifices in lives and personal wealth in behalf of the southern cause. Bearing up well under this burden, North Carolina within the first seven months of the war "provided the Confederacy with forty thousand soldiers, equipped and trained."[34]

Early in the new year, on February 7 and 8, decision makers in Raleigh and elsewhere in the Confederacy were confronted with a new enemy offensive. This incursion had been anticipated for several months; if successful, it would greatly extend Union control of North Carolina's coastline.[35] The federal expedition, which set out from Hampton Roads, Virginia, destined for Roanoke Island, consisted of some sixty vessels of various description, mostly coastal and under the command of Navy flag officer L. M. Goldsborough. Responsible for the Union army's role in the attack was Brigadier General Ambrose E. Burnside, whose troops — of some 11,500 men under his charge since January — were intended as assault forces against the ten-mile-long island dominated by swamps and flat land. General Henry A. Wise, commander of Confederate forces stationed there, became ill with pneumonia, leaving the island and its 2,500 defenders in command of Colonel H. M. Shaw. The Confederate fleet consisted of seven tugboats and river streamers, which accounted for a total of eight guns. Moving his fleet up Pamlico Sound in a single line two miles long with guns blazing, Goldsborough, by remaining close to the shore, escaped any effective Confederate firepower since their coastal weapons were permanently encased and aimed at the middle of the channel. Burnside, for his part, landed his three brigades at the island's southern end, then advanced his forces several miles before confronting a Confederate defensive line approximately a quarter of a mile in length and comprising some 1,500 men. These elements were overcome with comparative ease, and by afternoon on February 8, the Union offensive had reduced the island to submission and surrender.[36]

During the weeks which followed, Burnside and Goldsborough moved with ease, even impunity, to occupy virtually all of North Carolina's inlet seaports from Elizabeth City in the north to Beaufort in the south.[37] In fear and humiliation, North Carolinians heard of the fall of such state landmarks as New Bern, Washington, Fort Macon, and Plymouth. In Graysburg on February 22, Henry King Burgwyn penned a letter to Governor Clark in which he took the latter to task for the loss of the area that Burgwyn had sought to defend.[38] Referring to his previous personal request to be commissioned as brigadier general, Burgwyn acidly observed that a man of politics had received the commission in his place. Now, in this time of North Carolina's great distress, he again requested a commission, hoping this time to lead the defense between the Roanoke and Chowan rivers. Again, however, his request was refused.[39]

While Burgwyn was understandably concerned with the immediate threat to his own domicile, other disturbing southern military defeats were being reported beyond the state. Besides having just lost a significant section of the

Atlantic coast, Confederate military presence had been recently expelled from middle and western Tennessee as confirmed by the fall of Forts Henry and Donelson; hereafter, the trans–Mississippi was obviously included in any impending military and naval strike, as well as the city of New Orleans. All that remained, according to some professing expertise, was successful advance upon Richmond, and peace would result.

The likelihood of a renewed federal advance upon the state's interior explains Richmond's decision to rush troops into North Carolina after New Bern's capture. By March 31, 1862, the number of the infantry personnel throughout the state had risen to 24,030, along with 142 pieces of artillery.[40] To further improve the state's military position, a new structure of command was implemented which called for the replacement of General Gatlin by Major General T. H. Holmes, a native son and North Carolina's ranking general in the Confederacy. Brigadier General Samuel G. French succeeded Anderson at Wilmington, and recently promoted Brigadier General Robert Ransom, Jr., arrived on the scene from Virginia. His latest promotion had occurred in March following the loss of New Bern, and at Kinston he set up his new command.

Matt Ransom's duty along the Potomac quickly ended, for reasons also related to Burnside's successful coastal inland campaign. March found him stationed with his unit near Kinston, North Carolina; like many others in these uncertain times, he waited for whatever assignment fate wished to confer upon him.

The Thirty-fifth Regiment, which had been ordered to the area following its engagement at New Bern, was in the process of replacing its commanding officers. As determined by law, enlisted volunteers in North Carolina were entitled to elect their company officers, which included a captain, one lieutenant and two second lieutenants. These ranks in turn elected their field officers, consisting of a colonel, lieutenant colonel, and major. It was the colonel's responsibility to appoint a regimental staff comprised of a surgeon, quartermaster, commissary, and adjutant. In the election of the Thirty-fifth Regiment, the officers' unanimous choice for their colonel was Matt W. Ransom.[41]

Conditions of discontent and demoralization prevailing in the regiment were the result of its pathetic performance in the defense of New Bern. The colonel, Reverend James Sinclair, had been elected to his post under false claims of a meritorious military record. His incompetence for command, so recently indicated, roused a general sentiment that he should be replaced. His troops regarded him contemptuously as "a complete bag of wine and whisky."[42]

The Thirty-fifth's behavior in combat at New Bern, requires only narration. It was in January that the Thirty-fifth was ordered eastward to add strength to New Bern's defenses, and its first test in combat soon occurred under plans drawn up by Confederate General L. O. B. Branch. His line of defense was set up at right angles to the Neuse River, starting with Fort Thompson located on the stream and extending across the area to near Brice's Creek, placing his fighting units in this order: from left to right beginning at the fort, the Twenty-seventh, Thirty-seventh, Seventh, and Thirty-fifth Regiments followed by a militia unit; then the Twenty-sixth North Carolina Regiment, with the Thirty-third held in reserve. In support of these active units were two batteries, six pieces each. At the approximate midpoint of this line a railroad intersected, and at this junction a brickyard was situated. Here the militia was posted to guard this interval; to the left, the Thirty-fifth was stationed and commanded by Colonel Sinclair. Opening the attack in the early morning hours of March 14, Burnside, by repeatedly shifting his attacks, at last determined the line's weakest section. At the brickyard location he mounted a severe assault, under which the militia broke and dispersed. The Thirty-fifth Regiment, according to General Branch's official report, "quickly followed the example of the militia, retreating in the utmost disorder."[43] With the Confederate defense line severed and with exposed contingents being fired upon from the rear, General Branch moved his forces in the direction of New Bern and then retreated to Kinston.

Unwilling to accept a record tarnished by disgrace, members of the Thirty-fifth were anxious to improve their reputation. Clearly, to do so required better leadership. It was obvious to all that the qualities needed in a new leader — a cool head, a brave heart, and an exemplary record of experience and resourcefulness — were personified in Matt Ransom.[44] A major problem, of course, might be the unwillingness of Ransom's current regiment to part with him. As a matter of fact, the First Regiment was reluctant to accept Ransom's departure. There were a number of other persuasive reasons for Ransom to refuse the offer, and before reaching a final decision, he prudently requested the qualified advice of his personal friend and department commander, General Holmes. Very emphatically Holmes advised against acceptance of such a command, which would undoubtedly cost the life of the officer so appointed. The general observed that in subsequent battles the regiment, because of its humiliating conduct at New Bern, would require constant rallying by its commander, who would thus place himself in danger and probably die for his efforts. Thanking General Holmes for his interest and advice, Ransom took his leave by stating that although he had first doubted whether he should take the post, Holmes's assessment had made his duty plain.[45]

Among the arguments that might have been offered against Matt's new command was that two brothers perhaps should not be officers of the same brigade, with one subordinate to the other. Since arriving at Kinston, the brigade of Robert Ransom, Jr., as now assembled had included the Thirty-fifth Regiment. Matt, however, was convinced he could achieve a successful military mission under his brother's command, and to the proper regimental personnel he conveyed his acceptance of their offer.

Now the moment had arrived for Matt Ransom to take leave of his old regiment, and this proved to be an unusually sad occasion. Officers of the First came up with a very impressive sword, which they presented in ceremonial fashion to their departing lieutenant colonel. In a sincere letter of acceptance of May 11, 1862, Ransom replied:

> I accept, with emotions of pleasure and gratitude which I cannot express, the beautiful sword which the officers of the First North Carolina regiment have been pleased, through you, to present to me. Certainly the bestowal of no honor could have brought with it more gratification. The esteem of the chivalrous gentlemen with whom it has been my happiness to have been so long associated in the service of our country, so generously evinced, is a priceless attainment, and it will be my sacred duty through life to preserve untarnished this bright token of their confidence, and to transmit it as a sacred jewel to my sons. Around it will ever cluster pleasant memories of the cherished friends, the brave hearts, the patriotic spirits of that noble regiment, the gallant First. Cherishing in common with yourselves a holy purpose to assist in maintaining at all hazard the independence of our Country and the honor of our State, I remain gentlemen, most sincerely yours.[46]

The brigade as now organized consisted of the Twenty-fourth, Twenty-fifth, Twenty-sixth, Thirty-fifth, and Forty-ninth regiments, accompanied by two cavalry companies and five artillery companies. General Robert Ransom, Jr., being "very industrious and untiring in trying to perfect his Brigade," achieved the best of results in molding "a well drilled and disciplined command."[47]

Burnside's interior advance in the direction of Goldsboro was momentarily delayed, since Fort Macon had become his major concern. Located on Bogue Banks, the fort stood guard over Beaufort Inlet and was the only remaining Confederate installation on the Outer Banks not under federal control. No move could be made on Goldsboro until this southern stronghold, where Confederates might assemble to Burnside's rear, was eliminated.[48] On April 26, 1862, Union forces fulfilled that objective by taking the fort. Partly in response to this event, officers and men of the Thirty-fifth and other regiments of the brigade developed a longing to test their strength and recent training under conditions of combat. Little did they know that as their hopes were about to be realized, June orders would arrive to break camp, not to meet Burnside, but to return to Richmond.

To understand and possibly appreciate Richmond's decision at this critical juncture, it might be appropriate briefly to review the military scene unfolding north of the Confederate capital. On May 20, Union general George B. McClellan moved his formidable forces across the Chickahominy River. Six days later federal cavalry occupied Mechanicsville, only five miles north of Richmond. Southern military planners were aware that General McDowell was pushing his powerful Union troops south from Fredericksburg, which suggested that he and McClellan planned to join forces as soon as possible.[49]

These, threatening circumstances weighed heavily in favor of troop withdrawals in North Carolina. Nevertheless, an opposing point of view arose in the Old North State that officials were placing an excessive amount of emphasis on Richmond's defense plight in an already overburdened Confederacy.

Chapter V

Times for Steady Nerves

The entire command of General Holmes was breaking camp at Kinston and returning to Virginia. Although compelling reasons prompted General Lee to issue this order on June 20, 1862, it left North Carolina virtually defenseless against any further Union invasion. In these highly dangerous circumstances, North Carolina citizens responded with harsh criticism to what they regarded as callous neglect of their interests on the part of Confederate authorities. In the months just past, while their own troops had been in Virginia, North Carolinians had watched with consternation as federal forces overran the sound's region, then launched a campaign of attack against established eastern cities and towns. On May 26, 1862, they had witnessed the humiliating spectacle of Union brigadier general Edward Stanley being installed as military governor of those coastal areas under federal occupation.[1]

In the public mind there was some degree of conviction that the southern military situation had seriously deteriorated since the start of hostilities. Certain statistics and events seemed to support this view. In December of the past year, the command of General Joseph E. Johnston had numbered 62,000 effectives, but by February 1862 his total number of troops, after transfers and expiration of one-year enlistments, was reduced to 47,000 men stationed at Centreville, Virginia in the Shenandoah Valley, and along the Potomac.[2] In the West, alarming events continued to plague the southern cause for independence; the Confederate far-flung defense line seemed to be crumbling as indicated by defeats at Forts Henry and Donelson, followed by the Battle of Shiloh in early April, which was a prelude to the subsequent loss of Corinth, Mississippi. Really disheartening of course, was the fall of New Orleans on May 1, which deprived the South of its largest seaport. (Because of this deprivation in spite of obstacles resulting from a Union blockade, Wilmington, North Carolina, would become in time a main port of entry for the Confederacy.)

Other provocative issues exacerbated public unrest throughout North Carolina. With trade having been terminated between the two warring regions, the state soon found itself in short supply of numerous commodities formerly imported from the North. Clothing and medicine were scarce, as were two others items generally believed of equal importance, namely salt and sugar.

Attempts at coastal salt-panning operations ended abruptly when the sound's region fell to enemy occupation, and a lack of transportation to sugar plantation areas west of the Mississippi River made sugar one of the most sought-after food items. Tea and coffee quickly disappeared in markets and those left empty-handed made determined attempts to provide substitutes from locally produced parched cornmeal, rye, and potatoes. Critical shortages of drugs and medicines caused great public concern. Service personnel were vitally affected by limited reserves of the narcotics so necessary in treating the wounded, particularly amputees. Normally these pharmaceutical items were northern imports but now they had been declared contraband of war by Union officials and were thus subject to seizure. Once again, human ingenuity labored overtime as physicians and botanists attempted to produce effective replacements.[3]

On top of the popular dissatisfaction over these matters, the conscription act passed the Confederate Congress produced one of the most intensely debated questions before the state. This much-needed statute authorized the drafting for military duty of all men in the Confederacy between the ages of eighteen and thirty-five. Hereafter, military duty was no longer optional, and those now confronted with the necessity of entering the military against their wishes protested loudly that their personal rights were being violated. Fiercely they opposed the new law, which they denounced as unconstitutional and tyrannical.[4]

Amid disturbing conditions the summer of 1862 saw the Confederate government's popularity sinking dangerously low in the state of North Carolina.[5] Many citizens had come to question the credibility of state leaders who had earlier predicted a brief war. To some it even seemed that the groundwork had been laid for a revolution. Certainly there were politicians prepared and qualified to lead in that event.[6] Prominent among these was William W. Holden, editor of the *Raleigh Standard*. While favoring ad valorem taxes upon slave property during the political campaign of 1860, as a faithful Democrat he chose not to break openly with his party; but in opposing secession, he made his position widely known, irrevocably severing his ties with party leadership.[7] Holden's attacks on President Davis and his government were monitored by influential northern news publications, and some of his most vindictive editorials were reprinted in full on the pages of the *New York Herald* under the headline, "The Southern Confederacy virtually repudiated in North Carolina." *The Philadelphia Inquirer* was equally certain that the Old North State was "ready to return, is even now returning from her prodigal and ruinous career."[8] Spurning all appeals to champion themes of unity and harmony, the *Standard* continued its onslaught against secessionists and the Confederate administration. To weary, confused soldiers, Holden's messages were persuasive. Desertions were particularly heavy among troop elements from northern and western counties, including Chatham, Guilford, Randolph, Forsyth, Yadkin, Iredell, and Wilkes.[9]

Whether at peace or at war, North Carolina has generally managed to maintain its schedule for public elections, and the year 1862 was an election year. Zebulon Vance, having previously served in the Congress of the United States and being now on active duty as colonel of the Twenty-sixth Regiment, announced his willingness to run in the forth coming race for governor. Holden's failure to mount enthusiasm and support on his own behalf narrowed the contest to Colonel William Johnston and Vance. Few speeches were delivered by the two principal candidates; however, the media was extremely active, often vitriolic, in delivering personal attacks. "If Vance is the patriot and fine soldier claimed for him," questioned the *Raleigh Register*, "why does he not remain in the field?" " Ah," replied the *Raleigh Standard*, "If Colonel Johnston is the ardent Southerner he professes to be, why is it he is not in the field?" [He seems to prefer remaining at] ... "his office at Columbia managing his railroad."[10]

Finding Holden's efforts in creating dissension and division among the populace completely unacceptable, Vance, during his limited campaign, called "for the unity of sentiment and fraternity of feeling which alone can enable us to prosecute this war for liberty and independence."[11] Whether his appeals were successful remained to be seen; until July 31, when soldiers cast their ballots, would the elective process determine the state's next governor.

Months before these early stirrings of election excitement in North Carolina the Confederacy had held its own elections in order to replace the provisional government with a permanent one. Jefferson Davis was again elected and on February 22, 1862, again inaugurated as president, this time for a six-year term.

The moving of the Confederate capital from Montgomery to Richmond in May of 1861 had occasioned public debate, and as the war progressed, it began to seem that there might be some logic in the contention that the Confederacy's limited manpower and resources would become unduly absorbed in Richmond's behalf at the expense of other military objectives. Before the end of February 1862, President Davis was certain of an impending peninsula campaign by Union commander General George B. McClellan, joined by General Ambrose E. Burnside, who was expected to advance through Norfolk with Richmond's capture as an ultimate objective. With this ominous threat in mind, Davis informed General Joseph E. Johnston that the army in northern Virginia was to be withdrawn and that as many troops as possible should be placed in positions of support around the capital.[12] In compliance with his commander-in-chief's orders, General Johnston evacuated his defensive position at Centreville, Virginia, on March 9 and moved southward to take up a new position below the Rappahannock River.

Not all Confederate military movements were in retreat. General Thomas J. Jackson, or "Stonewall," who was thought by the federals to have also abandoned the valley, turned and attacked General Nathaniel P. Banks at

Kernstown, Virginia, on March 23. Immediate confusion resulted among high Washington authorities and notable federal commanders. Banks believed his adversary was in command of a sizable force, which prompted the Union commander to recall troops he had sent to Washington. Lincoln, sensitive to his capital's defense, ordered General Irvin McDowell to remain stationary in the Manassas area, preventing his juncture with McClellan on the peninsula. Although Jackson was repulsed at Kernstown, the engagement proved to be a strategic victory; Union troops engaged in battle with Jackson or stationed in Manassas with McDowell could not join McClellan to move on Richmond. The benefit to General Johnston was considerable.[13]

On April 5 McClellan began his slow, tedious operations on the peninsula. The first of May he was preparing a bombardment of Yorktown with General Johnston indicating a retreat; at this point, the overall Confederate military situation in Virginia was extremely critical. Johnston, with a force of 55,000, was confronted by an enemy nearly double his strength.[14] Norfolk was to be sacrificed, leaving Confederate general Benjamin Huger and his command of 10,000 with the single recourse of joining Johnston's main force. Any advantages which might have been incurred by these troops joining the main Confederate body were offset by the 12,400 Norfolk area federals now freed for reassignment under Brigadier General John E. Wool at Fort Monroe.

Spread out in the Shenandoah Valley and the Fredericksburg area were approximately 75,000 federal troops under commands of Irvin McDowell and Nathaniel P. Banks, with Union general John C. Fremont having at least 17,000 effectives in the western mountains of Virginia. If combined, all of these elements would constitute a powerful army, a possibility not overlooked by Richmond. Contending against this danger were very modest Confederate General Joseph R. Anderson was stationed below the Rappahannock with 13,000 men guarding McDowell; Stonewall Jackson and his command of some 6,000 roamed the northern Shenandoah; around Staunton, Virginia, General Edward Johnson was posted with a contingency of 2,800 to observe Fremont; and Major General Richard Ewell with his force of 8,500, strategically situated in the Blue Ridge, was free to give assistance to Jackson in the west against Banks or throw his support to Anderson against McDowell.[15]

In this current capacity as military adviser to President Davis, General Lee was determined to prevent the consolidation of the Union commands in northern Virginia. Such an event would surely guarantee Richmond's fall by reinforcing McClellan's already formidable forces on the peninsula. Against this grim contingency, General Lee on May 1 authorized Stonewall Jackson's Shenandoah Valley campaign.[16] Actually Jackson had already started his attacks of harassment on March 23 at Kernstown. Several weeks later on May 8 he defeated Brigadier General Robert Milroy, who commanded Fremont advance forces. Striking decisively again — this time at Fort Royal and Strasburg on May 23–25 — the highly resourceful Confederate general, after subsequent successful sharp encounters at Cross Keys and Port Republic, was ready to terminate his campaign by joining Lee's command in Richmond. In Washington, observers of the fierce activity in the Shenandoah knew nothing for certain except that a Confederate army, whose size could only be guessed at but whose aggressive capability had already been demonstrated, had reached the Potomac.[17]

In the meantime, by May 27 McClellan had pushed his way up the peninsula to Fair Oaks; in other words, he was about ten miles east of Richmond. Despite his conviction that his numerical strength should be increased, Washington had repeatedly refused to move troops in that direction because of the many uncertainties created by Jackson's activities in the valley.

With heavy rains swelling the already high Chickahominy during the night on May 30, General Johnston became convinced that the turbulent storm conditions seriously compromised McCellan's position. Concluding that his adversary's bridges were temporarily out of use, the southern commander decided to attack. For McClellan this could have developed into a very awkward, if not dangerous, situation. He had deployed two-thirds of his army under the commands of General Erasmus C. Keyes and General S. P. Heintzelman south of the river. Keyes was responsible for a one-mile front running southward from Fair Oaks, at a point on the Richmond and York River Railroad, to the crossroads of Seven Pines. Heintzelman's two divisions were deployed several miles to the rear in a flanking position at White Oak Swamp and a key bridge on the Chickahominy, which accommodated the main road from Williamsburg. McClellan and corps commanders John Fitz Porter, William B. Franklin, and Edwin V. Sumner were all north of the river, comprising an entire front of fifteen miles.[18]

With rain continuing to fall, General Johnston on the morning of May 31 moved out to make contact with the enemy. Originally he had planned to emphasize his attack north of the river, hoping to defeat the wing of federal forces that presumably were planning to lock into place with McDowell's troops when they arrived. Learning that McDowell was marching northward to the Shenandoah Valley, Johnston revised his plans by striking at the weakest section of the federal front south of the river.

For the Confederates, what followed was havoc and confusion. Misunderstood orders and poorly trained staffs were only two of the principal factors that undermined what had been a sound and reasonable plan. General James Longstreet misdirected his forces into taking a wrong road, creating a roadblock that prevented Huger's division from taking up a position of combat. With Longstreet unable to place many of his brigades into action, the intended firepower failed to materialize; instead there occurred what one writer has called a "straight slugging match in which much of the Confederate advantage was unused."[19] Very surprisingly, during this contest General Sumner, by crossing a bridge dangerously near collapse, delivered his entire corps south

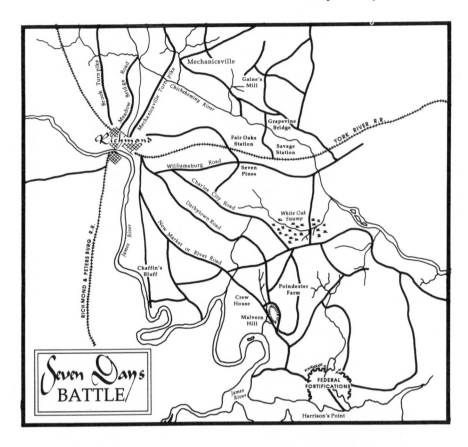

of the river to give strength to the faltering federal lines. Throughout the day a series of advances and retreats occurred on both sides, but at day's end, the Confederates seemed to have gained a great deal of ground — though at an alarmingly high price, which included the wounding of their ranking commanding officer, General Johnston. The incident occurred around sunset and afterwards, he was removed from the battle scene.

Early next morning the Confederates renewed their attack, hoping to sever McClellan's line of communications leading up the peninsula. Not only did they fail to attain this objective, but reverses on the field compelled them to abandon some of the ground gained on the previous day. Had plans and action been carried out successfully, they might have very well imposed a disastrous defeat upon McClellan's army. Instead, nearly everything went wrong, and the contest essentially ended in a draw.[20]

Nevertheless, the Battle of Seven Pines (or Fair Oaks, as it is also known) was certainly not without significance. At least one thing went right for the Confederates. During the heat of battle on June 1, President Davis appointed

Robert E. Lee commander of the Confederate Army of Northern Virginia. Casualty statistics indicated a willingness on the part of both sides to engage in any costly sanguinary ordeal which fate of circumstances might impose. Union losses stood around 5,000, with Confederates soaring up to 6,000.[21] This time, unlike Bull Run, there was little panic, but rather a kind of enlistment behavior generally associated with well-seasoned troops. Very importantly, although the southern army scored no higher that a draw in this battle, McClellan had been stopped in his peninsula campaign. Ending the final day of contest on June 1, Confederate troops retired to prepare defensive positions to await his next venture. However, having been thwarted in delivering what apparently was to have been a final blow in his campaign, McClellan would require more than three weeks to attempt another advance. The highly imaginative and resourceful Lee would use this time to great advantage, and the plans he would formulate would include a vital role for North Carolina troops.

Accompanying Holmes's entire command back to Virginia on June 20, Robert Ransom's brigade was comprised of the Twenty-fourth, Twenty-fifth, Twenty-sixth, Thirty-fifth, and Forty-ninth North Carolina regiments. During the Kinston assignment of standing guard against any menacing movement of Burnside, the brigade had taken on what might be described as an attitude of combat readiness, reinforced by the obvious proficiency of its officers. This transformation from raw recruits and newly commissioned officers into well-drilled and disciplined units was generally credited to the personal character and talents of General Robert Ransom, Jr. He was known as a strict disciplinarian — even as something of a tyrant by those who incurred his displeasure. If he had difficulty in his relations with other officers, it was quite possibly because their standards of conduct did not measure up to his.[22] At no time did Matt accept or receive special consideration or privileges; and, if the general seemed to overstress this principle, the colonel understood.

For Matt the long and largely monotonous journey terminating in the Petersburg-Richmond area offered time for thoughtful reflection on a number of serious topics. One highly troublesome matter involved General Burnside's future military movements. He might, as Lee speculated, move his forces up the James River against Drewry's Bluff.[23] However, if the Union commander should now decide to move inland into North Carolina from his present position at New Bern, he would encounter only faint, scattered resistance. The serious implications for the welfare of Pattie, the children, Verona, and friends and neighbors must have weighed heavily upon Ransom's mind. He might also have speculated on the as yet untested bond between himself and his men. All had gone well for Matt since taking command of the regiment and relations with both his staff and his troops were satisfactory. However, conditions that would try those relations were yet to be encountered. There still remained that critical moment when he would have to prove himself under enemy fire.

En route Matt gained information concerning the Battle of Seven Pines, now almost three weeks past. He learned, too, that a final struggle on the peninsula was in the making. In a few days he would learn greater details. News of a somewhat more personal nature included a report that James Johnston Pettigrew was wounded and captured in action around Seven Pines (subsequently, he would be exchanged and resume his military role). Just a short time ago, he and Matt had been students at the University of North Carolina, competing against one another for academic honors. Now they fought on the same side, but this time their very lives were at stake.

Arriving at Petersburg after an arduous, fatiguing journey of about 30 hours, the brigade soon learned that General Lee on June 21 had asked Holmes to procure the help of Ransom's brigade in action planned for the following week.[24] In response to this order, the last units of the brigade arrived east of Richmond during the early hours of June 25. Temporarily detached from General Holmes's command in order to provide extra strength to those limited forces defending the capital, the brigade now joined General Benjamin Huger's division on the Williamsburg Road.

During the day of the twenty-fifth, sharp clashes in the area occurred as a result of McClellan's probing attacks in preparation for a major advance. Carrying out these preliminary skirmishes, Union brigadier generals Philip Kearney and Joseph Hooker moved their forces through swamp and brush, stoutly resisted all the way, until they arrived that afternoon on a broad cleared field.[25] Here in front of them, they could see through drizzling rain freshly constructed Confederate breastworks. The subsequent sharp encounters at King's School House clearly indicated a strong Confederate determination to challenge the Union commander's strategy of regular advances. Toward evening General Lee arrived on the scene and ordered General Ransom's brigade to join in offensive action to take ground lost that morning. This accomplished, Matt's regiment along with others was detailed for night picket duty.

The day's local action, although comparatively modest in terms of involvement resulted in relatively heavy casualties, with Union losses at 516 and Confederate at 316.[26] Unknowingly and unwittingly, McClellan had struck at a drastically weakened Confederate line of defense. A determined assault could have overrun the line, with Richmond as a reward. Although McClellan might have overestimated his opponent's strength at this particular sector of the line, Generals Kearney and Hooker were not guilty of any such errors of judgment. Convinced Lee was involved in a plan of deception, they would have, if allowed, called his bluff. McClellan, however, was consistent in his inclination to exaggerate his enemy's strength. Standing before Richmond through most of June, he mustered 100,000 or more troops, believing himself outnumbered; he credited Lee's strength as 200,000, when in fact the Confederate commander could account for around 85,000 men.[27]

The thinly manned Confederate defense facing McClellan's overwhelming forces began at Chaffin's Bluff, crossing all major roads approaching Richmond in an eastern direction, and then connecting with the Chickahominy a short distance above New Bridge; thereafter it ran south of the river to Meadow Bridge. Within this defense perimeter east of the city Lee placed Major Generals Benjamin Huger and John B. Magruder. It was their job to portray themselves as having much stronger forces, and upon their performances rested the fate of Richmond. Having at their disposal only 25,000 effectives, of which Ransom's brigade was a part, they faced a foe able to muster at least 75,000 troops south of the Chickahominy; north of that stream a second part of the Union Army was stationed under General Porter with a force of 30,000.

Determined to extricate himself from his precarious situation, Lee decided to gamble by undertaking a counter-offensive. The ambitious plan he devised called for destruction of McClellan's Army of the Potomac. The dangerous risk of employing a limited number of combatants to protect Richmond was to be only for a brief period. Divisions of General D. H. Hill along with Longstreet's command would equal roughly 47,000 troops. These were to assemble near Mechanicsville, Virginia, to attack Union general Porter's smaller forces north of the Chickahominy. Also scheduled to join these assembled Confederate commands were the recently increased 15,500 effectives led by Stonewall Jackson, just returning from his victorious valley campaign. Jackson, in the coming strategy, was expected to envelop Porter's right flank, forcing him to abandon his fortified position and fight openly against superior numbers. By destroying this wing of the Union Army or by driving it across the river, Lee could also realize another major victory by seizing McClellan's supply line, the York River Railroad, which served the Union supply center located at White House on the peninsula.

As agreed upon by Lee and chief commanders, operations for the plan were to begin the morning of June 26. A cardinal principle of military science prescribes that one should never allow an opponent to engage in his own strategy of attack under conditions of his choice. General Lee intended to apply this maxim to its full extent. Willing to take great risks in exchange for victories, he was equally committed to seeking caution at every opportunity. Before undertaking the coming attack, he had dispatched Brigadier General J. E. B. Stuart with his 1,200 cavalry contingent on a scouting and harassment mission, encircling McClellan's army and returning to safety of Richmond's defenses on June 15. Vital information sought by the expedition included details of the Union right flank and what kind of protection was afforded to McClellan's supply route on the Richmond and York River Railroad.

By 3:00 A.M. on June 26, Jackson's troops should have been assembling around Ashland, Virginia, preparing to attack Porter's right flank in concert with A. P. Hill's frontal assault. Actually, Jackson was at least six hours behind schedule, and his men did not resume their march until 10:00 that morning. His patience taxed to the limits, A. P. Hill waited until 3:00 P.M., then ordered an attack in anticipation of Stonewall's arrival. Moving his five brigades through Mechanicsville, he then advanced about a mile to Beaver Dam Creek, and there he was repulsed by deadly artillery and rifle fire from Porter's entrenched forces.

Still hoping to salvage some semblance of success for the day, Lee, around 7:00 that evening, ordered General Roswell S. Ripley's brigade from D. H. Hill's division to cross the Chickahominy and attack the federal left flank. Those who managed to make the crossing found themselves too few in numbers to overcome their enemy's position, and by this time the darkness prevailed.

Though his army had fallen considerably short of the victory for which Lee had hoped, their failure was due not to a flaw in his plan, but rather to poor performance by subordinates in their assigned roles. Jackson never arrived to complete his important mission in the day's engagement. Rather than driving Porter's troops out of their entrenchments and forcing them to take to the open, the Confederates delivered a sustained frontal attack, the very kind of operation which was to be avoided if at all possible. During this day of confrontation known as the Battle of Mechanicsville, the federals suffered 361 casualties, compared to Confederate losses of 1,484.[28]

Ordered to retire, General Porter took up a new position at Gaines' Mill on Boatswain Swamp. Lee's attack on June 27 involved virtually the same plan as the day before, calling for Jackson to flank Porter's right at which time D. H. Hill would be involved in the frontal assault, with Longstreet taking a position in front of the federal left. At last Jackson arrived, but due to his lack of knowledge of the area and his inaccurate maps, he became lost while attempting to take up a position. He was forced to backtrack, consuming valuable time and forcing General A. P. Hill once again to conduct a frontal attack against a well-entrenched enemy without effective assistance from coordinate units. This time, Hill pounded away at his extremely able foe for over five hours. Finally, around 7:00, Lee ordered a general assault, which resulted in Porter's line finally breaking near the center. This breakthrough occurred as the Confederates were about to resort to bayonets; particularly effective was the sudden musket activity of Brigadier General John B. Hood's brigade, which had withheld its firepower during the earlier advance. Under partial shelter of darkness, the federals retreated across the Chickahominy. At a high price in human life and suffering, Gaines' Mill was a victory for Lee, his first. In this contest, twenty North Carolina regiments were involved.[29] Union casualties were 6,837, with Confederate loss at 8,750.[30] This engagement having unnerved McClellan, he complained in a letter dispatched to his superiors in Washington, "I have lost this battle because my force was too small." Thus far, only one of his five corps had been effectively engaged in combat operations, and these troops performed well.[31]

While the present campaign on the peninsula had failed to produce any decisive results, at least the Confederates were now entitled to new hopes that

Richmond was being delivered from Union capture. For Matt and his regiment, June 27 was another day of testing their stamina while applying continued pressure against a retreating enemy. By this time General Huger's advance forces had pushed to within a half-mile of the federal's rear defenses at Seven Pines. As Ransom and his men moved into their assigned positions, remnants of the Battle of Seven Pines were everywhere in evidence. From swampy bottom land arose repelling odors from decaying human and animal bodies, made worse by unrelenting heat and humidity.

North and east of Richmond the land becomes flat, with gently rolling features interrupted by swamps and marshes. From the standpoint of military strategy, the Chickahominy River is probably the most important terrain feature as it winds through areas of low elevation, becoming very difficult to cross in rainy weather. Between this stream and the James River lies White Oak Swamp, another difficult area that during the hostilities of June 1862 had been made more forbidding by heavy rainfall. While the fighting in this area had taken on dramatic qualities of suspense there was yet another front giving General Lee great concern.

Knowing full well that his military presence in Virginia was closely tied to the fortunes of North Carolina, Lee carefully monitored developments within that state. Greatly concerned that Burnside might attempt a renewed inland invasion, including capture of Goldsboro, the Confederate commander, since the first day of the current series of battles, had dispatched each evening a telegram to General James G. Martin at Kinston: "Any movements of the enemy in your front today?"[32] Undoubtedly General Lee was as relieved as the North Carolinians to learn that on June 28 Burnside had been ordered to give assistance to Union forces on the peninsula. With only a limited number of federal troops now occupying New Bern, Burnside's absence reduced considerably, at least for the moment, the possibilities of a renewed federal initiative in this sector.

For McClellan, who by now deeply feared that his army was placed in extreme jeopardy, decisions were required.[33] With General Porter now withdrawn from his position on the Chickahominy, and his army in disarray, McClellan's main base of supplies on the Pamunkey River at White House was dangerously exposed. Even before Gaines' Mill he had been convinced of the need to change his supply base. Although no military action of any consequence occurred on June 28, McClellan's army was greatly occupied in transferring military stores and goods on 5,000 heavily laden wagons destined for a new depot as Harrison's Landing on the James River. (In this move, McClellan was compelled to forego the Richmond and York River Railroad. Since the heavy weight of his siege guns required rail and water transport, Richmond's defenses were spared these giant weapons punishment.) Convinced that forces were outnumbered, the Union commander now issued an order, as yet unknown to Lee, to retreat to Harrison's Landing. To General Porter, he assigned the task of selecting a practical site where the terrain offered the best defense for retreating Union contingents. This highly competent Union officer, upon arriving at the foot of Malvern Hill and viewing its summit, very understandably concluded that it would be an ideal place to meet a contender.

By the evening of June 28 General Lee resolved to move with decisive force against his opponent. His uncanny military instinct told him that McClellan might be moving his troops toward the James, and if so , the Confederates might be able to attack with destructive force en route.[34] From the Williamsburg road, Magruder's troops were to attack the rear of the Union forces. Jackson's role was to apply unrelenting pressure at the rear, and to provide extra assistance, he would be joined by D. H. Hill's division. A. P. Hill's and Longstreet's divisions were ordered to strike out in a southwestern direction with the intention of intercepting Union forces at White Oak Swamp, ideally cutting off their retreat, or short of this, delivering a devastating flanking assault.[35]

Lee designated the early morning of June 29 as the start of his grand strategy; that which followed proved to be another day of confusion, delay, and frustration. Huger's division had just established a steady marching pace when they received a message from Magruder asking Huger to protect his right, as Magruder was battling a large Union force in his front.[36] General Huger was reluctant to comply with this request; it meant halting his division, and this he wished to avoid. In the end, however, he overcame his objections and came to the aid of a troubled officer whose judgment was highly questionable. To those alert and qualified officers in Huger's command, what followed must have been almost unbearable. Hours of waiting ensued, while incredibly, up ahead, the enemy continued its unhindered retreat. At last, orders arrived instructing the division to proceed on the Charles City Road, but by then, the federals had gained a substantial head start. As for Magruder, after cautiously advancing near the site of the Battle of Seven Pines, he had halted his forces and begun setting up a defensive position in anticipation of an overwhelming enemy attack. These decisions were wrongheaded from beginning to end, and only after hours of delay and at Lee's insistence did the overly imaginative divisional commander order a general attack in which he employed only two and a half of six brigades. His intended advance sputtered near Savage's Station.[37]

Lee's inability to impose a devastating assault during the Battle of Savage's Station rested again upon his subordinates' noncompliance. D. H. Hill and his forces, temporarily under the command of Jackson, failed to become involved in operations when the latter confined his activities to repairing Grapevine Bridge and crossing the Chickahominy on the following morning. Longstreet and A. P. Hill crossed the river, but so far north that the planned efficiency of their attack was lost.[38]

Even J. E. B. Stuart was subject to some degree of criticism concerning events of the twenty-ninth. He and his unit on this day hastily pillaged federal inventories at White House, rather than carrying out a much-needed intelligence mission. Meanwhile, the slow and overly cautious movements of Huger and Magruder, particularly the latter, profoundly affected the outcome of Savage's Station, allowing Union combatants an opportunity of continued escape to the James River.

June 30 offered no improvements in coordinating efforts among Confederate field officers. General Huger's progress on the Charles River Road was measured only by whatever success he had in removing fallen trees and other debris left on the road by yesterday's retreating federals. As Matt Ransom and his men labored at this agonizing task, there were many other reasons for frustration, including the realization that plans for implementing the day's attack were hopelessly behind schedule. Magruder continued to vacillate, and at White Oak Swamp, Jackson's conduct remained slow and indecisive.

As the regiments floundered on the narrow, abandoned country road, thoughtful minds in Ransom's brigade, must have perceived that they should instead have been moving into a position to support Longstreet and A. P. Hill, who had been locked in valiant and critical contest with General George A. McCall's division since around four o'clock that afternoon.[39] During that engagement's initial stage, the Confederates seemed to have scored with considerable success, breaking the federal line and even capturing General McCall, who was inspecting a forward position. Union generals Kearney, Hooker, and Sedgwick had quickly closed the gap, and the fierce fighting, including hand-to-hand combat, continued into the night. This was the Battle of Frayser's Farm, and when it was concluded, the Union line remained intact, thus virtually insuring McClellan's escape by way of Malvern Hill and thence to Harrison's Landing. Although the Confederates held possession of much of the contested area, once again Lee was forced to settle for a partial victory. D. H. Hill summed up the bloody confrontation as having "been a gallant fight ... but as an obstruction to the Federal retreat ... [it] amounted to nothing."[40] As for the federal army's intent to seek shelter at Harrison's Landing, the last remaining impediment to this object was swept aside. Confederate general Theophilus Holmes had been ordered to take his force of 6,000, accompanied by cavalry and artillery, to assume a position along the James and then employ tactics of delay against retiring federal troops. Exposed to some demonstration of federal firepower he finally got his artillery in place just as the last of McClellan's wagons rolled by.[41]

That night, June 30, a tired and pensive Matt Ransom bivouacked with his regiment at White Oak Swamp. He would have been more distraught had he known of General Lee's order that evening withdrawing General James G. Martin's brigade from Kinston to Virginia. Incredibly, the only troops stationed in North Carolina after this last withdrawal were two infantry regiments, one of cavalry, and three of artillery. The other forty-seven state regiments were on duty in Virginia.[42]

During the early dawn hours of July 1, 1862, in the heat and heavy humidity of this mosquito-infested area, Matt's Thirty-fifth got under way, accompanied by other regiments of the brigade. Orders of the day were the same as yesterday's: Pursue the enemy! Arriving where Longstreet and A. P. Hill had been engaged with the federals the day before, Ransom was appalled by the ghastly sight and stench of bodies and limbs strewn over the area, sometimes piled like cordwood in heaps. He heard the agonized moans of survivors pleading for relief and assistance. Battle litter of all kinds, including abandoned artillery pieces, picks and shovels, and knapsacks, covered the landscape. This was by far the most grotesque scene Matt had witnessed since taking up his Richmond duties.

That morning a meeting was held between Jackson, Magruder, and Huger near Glendale.[43] Meanwhile, during the previous night, four Union corps had taken up strong defensive positions at Malvern Hill, with McClellan's remaining corps under General Erasmus C. Keyes occupying Harrison's Landing about seven miles to the rear on the James.

According to Union strategy, one more stand involving rearguard action was necessary before falling back to the relative safety of Harrison's Landing. Preparations for this final stand on Malvern Hill were, for the most part, complete by the morning of July 1. Malvern Hill offered an excellent position, crowned as it was by a plateau of about one mile in width from which one had extended sight in every direction.[44] In front, the ground was of gentle decline, almost cleared, and apparently under cultivation. Extending behind these open grounds at the foot, the terrain was heavily timbered, laced with thick bush mired in swamp. Only one road made its way through the forest, and any challenging army would be compelled to organize its units for attack on open ground within convenient range of federal artillery. But using natural land features to their best advantage and by concentrating his powerful forces of artillery and infantry within the protection of earth works, McClellan had attained an almost invincible military position.[45] His right flank was covered by a creek, and his left was securely protected by federal gunboats on the James. The extremely talented federal colonel Henry Hunt was intrusted with setting up an artillery defensive pattern atop the hill. Batteries of mostly Parrott guns, deadly effective when massed, were extended with unusual expertise across the entire front; joining such weaponry were batteries of bronzed Napoleons, used as anti-personnel fire. To guard the area on the road's right side stood a repelling battery of thirty-two-pounder Howitzers. Not to be overlooked were fourteen siege guns, which included four-and-one-half-inch Rodman rifles, eight-inch Howitzers, thirty-pounder Parrotts, and two long-ranged ten-pounder Whitworths.[46]

With four-fifths of the Army of the Potomac defensively deployed before him, Lee briefly reviewed possibilities of a left flanking movement, hoping to place himself between Malvern Hill and Harrison's Landing. He quickly rejected the plan, for obvious reasons. The heavily wooded area in the midst of swampland had few passable places, rendering swift troop movements extremely difficult, if not impossible. Furthermore, recent operations requiring the Confederate commanders to act in concert had hardly produced impressive results. Referring to his record, Lee observed that McClellan would "get away because I cannot have my orders carried out."[47]

Before arriving at any final plan of attack, Lee dispatched Longstreet on a reconnaissance mission. Around noon the assignment was completed, and a report was delivered. Yes, Longstreet concluded, Malvern Hill was "formidable." However, it might be captured with effective employment of artillery fire by the Confederates. Longstreet's formula called for highly concentrated artillery near the Crew house on the right, and the Poindexter farm on the left. This arrangement, he hoped, would place the enemy batteries on the hill's summit in an intense crossfire. Once a number of federal guns had been neutralized and their lines of infantry exposed to shot and shell, a bold and determined Confederate charge might prevail.[48]

General Lee's orders for an attack clearly indicate that he agreed with Longstreet concerning the role of artillery. Consequently, no all-out assault was to occur until Brigadier General Lewis A. Armistead, stationed where he could watch the firepower and gauge its effect, signaled for a charge.[49] By three o'clock in the afternoon the charge had not yet taken place — not because Lee had changed his orders, but because the artillery success that was to precede the charge had so far proved unattainable.[50] Moving Confederate gunnery into favorable positions met with a number of problems. A host of terrain barriers blocked their way, and the few weapons which were put in place were almost immediately shattered by Union guns.[51] Lack of success in this effort may have caused Lee to consider again the possibilities of a flanking movement, and before returning to the center of his line, he ordered Longstreet to move his forces to the left.

It was between 2:00 and 3:00 when Matt was ordered to move his regiment down Quaker Road and take up a position in General Huger's line on the Confederate extreme right flank about one and a quarter miles from the action.[52] The ground where they settled bordered a belt of woods and a small stream. Here they stayed for several hours, during which the brigade was initiated in the battle by intermittent exploding shells.

Late in the afternoon, D. H. Hill, accompanied by several brigade commanders, went forward to inspect results of Confederate artillery action. He regarded the intended results as "almost farcical," and finding the firing had been, hopelessly inaccurate, he and his entourage began returning to their positions, believing no order would be given for a general attack.[53] Then suddenly on the right, one or two brigades rushed forward from out of the woods, shouting and firing weapons. According to young Lieutenant Colonel Henry King Burgwyn, Jr., who was present at the scene, these charging troops were in Magruder's command.[54] And, indeed, they were. The general had ordered his attack at a quarter to five, sending his troops into an area of the Crew House, a point McClellan considered invulnerable. By no means was General D. H. Hill the only officer who believed the sudden action on his right by Margruder was the decided-upon signal for mounting a full attack. To his officers he shouted, "That must be the general advance. Bring up your brigades as soon as possible and join in."[55] The Battle of Malvern Hill was about to begin in earnest.

As he helped direct Union defenses atop the hill, General Porter viewed events of that frightful afternoon as another Southern "reckless disregard of life equal to that displayed at Gaines' Mill, [where] with determination to capture our army or destroy it by driving us into the river, brigade after brigade rushed our batteries."[56] The persistent waves of attackers were caught up in blasts of devastating shrapnel, grape, and canister; those who miraculously survived, General Porter observed, were met with deadly weltering infantry fire.

The time had arrived when events of telling consequences were about to overtake Matt's regiment and brigade. The Forty-ninth, formerly attached to the brigade, had been reassigned because a bad relationship had developed between its commanding officer and General Robert Ransom; otherwise, all other units were present. All told, the number of effectives in the brigade that afternoon was about 3,000.[57] Around 5:00 a messenger arrived from Magruder requesting assistance in the current action. This General Ransom refused; instead he solicited instructions from his immediate superior, General Huger. This conduct of refusal was approved in Huger's reply. Within a half-hour, a second request arrived, and this time General Ransom correctly replied that any orders to him "must come through General Huger.[58]

By now the battle had reached a pitch of intensity throughout the line. Magruder's third request for aid arrived at 7:00, and because of its desperate tone, Ransom responded by ordering Colonel William J. Clark's Twenty-fourth forward. After receiving somewhat clarifying instructions, he ordered the entire brigade to advance preparatory to taking up a position on Magruder's active front. Colonel Clark's regiment had already moved ahead, followed first by Colonel Henry M. Ruthledge and then by Colonel Matt Ransom. Colonels Stephen D. Ramseur and Zebulon Vance were then sent at double-quick time to the battle front, and as these units arrived, General Magruder immediately ordered them into action.[59]

Matt advanced in front of his men with sword drawn, standard-bearers directly behind him hoisting the Stars and Bars and a beautiful recently designed state flag. In this moment Matt was allotted only a brief survey of the vast panoramic scene before him. Accounts he had read concerning battles of antiquity or even describing worst conjured-up details of Hades itself, failed to surpass what he was now witnessing. Literally thousands of men were locked in mortal combat; in a few hours 8,000 of them, by injury or death, would become statistics of carnage on this day.[60] Pressing forward "under as fearful fire as the mind can conceive," Matt encountered his first wound when a rifle bullet struck his right forearm.[61] Dazed and in partial shock, his wounded arm useless, Matt insisted on remaining in the front, to direct the regiment's progress up the hill. Then, after a few minutes, a piece of shell ripped through his right side, forcing him to the ground. Pain was immediate, and bleeding profuse. While lying on the ground, the wounded commander called for his lieutenant colonel, Oliver Cromwell Petway, and instructed him to take command. As he lay there helpless, not knowing the extent of his injuries, Matt received word that Petway had been mortally wounded.

With courage and determination as their only allies, members of the brigade, following Matt's misfortune, edged slowly up the incline. Soon, however enemy fire became so intense that the first three regiments, including Matt's, were forced to fall back under some hills for protection.[62] At this point General Ransom arrived with Ramseur's and Vance's regiments. By placing them to the right he created a line of the brigade approximately 200 yards away from enemy batteries. Around twilight the brigade was ready to attempt another advance. This time the line apparently undetected, reached a point less than 100 yards from the federal batteries, and here a loud shout went up from the charging Confederates. Quickly the federals wheeled around and met their attackers with "a perfect sheet of fire from musketry and the batteries."[63] Only about twenty yards from the federal guns, the brigade was again repulsed, and forced to fall back "before a fire the intensity of which is beyond description."[64] At seven o'clock, General Ransom withdrew the brigade to its earlier position. Here the men remained until after 10:00; at that time the entire brigade was ordered from the field, but possibly through lack of communications, some elements remained in place until morning. Most of these were inexperienced soldiers whose regiments had only been formed a few weeks before.[65] Of their performance, General Ransom offered nothing less than the highest praise.

Of all the regiments, Matt Ransom's probably suffered the highest casualties.[66] The brigade's total losses at Malvern Hill were 69 killed, 354 wounded and 76 missing.[67]

While the southern objective of destroying the Army of the Potomac was not realized, in Richmond there was little doubt the Confederacy had earned great victories throughout the series of Seven Days' Battles. The threat to the capital had been resolved. McClellan's peninsula offensive had been shattered and thousands of federal prisoners taken. Fifty-two artillery pieces, along with 35,000 stands of small arms and other vast supplies, had come into Confederate possession. There was, of course, a high price for these favorable results.

Confederate losses for the entire campaign stood at 3,286 men killed, 15,090 wounded, and between 900 to 1,000 considered missing; all told, roughly 20,000 casualties were involved. Federal losses were comparatively less: 1,734 killed, 8,062 wounded, and a staggering number of 6,053 missing in action, which included prisoners and wounded.[68]

Following the battle of Malvern Hill, McClellan was unquestionably disinclined to renew an all-out assault upon Richmond. Lee, on his part, because of bad weather conditions and other substantive factors, chose not to carry out major operations on the James River. The old West Point refrain melodically contends that "old soldiers never die, they just fade away," but this does not preclude the possibility that old soldiers can be led out to early pasture. In Washington City, Lincoln was looking for a replacement of McClellan. Meanwhile, three Southern major generals following the peninsula campaign were compelled to bid adieu to the Army of Northern Virginia. General Magruder received an assignment in Texas, and General Huger became Inspector of Artillery and Ordnance. General Holmes, North Carolina's ranking general, also was sent to the Department of the Trans-Mississippi. Jackson was neither sacked nor demoted. Lee could only hope his strange and singular subordinate would again, under better days and circumstances, rise to the level of his brilliant past performances.

Chapter VI

Increasing Prospects
for a Long War

Among the benefits available to wounded soldiers during the summer following the peninsula campaign were the medical and surgical services provided
by dedicated professionals of Chimborazo Hospital in Richmond. This huge
medical complex, one of the largest of its kind, would eventually take on a capacity for 6,000 beds, and a staff of physicians, surgeons, attendants, and admin-
istrators under the able direction of Doctor James B. McCaw.[1]

The fortunate convalescents, who had secured furloughs or permanent dis-
charges made their way, despite their physical handicaps, inside and outside the
Richmond train station, where crowds milled about, hoping to secure transportation. Following recent engagements east of the capital the sight of amputes
in these crowds was becoming more commonplace. Taking leave of these scenes,
Matt Ransom, with his injured side bandaged and his arm in a sling, set out for
North Carolina.

The military lifestyle to which Matt had so quickly adjusted was in complete contrast to the quiet restful environment at Verona. Home for care and
treatment of his wounds, he would rely upon a formula of recovery which
promised the best attainable results. This involved a resumption, however temporary, of a role he valued in the highest sense: being an affectionate husband
and father to his young, growing family. Matt, Jr., now seven, and five-year-
old Joe were completely overcome with excitement over their father's return.
Questions and more questions they asked about the war, and more would have
been forthcoming had not their mother intervened. Under a kinder fate, a third
child would have been present; an infant daughter, Martha, had recently suc-
cumbed to illness and been laid to rest in an area that would become the family cemetery, approximately one hundred yards from the house. Greatly her parents mourned her death, and even during moments of extreme peril in military
combat, Matt's thoughts would turn to the child he had lost.[2]

In July and August the land along the Roanoke River in Northhampton
County can be most inhospitable and unpleasant, marked by extreme heat and
humidity and enormous plagues of insects, especially mosquitoes. Nevertheless,

farmers must carry out their crop-tending operations to complete another year's harvest. Southerners have long since learned to adjust to prevailing environmental conditions. Very simply, they have mastered the technique of pacing themselves.

At Verona, Matt followed a relaxed schedule. His wounds steadily healing, he was allowed some enjoyable moments inspecting his farms and talking to the hands who worked the crops. During the cooler hours of the mornings, he spent time in letter-writing and reading. Physical features inside and outside the house made his environment as comfortable as possible by providing access to circulating breezes, accommodated by large rooms with vaulted ceilings and spacious swinging windows stretching almost from floor to ceiling. The kitchen was a separate building to the house's rear, sparing the main structure the heat generated by cooking.

Conditions outside Verona's tranquil setting varied widely that summer, but in one way or another, all were related to the war. Reports from Wilmington credited many deaths to an epidemic of yellow fever in the area. The disease was believed to have arrived with a blockade-running ship from Nassau whose infected crew members disembarked and used public facilities, thus initiating the local pestilence. In a matter of weeks, deaths reached as high as eighteen a day, with at least five hundred reported cases. One observer described an old battered hearse, drawn by a lean, worn horse, making its way down a street, the driver "a young colored man leaning over, too sick to hold the reins, and before the setting of another sun he was laid by the side of many of his fellow men."[3]

Aside from the grim realities of an epidemic, Wilmington, with its good harbor effectively defended, was rapidly earning a reputation for "the best blockaded ports."[4] A good way to understand the importance of blockade running might be to consider, at least in part, the cargo of a ship engaged in this enterprise. The *Modern Greece*, a large transport of around one-thousand tons, arrived on the night of June 26, 1862, a few miles off Fort Fisher, a major facility protecting Wilmington's harbor. (Being a larger vessel, she was not a typical blockade runner, but she was joined by others of her class and many smaller craft which served as willing and able accomplices.) Her cargo included 1,000 tons of powder, spirits, clothing, 650 small rifles, and 4 Whitworth rifles of 12-pound caliber. Whitworths were treasured items of warfare; a historian describes them as "not round, but octagonal having a twist throughout the length of the gun," with a five-mile range.[5] Early next morning, around four o'clock, the *Modern Greece* made a quick dash inland, but because of two federal cruisers in effective pursuit, she was compelled to beach herself. Although the ship was a total loss, much of her valuable cargo was salvageable.[6]

Less sobering than the epidemic and perhaps not so exciting as the exploits of blockade runners, an event in early August was nonetheless of great importance. Newspapers reported a sweeping victory by Zebulon Vance for the state governorship. In the counties he carried a total of 46, 756 votes to his opponent's 16,452, and he won the service vote on almost a two-to-one margin.[7] The governor-elect was formally sworn into office on September 8. In his inaugural address, concerning the current war, Vance pleaded, "On this great issue of resistance...let there, I pray you, be no dissenting voice in our borders."[8] In reality, however, Vance was requesting North Carolinians to abstain from a kind of conduct in which he himself indulged. His dissension in matters relating to Confederate officials was perhaps more frequent and more intense than that of any other southern governor. A strong Unionist before the start of war, Vance had taken his message to churches and street corners, where he begged citizens to "keep North Carolina in the Union! Let it not follow the example of other Southern states." Following Lincoln's election, the future governor remained a primary advocate of Unionism.[9]

Frustration and anger characterized much of North Carolina's public mood at this time, largely the result of being forced to adjust to the demands of war. How were North Carolina soldiers on meager limited government allowances going to support families already below subsistence level? The troops themselves were now confronted with critical shortages of shoes and clothing. The railroads, even at this early stage of the war, were showing serious signs of deterioration. With slightly less than 900 miles of tracks in the state, and with no new roads being built in the Confederacy after 1861, the future looked grim for this mode of transport. Ultimately the average speed of passenger trains would be reduced to ten or even five miles an hour; indeed, on the worst passages even the latter speed was regarded as a risk.[10]

Residents of the state's eastern counties were also legitimately concerned about the ever-present threat of Yankee plundering. Most notorious of the raiders were the "Buffaloes," native Union bushwackers engaged in terrorizing the countryside. During August 1862 this group confiscated a country estate above Edenton on the Chowan River. Soon this center became a refuge for runaways slaves, lawless whites, and Confederate deserters. In time, but none too soon for area residents, the Forty-second North Carolina Regiment would set the torch to this encampment.[11] Although some measure of relief resulted from this event, frightening raids and murder continued in this unfortunate region.

One of the most disquieting issues was North Carolinians' belief that in the current struggle their state was being required to assume a far greater burden than any other states in the Confederacy. When casualty statistics became public knowledge, citizens of North Carolina reacted with amazement, often followed by anger. In the recent peninsula campaign, North Carolina had suffered some 23 percent (about 3,800) of the total number of Confederate casualties. This was 35 percent in excess of the losses sustained by Georgia, the southern state with the next highest casualties, and 60 percent in excess of Virginia's.[12] In the minds of skeptics there was further evidence that Confederate authorities were unfairly biased toward North Carolina. At the apex of the Confederate military command were seven full generals. Not one of these was a North Carolinian. Out of nineteen lieutenant generals, the state could only claim two. North Carolina was limited to eight major generals and twenty-six brigadier generals; Georgia, which supplied fewer troops, was given thirty-six commissions of the latter rank.[13]

The intentions of those designing the emerging Confederate government were unmistakably clear. Presiding over this government was Jefferson Davis, former champion of state rights; he now found, since taking over his new post, that the most stringent nationalist policies were compatible with the recently established Confederate government. In the current military struggle, he recognized that the Confederacy required powerful central rule in order to effectively marshall its resources, already so heavily outweighed by those of the Union. Like his counterpart in Washington, Davis was willing to exert whatever power was necessary. This ruled out entirely the possibility that the rights of any state or citizen might interfere with the war effort.[14]

Whatever the local conditions during the summer months of 1862, the war front dominated the entire scene. Following the peninsula campaign during July and August, General Ransom's brigade was involved in construction of fortifications at Drewry's Bluff and trenches around Petersburg. Large numbers of troops and over a thousand slaves, mostly from North Carolina, were employed in this extensive project.[15] All of this activity was carried out in anticipation of a future Union threat south of the James River.

Early August witnessed the final withdrawals of McClellan's army from Harrison's Landing as it prepared to return to Alexandria, where it would join the forces of General John Pope, newly appointed commander of the Federal Army of Virginia. Union withdrawal and evacuation from the James brought on increased tension between Lee and D. H. Hill. Appointed on July 17 as commander of the Department of North Carolina, which also included an area from Cape Fear up to Drewry's Bluff on James, Hill was directed to hinder, damage, and even (if possible) destroy any river communications serving McClellan's army.[16] To have fulfilled such a Herculean task would have required resources of a magnitude not at Hill's disposal. This, however, was not the assessment of General Lee, who on August 17 requested the termination of Hill's current assignment.[17] President Davis complied by reassigning the remarkable North Carolina general to command of his old division. Leaving Petersburg on August 21, destined to join Lee's forces in Northern Virginia, he was about to add new fame to an already illustrious record.

Chastising subordinates is only a small part of the overall performance of senior officers, who are called upon to judge far weightier matters. Right or wrong, Robert E. Lee was at this time making crucial and highly involved decisions. Obviously ruling out any possibility of a renewed local federal offensive, he left only a limited number of brigades to defend Richmond as he began to move his forces northward into the valley. The first of these troops, under

Jackson, moved out on August 7, followed by A. P. Hill's division. Within two days Jackson arrived at Cedar Mountain near Culpeper, Virginia, and there encountered and overwhelmed federal troops before falling back on Gordonsville. Subsequent successes scored by Lee's army during the remainder of August revived many southerners' hopes of ultimate victory. Not since the start of hostilities had there been such optimism in the seceded states.

In contrast to their performances during the peninsula campaign, southern field commanders were about to demonstrate a high degree of proficiency in complying with orders in a well-coordinated, synchronized manner. Jackson had apparently recovered his superb qualities of military command. Emerging from Thoroughfare Gap, he proceeded to Bristol Station and from there to Manassas Junction, where he smashed General Pope's supply base. Groveton, which lay five miles northwest of Manassas, was his next objective, and here he encou r-tered heavy enemy resistance. On August 29, under extreme pressure, he resisted Pope's determined attacks but by this time relief had arrived with Lee, A. P. Hill, Longstreet, and Stuart joining in the fray. Pope, who had also been reinforced with troops of the recent peninsula campaign, struck at his foes again on August 30. Unable to assail Longstreet with sufficient force, the federal commander found himself the object of an all-out Confederate unified attack which swept him from his positions. From a practical standpoint, the Second Battles of Manassas and Bull Run ended on this day. The forthcoming southern victory at Chantilly would end Lee's campaign against Pope. Because of his tarnished record of defeats, this Union officer was relieved of his command on September 5, and against strong objections within his cabinet, Lincoln reappointed McClellan to command a reunited Army of the Potomac. Union casualties between August 16 through September 2 stood at 16,843 as compared to the Confederates' 9,112.[18]

Having no serious intentions of capturing Washington, General Lee gave his attention to more practical tactical objectives, such as severing the B&O Railroad and ideally the Pennsylvania; disruption of these communications would have the effect of isolating the Union capital. His initial plan included a possible advance of his army northward between the Catoctin and South mountains, posing a threat to Harrisburg, Pennsylvania. Operations such as these were in accord with the southern commander's disclosures in an earlier letter to President Davis. As concerned the summer and fall of 1862, the Confederacy could not "afford to be idle," Lee insisted. He further stated that, although the northern states were stronger in numbers of men and arms, the South "must endeavor to harass if we cannot destroy them."[19] A strategy of harassment was hardly a new concept in military science. It had long been a popular subject among academic theorists, and had actually been applied on occasions. But the concept almost always raises the question of how many wars have been won by employing only tactics of harassment. One hardly needs the mind of a Clausewitz to understand the serious implications of being unable to deliver a knockout blow to an opposing army. Armies that have received temporary setbacks on the field, without being permanently disabled, have a way of coming back for renewed engagements. On the peninsula the federal army, though tactically defeated, had pulled back in force, taking up something of an invincible shelter at Harrison's Landing. With the Second Battle of Bull Run, they had apparently repeated this performance.

If harassment was to be a vital component in Lee's current tactics he reasoned there was no better way to harass his adversary than to cross the Potomac and sample some of that alleged Maryland hospitality. Lee entertained no plans of establishing himself militarily in the North, and neither Baltimore nor any other metropolitan center was included among his objectives. Conditions of his army prevented any such ventures. Many of his troops were shoeless, ragged, and on limited rations, giving the appearance of an army of beggars. But, very importantly, apart from the plan of harassment, there were at least two compelling reasons to put this southern army on Maryland soil. First Virginia would be provided with a much-needed respite. Secondly, Lee always kept sight of the possibility that with his presence in Maryland, federal troops would be compelled to abandon their Washington defenses and come out fighting. Within the ensuing contest was the tantalizing prospect of a truly decisive victory, the kind of undisputed triumph that he had sought without success since his costly win at Gaines' Mill.[20]

Interestingly enough, the Maryland venture to which Lee attached so much importance almost failed to become a reality. On the eve of this upcoming campaign three of the highest ranking Confederate generals were contending with serious physical handicaps brought on by accidents or conditions of health. General Lee, as a result of a fall during combat on the last day August, suffered from a broken bone in one hand, and the other was badly bruised. With splints on both hands, handling a mount was out of the question, so an ambulance became his temporary mode of transportation. Jackson was assigned the same type of vehicle. He was recovering from back injuries incurred when his new mount reared and fell backwards upon its distinguished rider. Longstreet, who had come down with an infected raw blister on his heel, would be compelled to cross the river with the afflicted foot dressed in a carpet slipper.[21]

Having intently followed events in northern Virginia, Matt Ransom now anticipated further military conduct in which his regiment would be involved, Though not fully recovered from his wounds, he resolved to rejoin his unit at the earliest possible date. Accordingly, he accompanied his regiment on August 27 when he left Richmond, headed north to join Lee's army. The Twenty-sixth Regiment had been transferred to Pettigrew's brigade and its place taken by the Fifty-sixth North Carolina. The brigade of Robert Ransom, Jr., now consisted of the Twenty-fourth, Twenty-fifth, Thirty-fifth, Forty-ninth, and Fifty-sixth North Carolina regiments.[22] For the campaign ahead the brigade would be under the division command of Brigadier General J. G. Walker.

Matt's regiment reached the Potomac on September 7 and waded across at

Check's Ford, where the stream is waist deep and about a quarter of a mile wide. As the men set foot on Maryland soil, they were impelled to give the rebel yell. Marching to the Monocay River, they received orders to return to an earlier point of their march and blow up an aqueduct over a canal. On September 11, they re-crossed the Potomac at Point of Rock and subsequently occupied Loudon Heights, from which point their batteries could shell the federals at Harpers Ferry.[23]

On the evening of the eleventh after recrossing the river, Ransom's men and the other brigade units settled down for their usual meager rations. After their meal, as was their practice, they assembled around campfires for smoking and socializing, and when somebody volunteered his talents with a harmonica, many joined earnestly in the old ballads and spirituals. Others found their way to storytelling and joke sessions that continued long into darkness. Whatever such entertainment might lack in quality or style, it made up for in the relief it provided to the minds and hearts of very lonely men compelled to exist on the barest necessities under the proud title of the Army of Northern Virginia. So scarce was food that troops on extended marches relied upon green corn and wild fruits and berries for sustenance. In appearance, these soldiers bore little resemblance to the personnel of well-maintained armies. One young Marylander described them as "vermin-infested scarecrows" who were "hairy and sun-baked with nothing bright about them, but their weapons and their teeth." A visiting Kentucky civilian in the area called them "the dirtiest men" he had ever seen, resembling "a most ragged, lean, and hungry set of wolves."[24] The visitor noted further that a great many of these troops came from the deep South and spoke in a dialect difficult to understand; nevertheless, he understood enough to describe them as "profane beyond belief," a characteristic made worse by the fact that they "talked incessantly."[25]

Although outwardly drab and seedy, this formidable southern force moving into Maryland was not taken lightly by Union authorities. For a time the Army of Northern Virginia was scattered over a wide area under separate commands. On September 13, Lee was near Hagerstown, Maryland, with Longstreet and nine brigades. About twelve miles south were five more brigades under D. H. Hill at Boonsboro, located a few miles west of Turner's Gap, through which the National Road crossed South Mountain. The remainder of the army at this juncture consisted of three separate columns, one of which was preparing to attack Harpers Ferry under Jackson's command; Matt's regiment was a part of this force. The other two columns were still south of the Potomac. While Lee's army was divided in all these fragments, McClellan's Army of the Potomac was coiled in and around Frederick, Maryland. Perhaps at no other time in the war was a general provided with such an opportunity — the chance to take on small, vulnerable units of the enemy forces and obliterate them one by one.[26]

By a strange stroke of good fortune, the Union commander on September 13 came in possession of a written copy of Lee's plan of attack that had been lost earlier in the Frederick area. Private Mitchell of the Twenty-seventh Indiana has been given credit for discovering Special Order 191; responsibility for its loss has never been determined. Rather than acting speedily after receiving this vital information, McClellan did not move his forces through Turner's Gap and Crampton's Gap of South Mountain until the following day. The two passes are six miles apart, and at Turner's Gap, D. H. Hill fought a very stubborn defensive retreat, giving Lee time to decide whether he should stand or fight in this area behind a formidable line of defense along Antietam Creek. When Union forces began moving toward the mountain passes, Lee was on the verge of ordering his army to withdraw from its positions, and return to Virginia. However, D. H. Hill's successful rear-guard action and the surrender of 11,000 Union troops and huge quantities of supplies to Jackson at Harpers Ferry somewhat relieved of the urgency of the Southern commander's decision.[27]

Sharpsburg, Maryland, was a very small town, and Antietam Creek was a modest, unimpressive stream. Here, however, more men were destined to lose their lives than in any other place, on any other single day of battle, during the War Between the States. Antietam Creek runs north and south, and the confederate line extended down behind the higher ground overlooking the creek, with the terrain offering at least some advantages for a defensive posture; still, Lee would have preferred a deeper position.[28] Another great weakness of the Confederate position at Sharpsburg involved the very real possibility of losing the means of a quick retreat across the Potomac. With only one ford in the immediate area crossing the stream, Lee's army ran serious risks of annihilation. Perhaps the greatest disadvantage for the Confederates in this bloody encounter was the glaring superiority of union numbers. On this occasion Lee's army, because of straggling and dispersion of commands, was weaker than at any time since he had taken command. Even after his last troops arrived from Harpers Ferry, the southern army at Sharpsburg numbered around 40,000 men, while McClellan's stood at 87,000 and growing.[29]

Following the enemy's surrender at Harpers Ferry, Matt Ransom's brigade marched twelve miles toward the Shenandoah, and at 1:00 A.M. on the morning of September 16 crossed over into Maryland, their third crossing of the Potomac in nine days.[30] Arriving at Sharpsburg, General Walker stationed his division on the extreme Confederate right flank about one and a half miles south of town. The vital area covered by Walker overlooked a ford of the creek, and at the same time the entire unit remained in supporting distance of Brigadier General Robert Toombs on the left. Batteries were established on heights overlooking roads approaching Sharpsburg from the east, and along the wooded banks of the Antietam, sharpshooters were posted.

During the early dawn hours of September 17, in a misty, drizzling rain, federal skirmishers slowly made their way southward down the Hagerstown turnpike. On the left approaching Sharpsburg was a large field of bountiful corn measuring the height of a full-grown man; on the right, the land opened into

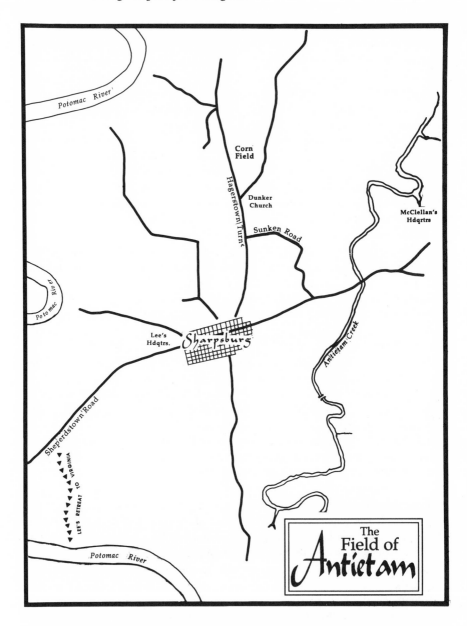

The Field of Antietam

rolling pastures, buttressed by nearby hills upon which J. E. B. Stuart had placed his artillery pieces. From this point on the pike up ahead a mile, the land assumed a slight incline where a whitewashed Dunker church stood. The federal plan of attack during these early morning hours called for occupation of those grounds in the church area in order to break Lee's left flank. For this action, McClellan called for a powerful attack in which one army corps would initiate the drive and two more would come in from beside and behind, capturing the southern force in a crushing movement.[31] The intent of these initial skirmishes was to feel the way for a subsequent attack by General Joseph Hooker's corps.

As the federal commander and his men moved down the pike, Jackson was waiting for the onslaught. Confederate artillery was placed around the Dunker church, with a heavy concentration of troops in the cornfield and west of the road. Upon detecting these infantry contingents, Hooker ordered three dozen fieldpieces to train their sights on the cornfield. The ensuing storm of Union firepower quickly destroyed the field and mercilessly disposed of the lives hidden within it.[32] Following this show of artillery, federal infantry advanced, fighting its way over an area strewn with dead and wounded bodies where a line of Confederate defenses once had been. Sweeping Jackson's remaining infantry aside, the federals moved up to the church. At this critical point, in support of the beleaguered Jackson, General John B. Hood's troops emerged from behind the church and out of the woods with muskets blazing away at their foes. (Hood's men had good reason to be angry — that night a meat ration had been distributed, and they had been preparing their first cooked breakfast in a week when orders were issued to advance.) Pursued by Hood's infantry, which now was assisted by several brigades of D. H. Hill, Hooker's forces were driven in retreat to their original position. Here the federals relied upon their heavy artillery to discourage any further Confederate infantry advances. The exhausted and disorganized Union corps limped from the field, as did its commander, General Hooker, whose foot had been pierced by a bullet.

Little time elapsed between this attack and the next. McClellan ordered General Joseph Mansfield's corps forward, driving the remaining Confederates from the cornfield. Although Mansfield was killed in this encounter, his men pushed forward and succeeded in disabling about half of Hood's forces while clearing out a segment east of the cornfield. They also managed to extend one arm of their unit as far as the church.[33] By now, however, the troops were demoralized and bleeding, and the Union drive came to a halt.

In accordance with the need of bolstering the Confederate left flank, around 9:00 A.M., Matt learned that his division was being ordered to support Jackson in the raging battle. Moving quickly with his regiment along the entire rear of the battle line, he observed some of the ghastly results of the early morning's gory contest. Wounded were being carried to the rear, and sounds of the moment included the booming of cannons, the whistling of shells, the pattering of small arms, and the hoarse yells of men from both sides as some advantage was gained. Apparently the second stage of the battle had now been reached. Hooker was repulsed, Mansfield halted; Jackson, having been severely tested, was now resting; Hood's brigade was ripped to pieces; and D. H. Hill's three brigades had been drawn in. Only a small force guarded the Confederate left, insufficient to repel an enemy brigade.[34]

At about 10:00 A.M., Walker's division arrived in the vicinity of the west woods. There they found Hood and Jubal A. Early grappling fiercely but inexorably losing ground to the sheer numbers of the union troops.[35] General Ransom's brigade had been deployed in a column of regiments. As one historian has described the action, "each regiment uncovered the one preceding it, was wheeled to the right and given the order to charge."[36]

The young, spirited mare on which Matt was mounted seemed restless and nervous. Matt looked back at the regiment for a final inspection, and all seemed well. His field officers, as ordered, had all dismounted except one, "little Clark," as he was affectionately known by the men of the regiment. Walter Clark, a boy hardly sixteen years old, was the regimental adjutant. His appointment had come about when Matt organized his staff after taking command of the Thirty-fifth. Highly intelligent and resourceful, the boy seemed headed for a bright future, and indeed, he was; years later he would serve as chief justice of the North Carolina Supreme Court. When going into the fight this particular morning, Clark for some reason was slow in dismounting, and suddenly a big, agitated mountaineer soldier rushed forward, pulling the young officer from this horse and shouting, "Git off'n this horse, you darned little fool, you'll git killed."[37] As he was pulled from his mount, a minnie ball struck Clark's hand, causing a minor wound but leaving a lifetime scar.

No serious problems developed during initial moments of the advance. Then, suddenly, to his consternation and horror, Matt observed that in their haste to fall in, several companies of the regiment had become confused and entangled. Were the situation not quickly remedied, disaster would surely result. Wheeling his mount around, Matt shouted to Captain D. G. Maxwell to send the colors forward. This officer attempted to comply, but when the color bearer was told to execute the order, he replied, "I'll be damned if I do it." Maxwell and First Lieutenant William H. S. Burgwyn advanced, carrying the colors. It was young Burgwyn who handed them to Ransom.[38] With his right arm still in a sling, Matt found that carrying the standard resulted in some considerable pain and awkwardness. Turning to his lieutenant colonel before undertaking the charge, Matt expressed a wish that should he be killed in this action, Pattie and the children might be informed of the circumstances of his death. Spurring his mount, off he dashed. The regiment pressed forward, never hesitating in spite of heavy losses, providing much-needed assistance in driving the enemy from a wooded area.[39] In this action, Union General John Sedgwick's division was entirely bested and beaten away by Walker's troops.[40]

Much to the relief of General Lee, commander General Edwin V. Sumner would send his remaining divisions into action in the same manner—one at a time.

For the next several hours the brigade of Robert Ransom, Jr., along with the Forty-sixth North Carolina, occupied their newly won area despite three determined infantry attacks and almost incessant artillery bombardment. The

Twenty-fourth North Carolina had become separated from the brigade, and General Ransom went in search of the unit with intentions of re-posting it. During his absence, Matt assumed command of the brigade, and while he held this post, the federals made a furious attack with heavy infantry at that point of the Confederate line.[41] Instantly responding to the challenge, and riding far ahead of his advancing brigade, Colonel Ransom at times was hidden from his men by the smoke of bursting shells and the sprays of the dirt which resulted from ploughing shot. Once the enemy had been repulsed, the colonel forged a deadly hot pursuit, and as he drove retreating federals across the field, his horse was shot out from under him. Quickly another mount was brought forward. The federals took up a position behind a post-and-rail fence. Having suffered so severe a punishment, they were in no mood for further infantry attacks for the moment.

There being a lull in the battle, General Jackson and General J. E. B. Stuart rode up to the regiment's position in the line. Arriving where Matt was standing, Jackson ordered an advance to take a battery that was in sight.

Ransom replied, "I will if ordered, but I shall probably fail."[42]

"But Colonel, I just observed your last charge, and I believe if you try again, you can take it!"

"Yes, I tried," Matt observed, "but upon arriving on top of the hill, I saw what seemed to be the greatest part of McClellan's army behind it."

"Have you a good climber in your command?" asked Jackson.

When Ransom called for volunteers, Private William S. Hood jumped up and asked for the assignment. He was barefooted, ragged, dirty, and lousy, but in spite of all that, records of the time describe him as a "handsome boy, only sixteen years old when enlisted; black eyes, long black hair, fair skin, indeed a noble type of a Southern lad."[43]

Jackson selected a tall hickory tree and told Hood to climb it. When Hood had almost reached the top, the general, sitting on his horse beneath the tree asked, "How many troops are over there?"

"Oceans of them," Hood shouted back in amazement.

"Count the flags," the general ordered.

The boy began counting federal regimental flags. "One, two, three..." and on and on continued the counting, with Jackson repeating each number as called, until thirty-nine was reached. By this time Hood had become a prime target for federal sharpshooters, who were peppering the tree with a steady stream of rifle fire.

"That will do, come down sir!" Jackson ordered. Needless to say, Hood required little encouragement. The general then turned to Ransom and asked, "What made you charge that battery with all of those troops defending it?"

Ransom answered, "I saw a large body of overpowering enemy troops preparing to charge us, and in order to discourage them, I decided to attack first. I did not know, however, the strength of the enemy until I reached the hill where the battery was located and saw the force of the enemy behind it."

Jackson departed as unceremoniously as he had come — wearing an old, worn uniform with a slouch hat pulled down over his eyes, and "riding a mighty sorry-looking claybank horse." The general's parting words were to listen for the rattling of his small firearms, since this would be the signal for an attack upon the enemy at that point of the line.[44] This attack however, was never made.

Following General Sedgwick's failure to break through the line where Matt's regiment was posted, the next determined Union thrust was aimed at the Confederate center. The terrain here featured a zigzag sunken lane where D. H. Hill's forces had established a strong position. The fighting was furious, and once again, federal forces were repulsed at great loss. At this point, General Sumner ordered his third division into battle. By now the Confederate defenses had become desperately weak, with so few manning the remaining guns of a wrecked battery that members of Longstreet's staff were compelled to give assistance. D. H. Hill himself, after picking up a musket and waving it over his head, attempted to rally stragglers. "So desperate was this hour that it could have been the breaking point for the entire Confederate army."[45] However, the Union failed to rise to the occasion. Having lost its momentum, Sumner's exhausted third division ground to a lasting halt, but not before losing its commander, Brigadier General Israel Richardson. In the rear, fresh and ready to fight, Union Brigadier General William B. Franklin was standing by. McClellan, however, continued to hold Franklin's corps in reserve, as he was convinced General Lee was preparing to amount on offensive on the Union right flank.

Actually, any hopes of mounting a southern offensive on the Union right flank was of brief duration. On Matt's front during mid-afternoon, the scene was marked by intense skirmishes on both sides, accompanied by artillery duels. Beginning around noon and thereafter, General Ransom received a series of orders from Longstreet to advance against the enemy, but since these orders were contradictory to those of Jackson, they were not obeyed and were deferred for final decision. By 4:30 P.M., after probing the federal right to find it securely posted and protected by heavy batteries of reserve artillery, General Stuart abandoned any idea of launching a serious attack. This decision was reaffirmed subsequently by consultations among senior Confederate commanders.

After General Sumner's final attack, which resulted in a very near collapse of the Confederate center, McClellan ordered his next major thrust on Lee's right flank. In charge of this offensive, General Burnside had at his disposal an impressive corps of four divisions. Like its predecessors on that day, however, this Union corps was completely without coordination, and the divisions were ordered into combat singly rather than as a powerful joint effort.[46] Furthermore, Burnside began his attack late in the afternoon and was extremely slow in executing his orders.

Yet this next federal move carried a great deal of importance. If Union troops were successful, Lee would be in desperate straits for having lost access to an immediate escape route across the Potomac. Indeed, by 4:00 P.M., a Union victory seemed imminent. Federal forces had gained most of the high ground south of Sharpsburg; all that remained was to push 1200 yards further west, and Lee's line of retreat would have been severed. On the northern side of town, federal flags were visible, which indicated the blue uniforms were approaching Shepherdstown Road. Then something of great consequence occurred. Throughout confederate ranks, thrilling news was rapidly spreading that A. P. Hill was on the way. And, in fact, after a rapid seventeen-mile march from Harpers Ferry, according to one historian, he did arrive. His arrival highlighted one of the strange features of battle. From the moment the two armies confronted each other here, Lee had been given forty-eight hours to reassemble his scattered forces, and this last piece slipped into place just when it was most needed."[47]

Hill ordered his forces to the right, and while riding ahead of his brigade directing fire, the very able General L. O. B. Branch was killed. By this time, the entire federal attacking wing, sagging and gapping but still in an unbroken line, was being driven downhill to the Antietam's banks. Here partial shelter was provided by low ridges near the creek. By sunset, weapons were virtually silent, and by darkness, the terrible battle was over.[48]

During the intense contest on the Confederate right, Matt's position was relatively calm; this was indicated when around 5:00, Longstreet ordered General Ransom's brigade toward the right to reinforce the Confederate center. At this time the enemy seemed to be preparing an offensive move. No attack occurred, but federal artillery delivered a constant barrage against the southern line. In General Walker's words, "Our own batteries [were] replying but slowly, for want of ammunition."[49]

For Matt Ransom this had been a long and undoubtedly memorable day. From early dawn into the darkness of night, through fourteen bloody hours of battle, Matt on no occasion went under cover for shelter. So many times during the day he thought of little Martha. To Pattie he confided in a letter that the child's "little soul seemed to be with me, saving me."[50] Miraculously, Matt came through this ordeal without a scratch; not even a thread of clothing was touched. Most importantly, he would hereafter be spared any doubts concerning his role as a commander of troops on a battlefield. His professional conduct during the day was genuinely praised by fellow officers and in General Walker's official report. His brother Robert's report was apparently another matter, for feelings of disappointment when he wrote Pattie that he "was not quite" ignored in this work. Evidently Robert slighted Matt because, he was told, "it would not seem right for one brother in these circumstances to praise another." Had their cases been reversed, Matt confided, "I would have put him in the stars. I know he means right and have nothing to say."[51]

After the Sharpsburg engagements both sides appraised their positions, and neither resumed offensive action. Troops and officers of the southern side regarded the contest just concluded as a draw. This was certainly Matt's view.[52] General Lee marked it an incident in a campaign, not the end of one.[53] The coming withdrawal of his forces back across the Potomac into Virginia he viewed as a tactical move, to be followed by a renewed invasion by way of Williamsport, striking Pennsylvania, moving thence to Hagerstown, and requiring McClellan to meet another grave threat.

During the night of September 17, some five thousand stragglers joined the Confederate line, giving Lee possibly enough strength to hold his position the next day. Nevertheless, it was a very weak army that returned to Virginia. Shortly thereafter, it became increasingly apparent that the army was far worse off than Lee had assumed. The lower Shenandoah Valley had become a major route of retreat for swarms of men who had deserted their units and were headed southward for their homes. By September 22, the Army of Northern Virginia had dwindled down to approximately 36,000 men exclusive of cavalry, and the morale required much improvement. By this time hard reality persuaded Lee to give up any hopes of an immediate northern campaign. He would leave the next move to McClellan, provided McClellan decided to move at all.[54]

At Sharpsburg only the Union command was capable of delivering massive coordinated attacks, and these tactics were not employed. Only singular piecemeal operations were put into play, wasting Union advantage over weaker forces, which were able to thwart fragmentary assaults. During three separate major federal attacks — Hooker's assault on the Confederate left, Sumner's against the center, and Burnside's the Confederate right — McClellan failed to use rested massive reserves. While all of these Union attempts were partially successful, they failed to accomplish the intended result of destroying Lee's army. Ironically, a victory by Lee would not have radically changed the balance of power, since the South was not capable of any follow-up.[55] At any rate, McClellan had not achieved a decisive victory, and he left his opponent the option of returning to his base to contemplate and prepare for future operations.

The Maryland campaign proved costly in terms of human life. Casualties for the Confederacy numbered 13,109, compared to Union reports of 14,756; counting federal personnel surrendering at Harpers Ferry, the number increases to 27,278.[56] The Confederate losses were more than Lee could afford, and in this instance he lost many of his best troops. Very importantly, in terms of war, Lee's attempt at bringing the war to an early close by means of an invasion had been rebuffed.[57]

On September 18, Matt remained with his regiment in the same woods they had defended the previous day. Late that night they slipped away to cross the Potomac at Shepherdstown. From there the march continued toward Martinsburg, and thereafter to the neighborhood of Winchester, where the brigade remained until October 23.[58] Late on afternoon during the Winchester bivouac, Robert Ransom, Jr., galloped past the regiment, followed by Private Hood. The young man's spurs were tied to his feet, he was riding one of the general's horses. Recognizing members of his old company, Hood raised his old, greasy cap and saluted as he passed. From this time forward, a warm, strong, soldierly relationship developed between the boy and the two Ransom brothers.

Here in camp the men were fond of recalling incidents of the recent battle, and one story concerned Private Hood. Before the boy made a name for himself by counting regimental flags for General Jackson, he had also volunteered to undertake a scouting mission for Matt. Hood was absent for at least an hour on his assignment, and upon his return, he gave such a good report that Colonel Ransom requested the name of the boy soldier. Later, to his immediate commanding officer, Hood provided a vivid account of his reconnaissance duty. While out on the field among the dead and wounded, the young soldier had come across a badly injured federal field officer begging for water. Without hesitation, Hood handed over his canteen of water. The officer than offered his gold watch with chain and all money on his person in return for being removed behind Confederate lines for medical attention. Sympathetically informing the wounded man his proposal was impossible, Hood then sought out federal pickets, alerted them to the officer's condition, and guided them to his location. Placed upon a stretcher, the officer was then carried back to his own lines. In helping the officer, Hood had risked capture, but because of his compassion and selfless bravery, the federal soldiers treated him with kindness and even provided him with coffee before sending him back to his own camp.[59] Of course the youngster's gallantry during the day brought him considerable good fortune; he became one of General Ransom's couriers.

Events during battle some times take on the very romantic, even fairy-tale qualities. One such incident at Sharpsburg occurred during the late afternoon, after Matt and his regiment had completed a charge driving federals from a battery atop of a hill. Despite this success, artillery fire forced the regiment to retire. The retreat covered a distance of about three hundred yards and ended on higher ground in the woods. Shortly afterwards, from this vantage point, the men of the Thirty-fifth witnessed a most interesting spectacle. A federal officer mounted on a bob-tail horse rode up to the very battery which had been under siege but was now completely abandoned. Apparently his mission was to inspect the installation and view his attackers' position. By now at least a hundred rifles were firing upon him, yet he "sat unconcernedly upon his horse." In a gesture of respect and fairness, Matt shouted, "Cease firing; don't shoot that brave man."[60]

Another Sharpsburg incident revealed even more of Ransom's personal sense of fairness and values. Endowed as he was with a keen intelligence, he quickly recognized and responded to this same quality in others. Competent intellect combined with good character — this, in Matt's mind, constituted the epitome of a good man. During the Battle of Sharpsburg a young officer in the regiment performed with unusual bravery and skill. Observing this behavior, Matt was greatly impressed and wished to reward the man for his fine conduct. The lieutenant's name was John J. Case. Though Case was popular with his men, his fellow officers looked down on him because he had little social standing, was ignorant of letters, and before the war had (barely) made his living as a tailor. Since the captain of Company G had been killed, that position was now open to a new appointment. Case as a candidate was opposed by a number of other officers. Ransom found the condescending views of his subordinates unacceptable, and he championed the cause of the lieutenant who subsequently received his promotion to captain.[61]

Matt's wounds from Malvern Hill were not really healed before the Maryland campaign, and now good judgment and discretion compelled him to return home for further rest and treatment. On October 14, he made an eloquent address to his regiment, and on this occasion he commended his men for their fortitude in carrying out many strenuous, weary marches; he especially praised their bravery in the late battle. These sentiments he promised to pass on to their brigade commander. His departing words included an assurance that he intended to "return at the earliest moment."[62]

Chapter VII

Moments of Hope
and Moments of Despair

As the old year moved into a new one, the plantation area around Jackson and the neighboring counties to Northhampton were becoming increasingly important in providing the Confederacy with vital food supplies — particularly on those occasions when Richmond held less than ten day's rations for Lee's army.[1] The precious cargo that arrived by way of the Weldon and Petersburg Railroad provided Lee with the option of remaining in Richmond; without this extremely important line of transport, his military presence in the capital city would have been impossible.

Within neither Northhampton County nor the state had there been any insurrections or slave uprisings as a result of Lincoln's preliminary Emancipation Proclamation on September 22, 1862, and his formal decree on January 1, 1863.

Up north the public witnessed the interesting spectacle of such prominent personalities as Senator Charles Sumner of Massachusetts, George Julian of Indiana, and Salmon P. Chase assuring their fellow citizens that the President's proclamation would not encourage mass migrations of blacks; on the contrary, their argument ran, these former slaves would now prefer to remain in their southern abodes. On the subject of Africans, Senator Sumner assured a Boston audience that "the North would be free of their presence."[2]

Much to Ransom's satisfaction, he found on returning to Verona that conditions there far exceeded his cautious expectations concerning farm operations and productivity. Crop averages had not only been increased during the growing season, but yields of cattle, hogs, gardens, and orchards had reached such high levels that canning and food preservation were among the servants' major undertakings. Clearly, on the Ransom farms there would be no food shortages or hunger.

As his wounds continued to respond favorably to local professional treatment and Pattie's care, Matt followed carefully, through correspondence and other means, any important events involving his regiment. On October 23 the Thirty-fifth moved with the brigade from Winchester, Virginia, and marched through Culpeper Courthouse, arriving near Fredericksburg on November 23. Here the men went into camp preparing to do battle at this place.[3] There were certainly clear signs of an impending military offensive by the federals, whose forces numbered 122,000, and engineer units began placing pontoon bridges across the Rappahannock on December 10. The Union had difficulty restraining Confederate sharpshooters at Fredericksburg, but in spite of obstacles, by December 12 two federal divisions were able to cross the river, one inside the town and the other just south of it. By the morning of December 13, with preparations completed, active firing began along the entire Union line. In command was General Ambrose E. Burnside, who had recently replaced McClellan following the Battle of Sharpsburg. The Union commander's plan for the moment included capturing and moving through Fredericksburg, and then to Richmond; all of this was to be accomplished before Lee could assemble widely scattered forces.

Terrain features in and around Fredericksburg are ideally suited for defensive warfare, and Lee was determined to profit from these advantages. The town is situated on a river bend, and in its rear, the land is marked by low-lying hills extending from Mayre's Heights southward to Prospect Hill. By outmarching the new federal commander, Lee was able to station his army of 78,000 on high ground in a line one or two miles south of the Rappahannock, in effect paralleling this stream for some six miles. It was, however, along the town's heights that Confederate planners set up an unassailable position involving 306 guns, with Jackson in command of the left of Mayre's Heights, and Longstreet in charge of the right. Combatants in this sector experienced the most severe fighting, especially where a sunken road offered excellent cover for deployed Confederate forces. In this location the division of General Robert Ransom, Jr. along with an extra brigade, defended the immediate batteries and Willis's Heights while at the same time supporting troops along the sunken road. At this point of the line, from about 11:00 A.M. until dark, the federals made fourteen unsuccessful charges at a frightful cost of human life. Before the battle ended at nightfall, Burnside was confronted with 6,300 casualties, and the entire expedition cost 10,208. It was now a Union commander's turn to retreat across a river with a defeated army. The Confederates, for whom this had been a defensive fight, counted their dead and wounded at 5,209.[4]

A high-ranking confederate officer was almost included among southern casualty statistics. During an intense artillery barrage on December 13, General Lee came close to losing his own life. He was standing about fifty feet behind a giant Parrott gun when it exploded, and a huge fragment of the cannon, weighing perhaps seven hundred pounds, landed just a short distance from where he stood. Briefly glancing at the object, he showed neither surprise nor concern, and then returned his attention to other matters.[5]

Before the Federicksburg engagement General Lee had again assumed his habitually dignified, courtly appearance. He had partially recovered from the injuries of his recent fall, and thus had been relieved of the splints on both hands as well as an arm sling. Able to dress and undress himself, he had regained use of his right hand, though swelling and pain persisted.[6] His real pain concerned an entirely separate matter, never discussed with friends or associates. During the previous October, his daughter Annie, who raked high in his favor, had passed away with fever while visiting Warren Sulphur Springs in North Carolina.

To Matt's great relief, his regiment incurred few casualties at Fredericksburg, and he was delighted over his brother's much-enhanced reputation as a military commander. On his own impulse and initiative, Robert Ransom, Jr., following the battle, had solicited financial contributions, from his officers to aid the destitute citizens of Fredericksburg, whose straitened circumstances had been brought on by the recent military contest.[7]

Because of the Union Army's debacle in Virginia, a decision was made in Washington to replace Burnside with General Joseph Hooker. In his continuing search for the right general, Lincoln indicated serious doubts and reservations about his new appointment. "I think it best for you to know that there are some things in regard to which I am not quite satisfied with you, "he wrote candidly to General Hooker in a letter of January 26, 1863.[8]

Lincoln was confronted with a host of other problems, some of which were not dissimilar to those experienced by Richmond. Mass desertions in the federal army undoubtedly ranked high on his list of matters deserving immediate attention. The magnitude of this dilemma increased when many families began sending their service kin parcels of civilian clothing through the mails. Both service and public morale in the North were desperately low. "We are on the brink of destruction," Lincoln confided to a friend.[9] Adding to his difficulties were the disastrous fall election results for the Republican party; this defeat at the polls; according to some analysts, could be attributed to the Emancipation Proclamation. In his annual message to congress in December, Lincoln joined with other prominent northern spokesmen in attempting to combat his countrymen's growing anxiety over the possibility of newly freed Africans migrating in great numbers to the North. They would do this only if they felt compelled, the President contended. He confessed that black people had previously fled north to escape bondage, and that at the moment, they might seek to escape both bondage and destitution. "But if gradual emancipation and deportation be adopted, they will have neither to flee from." If given an opportunity, Lincoln confidently stated, these former slaves would gladly continue working under old masters for wages until "new homes can be found for them in congenial climes with people of their own blood and race." In his concluding point on this sensitive subject, Lincoln asked, "In any event, can not the North decide for itself whether to receive them?"[10] Apparently the president "was suggesting that the Northern states might resort to exclusion laws such as some of them used before the war to keep Negroes out."[11]

While Lincoln contended with issues under his own jurisdiction, there were no signs of the Union's military posture being badly eroded or subject to significant threat — certainly not in North Carolina. As the new year opened, reliable reports indicated a sizable increase of federal troops around New Bern, and warships were reported at Beaufort. So tense had the situation become that serious hostilities were expected daily. Matt was convinced the enemy intended to extend its grip over eastern North Carolina, and this of course included his own domicile. During December Union general J. G. Foster led raids from New Bern upon Kinston, Whitehall, and Goldsboro; nor did he neglect the countryside, which was terribly devastated. He was really intent on destroying the Wilmington and Weldon Railroad at Goldsboro and the Neuse River bridge. Before year's end, damage to the railroad and bridge was repaired, making both facilities operative; finally, Foster's troops were driven back by Confederate general G. W. Smith.

Another area incident demonstrating not only strong local resolve, but also humor, occurred on December 10 when Lieutenant Colonel John C. Lamb, leading several companies of the Seventeenth North Carolina and a squadron cavalry, attacked the town of Plymouth, then under federal occupation. Before daybreak the Confederates pushed downtown, dispersing their foes, and then they turned their artillery on the lone river gunboat *Southfield*. After being disabled, the vessel dropped downstream. At this point, Captain Barnabas Ewer, federal commander of the Plymouth garrison in panic and fright deserted his forces and went aboard the departing *Southfield*. When asked where he left his men, he replied "he did not know, but hoped most of them were in the swamp."[12]

The dismal outlook confronting eastern counties was somewhat improved as the new year began to unfold. On January 3 Matt's regiment marched through Petersburg en-route to Kenansville, where it would join other troops being stationed in North Carolina. Ten thousand troops were assigned to General Whiting at Wilmington. Other forces comprised single and parts of regiments encamped at Magnolia, Kinston, Weldon, and Hamilton. Eventually, at least 30,000 soldiers were present for duty in the Old North State. The explanation for this new Confederate strength in North Carolina involved Lee's decision, following his victory at Fredericksburg, to place two divisions under Longstreet south of the James River. These forces were not only expected to engage in combat activities, but they were to be involved in vital food gathering for a short-supplied Army of Northern Virginia. In attempting to relieve some measure of the forage needs, Lee sent a number of cavalry horses southward for winter grazing. Some of these were dispatched to western North Carolina, causing Governor Vance to voice a strong protest. If these animals were not removed, the governor threatened to employ local militias to drive them out. Confederate officials assured Governor Vance the problem would be of short duration, but if the animals were returned to Virginia immediately, they would likely starve. As historian Samuel Ashe puts it, "The horses stayed; nobody starved."[13]

Taking over his new command of the Department of Virginia and North Carolina on February 25 at Petersburg, Longstreet expected to accomplish a number of important objectives. Above all, he wished to insure the continuance of those vital supply lines in North Carolina, and from this eastern area, with Lee's encouragement, he planned to gather provisions. By making heavy demonstrations against Washington, North Carolina, Longstreet hoped to discourage any further federal military initiatives in that part of the state.

Under the new command arrangement North Carolinians were proud and relieved when their native son General D. H. Hill joined Longstreet's command to take up his post at Goldsboro. It was no secret General Hill was among those who viewed Richmond's past policies toward the state as apathetic and ineffectual. In December during Foster's raids he had strongly urged an ending of such harassment by mounting a major offensive against federal forces and driving them completely from North Carolina. Two days after taking over his new assignment, he again proposed this idea, pointing out that Lee's forces on the Rappahannock would be idle for an indefinite period and could be used to great advantage in the area under his command. This argument seemed to be reinforced by weather conditions during January and February. Heavy rain and snow helped create a mud-bound federal army, which was even further mired in the problems of organizing a new command and deciding future strategy. Rather than sending a good part of his army, Lee sent only two divisions. At a later time, Hill observed, "I was unheeded." [14] Often exhibiting a gloomy disposition, General Hill made repeated predictions of a Northern victory. These did not set well with Lee, who feared his subordinate "croaked too much."[15]

The Confederate offensive began on Friday, March 31, when General Junius Daniel's scouts exchanged fire with federal pickets on what was known as the lower Trent road about ten miles from New Bern. Falling back two miles, the federals took up a defensive position at Deep Gully but were driven from it; even after reinforcements arrived, they retired next morning to New Bern's defenses. Such Confederate successes were not repeated at Fort Anderson, which was an earthwork directly opposite New Bern on the Neuse River's northern bank. The installation, being flanked by swamps, could be approached only by a causeway leading into the fort. During early morning hours on the fourteenth, General Pettigrew's troops stormed across this causeway; then, with light batteries, they delivered intense, effective fire on the fort. Fearing a frontal attract would prove too costly on both sides, Pettigrew hoped to demoralize his enemy by heavy artillery fire, and then demand surrender. This approach embodied all the elements of a serious blunder. Federal commander Hiram Anderson, Jr., entertained no thoughts of surrendering his command, and to gain time, the crafty officer requested a ceasefire. Against his officer's advice, Pettigrew granted a truce. During this interval, Anderson, while pretending to be in consultation with superiors over surrendering the fort, was in fact waiting for federal gunboats to move into effective firing positions against the Confederates. After realizing he had been deceived, Pettigrew renewed his artillery attack, but it was much too late. Under fire from Union gunboats and superior artillery, the Confederates could not hold their position, and a withdrawal followed — much to the displeasure of the rank and file, particularly Henry King Burgwyn, Jr., who was present as commander of the Twenty-sixth North Carolina.[16]

Another Confederate expedition also proved disappointing under B. H. Robertson, whose troops were under orders to sever a local railroad. Because of the failure of Pettigrew and Robertson to fulfill their assignments, General Hill felt compelled to abandon any further attempts to capture New Bern. Heavy rains prevented a surprise move against Washington, North Carolina, and for the time being, the Confederates could accomplish nothing.[17] By March 30 the city was under siege, but a full-scale assault would have been contrary to Lee's orders, which called for only "demonstrations."[18] General Hill complained bitterly to Longstreet and Governor Vance concerning the many hindrances of his command. Other than gathering stores of corn and bacon, he could account for little success during his two months' duty in North Carolina. Inclement weather, poor performance by subordinates, and bad luck conspired to foil his campaign.

A telegram from Longstreet to General Ransom on April 19 indicated Matt's leave of absence would soon end. "In case you are likely to give battle," Robert Ransom, Jr., was instructed, "telegraph for Colonel Ransom."[19] On May 22 the brigade, along with Cooke's command under D. H. Hill, engaged the federals below Kinston, driving them back to New Bern. While Matt felt a strong sense of urgency for returning to his regiment, there were other pressing matters on his mind. Pattie was expecting another child within two months.

Matt's patriotic sense of duty to the Confederacy was hardly shared by many others who were determined to leave their military experience behind them forever. By May 1863, desertions in the Army of Northern Virginia had reached alarming numbers, much to the disturbance of Confederate authorities, especially Robert E. Lee. Following mountain regions of northern Virginia down to western North Carolina, South Carolina, Georgia, and Alabama, bands of deserters, generally well armed, lived off the land by robbing and plundering. Governor Vance estimated this lawless element in North Carolina as being at least 1200 in number.[20]

In spite of these problems, early in May there came a great military victory for the South. Between May 2, and 4 at Chancellorsville, Virginia, General Lee again demonstrated his unique talents of command; he achieved a victory many consider the most outstanding of his career.[21] His adversary, General Hooker, lined the Rappahannock River at Fredericksburg with upwards of

130,000 men. Without Longstreet's two divisions, then occupied in eastern Virginia and North Carolina, Lee's total forces were about 60,000 effectives.[22] By a series of rapid movements starting on April 27, Hooker moved four army corps across the Rappahannock, concentrating on Lee's left flank; at the same time, still maintaining a powerful center line, he also dispatched General Sedgwick across the river to challenge Lee's right flank. With the Union army thus poised for offensive operations, Lee left 10,000 troops under General Early at Fredericksburg to face Sedgwick, and then, with the remainder of his forces, he headed for Chancellorsville. Here the Southern commander at great risk divided his strength by ordering Jackson, with about 30,000 men to move around Hooker's right flank. Lee, with less than 20,000 men, resorted to a series of tactical skirmishes intended to deceive his enemy concerning Confederate strength on that particular front. During late evening hours on May 2, Jackson, having completed his march, fell upon Hooker's right flank, smashing one corps and leaving another in a bad state.

Jackson's corps was now in desperate need of realignment and rest, and a more conservative general would most likely have halted operations in preparation for the next major move. However, Jackson was determined to place his troops on the Rappahannock's banks before night ended, for he saw the prospects of annihilating Hooker's entire army. Riding ahead and in front of his line with staff members, he attempted to explore the best possible roads for his pending operations. Having completed their mission, he and his group — under night darkness, unannounced, and unidentified — approached a point of the Confederate line which had just been alerted to accept a Union cavalry attack. Believing Jackson and his mounted aides hostile parties, a North Carolina regiment opened fire. The general received three bullets in his body almost simultaneously. One struck in the right hand; another entered the wrist of his left arm and passed through the left hand; the third shattered a large bone of the upper left arm and would require amputation. Removed from the field for treatment, the stricken warrior struggled with great physical pain for several days before a charitable death arrived.

When the battle resumed next day, Hooker's fortunes continued to grow worse. Fearing destruction of his army, he withdrew his forces across the river, where they sought safety and protection throughout May 2. It was then time for Lee to contend with General Sedgwick's corps, for they had driven General Early from the very heights of Fredericksburg which Robert Ransom, Jr., had so recently and successfully defended. No match for Lee's veteran attacking forces, Sedgwick likewise retreated and crossed over the Rappahannock during the night of May 4. Next day Lee pressed beyond Chancellorsville, and Hooker drew his army back north of the river with no intention of renewing hostilities. The battle was over, at a price of 17,287 Union dead and wounded. Confederate losses were 11,423, much higher than the South could afford, particularly one casualty — Stonewall Jackson, who died on Sunday, May 10, 1863.[23]

On May 12, 1863, thousands of citizens at Richmond turned out to pay their final respects to their hero. With flags at half mast, places of business and offices closed, and church bells mournfully ringing, throngs of silent figures stood along the streets waiting to catch a glimpse of the Confederate flag-draped coffin. Behind the hearse and riderless horse were the pallbearers, all general officers, followed by President Davis in an open carriage, then by members of his cabinet, with state and city officials included in the procession. At Lexington, Virginia, the famous, fallen soldier was laid to rest. Stonewall Jackson was dead, and many of his admirers found themselves questioning and reconsidering the hopes they had pinned to this hero.[24]

While jubilation was the initial public reactions to Chancellorsville, the reflection that followed offered a very different appraisal. At best, this ordeal appeared to be just another bloody victory. Actually nothing decisive had occurred. Nothing had really changed insofar as hopes for a southern victory were concerned. The Confederate government and army were still faced with the same mounting problems. As a matter of fact, General Lee, who absented himself from Jackson's funeral because of duties at the front, informed his superiors he might be compelled to retreat and take shelter at Richmond if reinforcements failed to arrive.[25] McAllen and now Joe Hooker had been prevented from carrying out their designs against Richmond, this was only a temporary relief. Federal siege troops would return. There was no resolution in sight.[26] The government was calling upon people to make greater sacrifices, and events about to occur bore testimony to this need.

After Chancellorsville Lee began making preparations for the second northern invasion, and for this, he would be compelled to call up his troops then stationed in North Carolina. Lee's motives for this venture were not shared by his subordinates. General D. H. Hill took sharp issue with his superior, who regarded the coming campaign was a practical means of obtaining new recruits, acquiring much-needed supplies, and promoting the northern peace movement. It would have been far better, the sharp-tongued North Carolinian argued, to have left an ample garrison behind to protect Richmond, and with a large army segment to have gone west in behalf of Vicksburg. Much later, Hill would remark that "the drums that beat for the advance into Pennsylvania seemed to many of us to be beating the funeral march of the dead Confederacy."[27]

Generals Beauregard and Longstreet shared equal concern over events in Mississippi, and each offered a plan. Beauregard would have sent an entire corps of Longstreet's men under Lee's active command to Tennessee, and there to defeat William S. Rosecrans. Such a victory promised the results of regaining the state and possibly Kentucky. Moreover, a Union defeat of this kind would seriously compromise Grant's campaign against Vicksburg. Longstreet's formula was virtually the same, except he would not have sent Lee west to assume active command.

While Hooker was losing at Chancellorsville, Ulysses S. Grant was winning the towns of Port Gibson and Grand Gulf in Mississippi and following with a determined thrust into the state's interior. Just how seriously Richmond regarded these western developments became clear when Lee was informed that he might need to dispatch a division of Longstreet's troops to Vicksburg. For Lee the idea of dispatching Longstreet's men anywhere was a tender subject; those same men had been sorely missed at Chancellorsville, and only now were they coming back to his command.[28] An avid reader of northern newspapers, Lee paid close attention to those reports of Hooker being reinforced. To him this could only mean Virginia would again become major theater of operations. Under such circumstances, the Army of Northern Virginia should be strengthened, rather than weakened by troop detachments. Concerning Vicksburg, Lee made his point with clarity and force to his superiors. As a matter of priority, he asked which rated first, Virginia or Mississippi? No real discussions or guiding policies came from Richmond relative to the western theater of operations. Joseph E. Johnston was in nominal command, receiving only minimal or incidental support; he and his subordinates were expected to carry on alone as best they could against Grant and Rosecrans.

In a letter dated May 25, General Lee thanked D. H. Hill for his efforts in harassing the enemy over recent months, and expressed hope that forces within North Carolina were sufficiently strong to defeat enemy elements and drive them from the state. While Lee wrote this letter, he was withdrawing troops under Hill's command. With his troops disappearing into the Army of Northern Virginia, Hill was placed on the defensive, even as Union general Foster at New Bern found himself more able to move out of his fortified area.[29] By the end of May, North Carolinas was again without a sufficient number of troops to protect its eastern counties. Fortunately, the months of June witnessed very little, if any, hostile Union activity in the area.

After returning to Petersburg around June 1, Matt's brigade was in need of a new commander. On May 26 Robert Ransom, Jr., had been promoted to major general. The brigade post was vacant for only a brief period; on June 15, when Matt returned to active duty, he assumed his brother's former command as brigadier general.[30] This choice was unanimously recommended by officers of the Twenty-fifth, Thirty-fifth, Forty-ninth and Fifty-sixth regiments, over three senior colonels in the brigade. Officers of the Thirty-fifth as a group called upon their new general, delivering congratulations while expressing regrets over losing him as their immediate commander. Spokesman for the delegation was Surgeon O' Hagan, of whom Matt remarked to a friend "that he was so much embarrassed by the complimentary things said of him by the eloquent doctor that in his reply he made the meanest speech of his life."[31] Next month the new general's brigade would join with those of A.G. Jenkins and John R. Cooke to forming Robert Ransom's division of the department of Richmond. Under D. H. Hill's command, while Lee was absent at Gettysburg, the division met and defeated federal forces advancing from Williamsburg and briefly threatening Richmond.[32]

News from the battlefronts in July 1863 was extremely discouraging to North Carolinians, and to Matt Ransom, for personal reasons, very painful. The Battle of Gettysburg just fought cost the Confederate army 20,000 dead and wounded.[33] The Twenty-sixth North Carolina suffered an 88 percent casualty rate in this encounter — the greatest loss to any regiment for the whole war's duration.[34] On this occasion, while leading this remarkable unit, Henry King Burgwyn, Jr., the "boy colonel" of twenty-one years, fell mortally wounded; a bullet had pierced both lungs. His father had recently been a frequent visitor at Verona, and in his turn, Matt had become a regular guest of the Burgwyns at Thornburg during his convalescence. Very often, Mr. Burgwyn, Sr., had spoken of his oldest son with parental pride and affection; now he was taken. Another son, William Hyslop Sumner Burgwyn, better knows to family and friends as Will, was currently serving as a commissioned Confederate officer in the Thirty-fifth North Carolina; there was yet a younger boy, still in his teens, who would tender his military services to the southern cause. For the Burgwyns, doing one's duty was no meaningless platitude.

Another event following the Gettysburg ordeal also proved to be a sad experience for Ransom. On the morning of July 14, as the retreating Confederate army was crossing the Potomac at Falling Waters, a slight skirmish ensued with Union cavalrymen. Before it ended, James Johnston Pettigrew became another fatality of the war. It seemed to Ransom, upon learning of the tragedy, that a symbol of his youth had suddenly slipped away. The two men during their boyhood rivalry at Chapel Hill were never friends, but from that time and through the years that followed they had shared a healthy, profound respect for each other.

Of the two major battles fought in July 1863, Gettysburg would go down in history with far greater recognition. Volumes of related literature are available today, dealing with every conceivable aspect of this event. Sometimes it is called a turning point of the war, the high tide of the Confederacy; with dramatic emphasis, the battle has been declared the greatest ever fought in North America in terms of numbers and casualties. Yet, in a real sense, Gettysburg was another indecisive battle. Lee, on his part, expressed a willingness before his superiors to assume full responsibility for his failure; of course, this gesture was refused. Very importantly, he was allowed an opportunity to pull his army back into Virginia, and the war would continue indefinitely. Vicksburg, on the other hand, was not an indecisive battle. At least 30,000 troops surrendered to Union victors. The Mississippi River in a matter of days would be entirely cleared, and the shrinking Confederacy would be cut in half.

Leading these Union operations, Ulysses S. Grant bore no resemblance to the federal commanders previously charged with eastern campaigns. Unlike

McClellan, this general was not subject to delusions concerning the numerical superiority of opposing forces; he did not panic at the sight of large amounts of blood, particularly from his own men. His patience and tenacity were more than illustrated by his siege of Vicksburg, which lasted from the middle of May until July 4, 1863. This very will might be the man for whom Lincoln had been searching since the start of hostilities. One point was certain; If this general one day should assume command over Union forces along the Potomac, it would certainly qualify as a tragic event for the rapidly dwindling and poorly sustained Army of Northern Virginia.

The summer of 1863 offered little relief for many of the problems confronting North Carolinians. By withdrawing troops from the state for duty elsewhere Lee had essentially paralyzed any efforts by Governor Vance to confront some of the most pressing matters of violence on his home front. In eastern counties private homes and property continued to be sacked by federal raiding parties, and the booty sent north in gross amount. In western regions of the state Confederate troops for all intents and purposes fought a second civil war, in which the enemy was comprised of bushwhackers and deserters from their own ranks.[35]

Southern defeats at Gettysburg and Vicksburg produced a very despondent public attitude throughout the state, which editor William W. Holden skillfully utilized in his peace campaign. Wishing to bring an end to the war, he had at first urged Confederate officials to initiate peace discussions; after President Davis refused, Holden struck out on a new approach which included independent state efforts to achieve peace. In public peace meetings — possibly a hundred were held in about forty counties — speeches were made and resolutions passed censoring Confederate policies and the war. Representatives from these meetings demanded that the government in Richmond make peace.[36] The meetings seemed to provide a greater impetus to a growing public resolve to call a state peace convention. Since Holder and his followers gave active and open support to the convention process, with its implications of North Carolina deserting the Confederacy and returning to the Union, Confederate and conservative groups in the state became greatly alarmed. Governor Vance's role was most awkward. On the one hand he wished, for political expediency, to avoid appearing submissive to Confederate authorities; but at the same time, he was determined to continue giving loyal support to the war effort. The conduct upon which he settled was in keeping within successful record of endearing himself to citizens. While opposing Confederate policies which created the greatest public criticism, at the same time he countered negative and defeatist attitudes in the state.

As to complaints regarding Richmond's conduct of the war, the most persistent charge continued to be that North Carolina was carrying an unfair burden of human loss and injury in combat. At Chancellorsville, there were 124 Confederate regiments, of which 24 were from North Carolina. Thus, the state made up one-fifth of the Chancellorsville force, but it sustained about one-third of the total confederate losses.[37]

During the middle of July General Foster made his next offensive move out of New Bern when he ordered his chief of staff, General Edward E. Potter, to lead a sizable cavalry force against Greenville, Tarboro, and Rocky Mount.[38] Already, on July 5, a devastating raid had been conducted against the Wilmington and Weldon Railroad, destroying in excess of a mile of track at Warsaw. On July 19, General Potter approached Greenville, which his men subsequently overran, destroying property estimated at $300,000, robbing citizens, quenching thirst's at local taverns, and, as a grand finale, burning the Tar River bridge.[39] Resuming his march late in the afternoon, Potter by midnight arrived at Sparta, which was around eight miles from Tarboro. Here, a battalion was detached and dispatched to Rocky Mount with orders to burn and destroy the railroad bridge and government property there. Arriving at Tarboro with his main force between 7:00 and 8:00 A.M. on July 20, Potter encountered only limited resistance, and then proceeded to destroy an ironclad on the stocks, two steamboats, a number of railroad cars, and at least 100 bales of cotton. Learning that a Confederate force was opposite the river, Potter began a retreat to New Bern by way of the same route he had come, but not before burning the local Tar River bridge. Not until the federals arrived back at Sparta were they seriously pursued during their return to New Bern, where they concluded their trip on July 23.

With these disturbing events in his mind, along with the knowledge that federal troops had carried out their assignment in Rocky Mount by burning the bridge, Matt Ransom read a telegram received late in the afternoon on July 27 from his friend and neighbor Mr. John Long. The message informed Ransom that Colonel S. P. Spear, with a large Union cavalry force accompanied by artillery, was advancing from the town of Winton to Bertie County, destined for Weldon.[40] Immediately General Ransom dispatched a message by courier requesting permission to intervene in the latest Union invasion. Gaining approval for his mission, Ransom ordered the Thirty-fifth regiment during that same afternoon to proceed to Garysburg on the next southbound train.[41] He and his staff in the meantime moved out ahead of the unit after procuring a locomotive, and arrived at Weldon just at daybreak on the twenty-eighth.[42] There were, as Ransom discovered at Garysburg, four companies of the Twenty-fourth North Carolina and a section of two guns of the Macon light artillery class. These troops and artillery pieces he ordered to Boon's Mill, about eight miles in the direction of Jackson on a road that passed by Verona. Orders were left behind directing newly arriving troops to follow the earlier contingent.

Lacking a cavalry force, Ransom was compelled to rely upon his own resourcefulness. He ordered Captain Will Burgwyn, brother of the slain "boy colonel," to mount a squad and scout the area. At this time, the general and members of his staff set out for Jackson, a distance of about nine miles, where they hoped to gain information concerning enemy movements. Mounted on his thoroughbred Ion this morning, and taking a lead position, Ransom set the pace for those who followed; early as the hour was, the heat and humidity were already taking their toll in human energy. From the road, General Ransom gave only a quick glance at his home as he passed it on his journey. Not only were Patties's and the children's welfare at stake, but the fate of an entire community would be determined by events on this day.

The party now approached a bridge over a waterway which ran from a tree-shaded pond to a grist mill. Called Boon's Mill, it was a place of local strategic importance, as indicated by the rifle pits that had been thrown up to command the bridge. After a distance of about three more miles the general and his aids reached Jackson, and here he learned that federals were coming up rapidly toward town. It was now around noon. Shouting for his staff to follow, the general on his powerful mount headed at a sustained gallop for Boon's Mill, where he intended to make a determined stand. Ransom and his entourage had gone no more than a half-mile when suddenly a great shout and commotion arose behind them. Halting their mounts to investigate, they caught a glance of pursuing Union cavalry charging over a hill at a distance of about two hundred and fifty yards. It was now a question of whose horses were faster.

During the chase that followed, federal cavalrymen delivered a steady stream of gunfire at their mounted targets. The Confederates, turning in their saddles, returned their share of firepower. One federal trooper fell fatally wounded from his horse on the road directly in front of Mr. Henry Boone's home. The noise of the battle had drawn Mr. Boone outside, and he was standing just a few feet from where the federal cavalryman dropped to the ground. Still in heavy grief over the death of this son, Augustus, at Malvern Hill, Mr. Boone suddenly unleashed his emotions by clapping his hands and shouting, "Good, and I hope they get another one!"[43] Hearing this remark, a Union mounted rider with revolver in hand screamed, "Mister, if you don't get back in that house, the same thing will happen to you!"

When the race concluded, it was clearly evident that Matt's men had risen to the occasion as they were trained to do. Seeing many of his men bathing in the pond as he charged across the bridge, Ransom shouted for the planks to be taken up, and ordered all troops to fall in ranks.[44]

As advance elements of Colonel Spear's forces arrived they were for a brief period disorganized, and they needed to reform before launching a serious attack. This time interval offered the Confederates an opportunity to take up a defensive position to meet whatever challenge was forthcoming from their enemy. Tactics of deception are traditional in conducting warfare, and in this rural, almost isolated setting, Ransom and his officers tried to use such tactics to their best advantage. Hoping to create an impression of a much larger force, they moved quickly and constantly throughout their lines, as Will Burg-wyn would remember years later, in shouting "stentorian tones," and giving "certain well-known commands" heard only in Lee's army.[45]

Spear's first efforts of attack involved bringing up his artillery, and for over an hour he pounded the Confederate position. He then dismounted his cavalry and attempted to advance down the road to the mill, where he was met by heavy, rapid fire and forced to retire. Fortunately for the Confederates, about this time two guns of Macon light artillery arrived as the federals were preparing simultaneous attacks upon both of Ransom's flanks. Although some Federals, concealed by thick swamp undergrowth, managed to make their way across the pond and were able to take up a position to the rear of General Ransom's men, they were quickly dispersed by grape and canister fired from the two Confederate artillery pieces. By now the fight had lasted some five hours. Effectively repulsed, and convinced they had met a much larger body of troops than was actually present, Colonel Spear abandoned what he had earlier thought would be an uneventful expedition to Weldon, where he had intended, among other things, to destroy the bridge. Late that afternoon, he disengaged his forces, and under cover of night they retreated through Jackson.

In this important skirmish, part of which was fought on land belonging to Verona, the federal commander had at his disposal one brigade of cavalry and nine artillery pieces. At the mill, Ransom's command consisted no more than two hundred infantry and two small artillery pieces.[46] Yet, General Ransom and his modest band of troops not only saved the Weldon bridge, but also spared another large section of the state from falling under Union occupation. At the very same time as the Boon's Mill contest was begin fought, not too many miles distant from Winton, General Foster, with a considerable force, was waiting upon the outcome of Colonel Spear's expedition. That outcome was surely not to his liking, for the rich farmland that by and large kept the Confederate army fed would remain in southern control. Indeed, that area's crops of 1863 and 1864 were saved as though no war had ever troubled them.[47]

Verona on past occasions had been the scene of many joyful social events in which guests were offered unlimited hospitality, but surely the most memorable affair of all occurred on the morning of July 29, 1863. Out of gratitude and respect to his men who had won the previous day's victory at Boon's Mill, General Ransom invited members of the Twenty-fourth Regiment to be his guests for breakfast. Apparently orders went out that every man should have his fill, because, as a contemporary noted, "some of the boys said here was the most fried bacon they ever saw at one time."[48]

Among those present at Verona was William Hood, the youngster who had climbed the tree for General Jackson at Sharpsburg. The seedy appearance that had characterized him at that time had apparently been transformed following his assignments as courier to General Robert Ransom, Jr., and now to Matt Ransom. What was more, this boy, who hailed from Clear Creek township in Mecklenburg County, could boast of a penmanship of unusual quality and style, and he was often detailed to assist in clerical duties such as making out reports and payrolls. Having already won the hearts of the Ransom brothers, here at Verona he likewise impressed Mrs. Ransom — all without the slightest planning or intention on his part. Cheerful, unpretentious, with a bright clear mind and handsome face, he invariably won immediate acclaim, among all he met.

Only a few days following the Boon's Mill encounter, an expected guest arrived at Verona. On August 3 another child, Thomas Exum Ransom, was born.

Chapter VIII

When Will This All End?

Months and now years had passed since the start of this bloody contest, and as a consequence, thousands of southern mothers, wives, and young girls were left with only memories of the men who had gone off to war — gone forever, they became cold statistics of hard-fought battles. In periods such as these, people often seek relief and shelter, sometimes survival, in their religious heritage. A general public conviction still prevailed in North Carolina that Lee's army was divinely blessed and therefore unconquerable; eventually the enemy would be forced to abandon its present belligerent course and accept southern independence. However, there persisted the agonizing question of how many more men on both sides of the conflict would have to be killed before the struggle ended. During this time, an intense religious crusade enveloped the southern army, resulting in thousands of conversions to Christianity. Services resembling camp meetings were held daily and on Sundays, with large attendance by both officers and men.[1]

Matt Ransom's brigade during the winter months of 1863-64 was assigned to the Department of North Carolina under Major General George Pickett.[2] During the cold season and into spring weather, General Pickett, along with his wife and staff, took up comfortable quarters at Verona.[3] The general's official presence in North Carolina was the result of a decision by Confederate authorities to demonstrate another military move against Union forces occupying New Bern. Brigadier General Robert F. Hoke was Lee's choice to head the campaign, but it was finally decided that an assignment of this magnitude should be handled by an officer of higher rank.[4] Operations got under way on the morning of January 30, 1864, when a force of at least thirteen thousand marching troops and fourteen navy cutters — taking a river route — headed out from Kinston in New Bern's direction.

Picket's plan of attack largely duplicated an earlier one Hoke had suggested to Lee. Brigadier General Seth M. Barton's command included his own brigade, that of Brigadier General J. L. Kemper, and three regiments under Matt Ransom. These groups were supported by eight rifled pieces, six napoleons, and six hundred cavalry, all of which were to move across the Trent River near Trenton; from here, Barton was ordered to follow the southerly side of the stream to Brice's Creek below New Bern. Crossing over that creek, he was expected to capture intervening forts along the Neuse and Trent Rivers, moving against New Bern by way of the railroad bridge. This plan, if carried out successfully, would have the effect of isolating the town by severing all land and water approaches from Morehead City and Beaufort. While these operations were in progress, a Confederate column under colonel James Dearing, consisting of the Fifteenth and Seventeenth regiments as well as Colonel J. N. Whitford's regiment, accompanied by three pieces of artillery and three hundred cavalry, were to move north of the Neuse while capturing Fort Anderson and Barrington ferry. The third column, commanded by General Hoke and accompanied by Pickett, was to become active in an area between the Trent and Neuse rivers, overcoming enemy troops at Batchelder's Creek by surprise, neutralizing guns of the star fort near the Neuse, and then moving against New Bern from that direction. A simultaneous attack by these three columns was set for Monday morning, February 1. To facilitate this assault, Commander John Taylor Wood planned to descend the Neuse with the intention of intercepting and capturing federal gunboats, meanwhile, General Whiting, commander of Confederate forces at Wilmington, was to give an impression of moving against Swansboro in hopes of distracting the enemy.[5]

In attempting to carry out his assignment, General Hoke arrived too late at Batchelder's Creek; the enemy, having been alerted, destroyed the bridge. However, later that day the Confederates succeeded in making a crossing, and they routed the federals, who retreated one mile from New Bern. Here, Hoke halted his advance and anxiously waited for sounds of General Barton's guns opposite the Trent River. For a whole day he waited, and during this time, two trains arrived in New Bern from Morehead City. The arrival of these trains would have been impossible had Barton succeeded in his objective.

General Barton conducted his command in an orderly and successful fashion until he arrived at Brice's Creek on the morning of February 1. With an element of surprise in his favor, he could have dismounted his large cavalry force, and by combining it with his infantry, he might have launched a heavy assault against the federal works. Instead, he called upon his artillery, and in company with General Ransom and Colonel William R. Aylett, he made a reconnaissance. The obstacles he observed were more serious than he expected; in fact, he was forced to conclude that the odds against his troops were insurmountable. In a communication to General Pickett, Barton asserted that he had been misled by underestimates of enemy strength, and he announced that he had no intention of advancing.[6] In reply, General Pickett ordered Barton to join his forces with those preparing for a frontal assault upon New Bern. To this new attack approach, General Hoke objected so heatedly that Picket threatened his subordinate with arrest and court-martial.[7]

Upon learning that General Barton could not deliver his forces before New Bern until the fourth, and possibly not even by then, General Pickett decided it was futile to continue any further campaign operations against the city. Equally discouraging news had reached him concerning Colonel Dearing, who had found Fort Anderson too well fortified for his forces to capture.[8] By orders of General Pickett, Confederate forces withdrew from New Bern on February 3. Considerable blame for the ill-fated venture naturally fell upon the commanding general. Pickett, in turn blamed his subordinate commanders. However, many believed the Confederates would have met with success had Hoke, rather than Pickett, been in charge.[9]

In a letter to his wife dated March 8, 1864, Matt Ransom indicated he was not likely to return to Verona soon, and he complained of pain from his injured arm. However, any physical discomfort he may have experienced did not prevent him from leading his brigade and cavalry force on the following day against Suffolk, Virginia. Here, he drove the federals from town, "capturing a piece of artillery and quarter-master stores of much value."[10] By this time few goods and commodities were slipping through a tightening Union naval blockade of Wilmington, and there were few other sources for imports, particularly medicines. Quite understandably, the capture of enemy stores was always welcome news to a population feeling the rigors of war.

On the very same day that Ransom carried out his attack on Suffolk, there occurred in the White House a ceremony which, though brief, had great bearing on the future conduct of the Union war efforts. Under a revived commission, the title of which only George Washington had held, Ulysses S. Grant assumed command as lieutenant general over the Northern armies. Upon making his debut in the national public arena, the new appointee appeared to many as shy, and very plain in appearance. His friend General William T. Sherman was concerned that Grant's simple nature would make it difficult for him to deal with dishonest and deceitful elements in Washington.[11]

Inclined to reduce military tactics and strategy to simplified formulas, General Grant regarded his mission as having two primary objectives: to destroy the Army of Northern Virginia commanded by Robert E. Lee, and the Army of Tennessee commanded by Joseph E. Johnston. With Richmond behind him, Lee's army was defensively encamped below the Rapidan River. Johnston had taken up a position near Dalton, Georgia, and behind him lay Atlanta. General Johnston's fate was to be the responsibility of William T. Sherman, whose forces were to move out of Tennessee headed southward, with the objectives of capturing Atlanta, and then pushing to the Georgia coast. Here, Sherman would turn northward and eventually rendezvous with Grant's forces. While this awesome southern campaign was being conducted, two federal armies — the Army of the Potomac under Grant's strategy and the Army of the James under General Benjamin F. Butler — were to be occupied in the Richmond operations. From the very outset of his command, Grant chose to exploit his advantage in troop numbers and resources. The plan called for pinning Lee down, depriving his forces of all mobility in an ever-increasing bloody contest, even if half of the Army of the Potomac were destroyed in doing so. In the upcoming campaign the eighteenth-century emphasis upon capturing cities would be incidental and subordinate to more realistic goals. Grant informed General Meade, "Lee's army will be your objective," and told him wherever "Lee goes, you will go also."[12]

The Southern high command held mixed opinions pertaining to Grant's appointment, but Longstreet's views offered the most ominous projection. At West Point he had developed a strong friendship with Grant; later, he attended Grant's wedding, and through family marriage actually became related to him. "We must make up our minds to get into line of battle and stay there," Longstreet admonished, because "that man will fight us every day and every hour until the end of the war."[13]

Apparently, Lee was experiencing a calm moment along the Rapidan River, and on April 12 Confederate army headquarters in Richmond issued orders for Matt Ransom, and his brigade to proceed immediately from Weldon to Tarboro for special duty with General Robert Hoke. The brigade was "to carry at least five days of provisions and ammunitions for active field service."[14] Hoke, a native North Carolinian, had achieved an outstanding combat record, rising from private to brigadier general by age twenty-six. In temperament and abilities he and Ransom shared much in common, and the two men enjoyed a cordial relationship during these next critical days.

In essence, Hoke proposed a well-defined plan for a combined land and water assault against the federals in Plymouth, North Carolina. A port town situated on the Roanoke's southern bank about eight miles west of Albemarle Sound, it was established in 1790, incorporated in 1817, and served as Washington County's seat of government.[15] Its recent history was exceedingly turbulent. Early in 1862 federal troops had garrisoned the town. In December of that same year, Confederates had attacked and defeated Union troops there, but the federals had returned the following year to build up a rather impressive supply depot.

Plymouth was now surrounded by professionally constructed defenses manned by just under three thousand men, supported by river gunboats. A successful assault against such strength required a carefully combined military and navel operation carried out under the most skillful tacticians. The line of defense lay westward on the river, then ran south, forming a semicircle as it turned north to terminate east of town on the river. Confirming this perimeter of defense, at a point about two miles above Plymouth, was Fort Gray, equipped with a heavy battery of fifty men of the Second Massachusetts heavy artillery. The Eighty-fifth New York also supplied one and one-half companies of infantry support. At a distance of about one mile southwest of Plymouth was Fort Wessells. To this installation were assigned forty-two infantrymen from the Eighty-fifth New York and twenty-three effectives of the Second Massachusetts heavy artillery. Giving added strength to this fortification were a light thirty-two-pounder and an iron six-pounder cannon. Surrounding protection included a ditch spanned by a drawbridge and felled trees in the immediate vicinity. Federal entrenchments around the town were appropriately anchored to well-defended fortified points such as Battery Worth on the west side, where a two hundred-pounder Parrott was mounted. To the south stood Fort Williams; on the east were Conaby Redoubt and Fort Comfort. Those entrenchment's east of town, curving downward to Fort Williams, were manned by the One hundred and first Pennsylvania, the Sixteenth Connecticut, and five companies of the One hundred and third Pennsylvania. To the west of Fort Williams two companies of the Eighty-fifth New York were posted, as well as the Twenty-forth New York independent battery with the remainder of the line (extending to the river) comprised of pro–Union refugees, blacks, and portions of two companies, which included some Confederate deserters. On hand to perform any cavalry duties was a detachment the Twelfth New York cavalry. In command of this federal garrison was a fifty-five-year-old Connecticut native and career army officer, Brigadier General Henry W. Wessells. Federal naval assistance was to be provided by Lieutenant Commander Charles W. Flusher from his gunboat *Miami*. Other craft in his command included *Southfield* (formerly a New York ferryboat now converted to a gunboat) and three smaller vessels, the *Whitehead*, the *Ceres*, and the *Bombshell*.[16]

Wishing to eliminate or at least reduce possibilities for a miscarriage of his plans, General Hoke established personal contact with parties responsible for construction of the ironclad *Albemarle* at Edward's Ferry in Halifax County. He was promised the vessel's presence and active involvement during the coming assault on Plymouth. This assurance was given by none other than the ironclad's commander, James W. Cooke, who conceded that because of the rush for time his craft might have to sail before construction had been completed. Scarcity of iron had prevented steady work on the *Albemarle*, and to contend with this problem, search parties had combed the entire area for bolts, bars, and metal of all kinds. The keel was built in a cornfield, with an ordinary blacksmith shop serving as a construction site. Plans called for a finished vessel 152 feet in length, 45 feet in width at the beam, drawing 8 feet of water.[17] The prow was of solid oak, tapered for ramming, and covered with two inches of iron. The 60-foot octagonal casemate was amply protected by two layers of 2-inch plating. Propelled by two engines of 200 horsepower,each and armed with two 100-pounder rifled cannon, the *Albemarle* was destined to become a formidable floating fortress.

On April 15 General Hoke left his headquarters at Tarboro, and with his forces headed for Plymouth. Infantry units included Brigadier James L. Kemper's old Virginia brigade of the Fifteenth, Seventeenth, Eighteenth, Twenty-ninth, and Thirtieth regiments, which were now commanded by Colonel William R. Terry. Hoke's brigade consisted of the Twenty-first Georgia and the Sixth, Twenty-first, Forty-third, Fifty-fourth, and Fifty-seventh North

Carolina regiments, led by Colonel John T. Mercer of the Twenty-first Georgia. General Ransom's brigade was composed of the Twenty-fourth, Twenty-fifth, Thirty-fifth, and Fifty-sixth North Carolina regiments; Ransom's Forty-ninth remained behind on picket duty and was replaced in the pending campaign by the Eighth North Carolina of Brigadier General Thomas L. Clingman's brigade. In charge of the single cavalry regiment was Colonel James Dearing. North Carolina, Georgia and Mississippi each contributed one artillery battery; all remaining artillery hailed from Virginia.[18] Leading the marching columns was Kemper's brigade followed by Ransom's and Hoke's units. Leaving Tarboro, the force journeyed to Jamestown and from there they followed the Jamestown road, making a southwesterly approach to Plymouth. By April 17 the Confederate column was only five miles from its destination and siege operations were about to begin. So far, at least, the Confederates enjoyed one great advantage in being able to conceal their movements preparatory to an attack.

The federal command at Plymouth had concluded their enemy would remain inactive for at least the next several weeks. The monotony of camp life was relieved only by the occasional raiding detail. General Wessells assured his superiors the local front was without any immediate dangers and the ironclad under construction posed no immediate threat. Such optimism seemed confirmed on Saturday, April 16, when the Twelfth New York cavalry, after a scouting assignment, reported no enemy elements in the vicinity of Plymouth. In the midst of all these encouraging signs, General Wessells did not retain the gunboat *Tacony*, recently sent to reinforce his local flotilla, but allowed it to return to New Bern. This was a decision he would soon greatly regret.[19]

April 17, 1864, dawned as a typically delightful spring day in eastern North Carolina. It was a Sunday, and church services in Plymouth were attended by both soldiers and local civilians. During the first part of the afternoon, enlisted Union personnel visited, napped, wrote letters, and leisurely puttered around their personal quarters. At four o'clock, quiet prevailed over the town. Bugles of the cavalry and drums of the infantry were expected to sound on the next hour, signaling a regularly scheduled dress parade. But suddenly the stillness was broken by distant, rapid musket fire coming from a picket line. This was shortly followed by a mounted cavalryman rapidly making his way into town with hat in hand, shouting, "The Rebs are coming!"[20] And indeed they were. Colonel Terry's forces and two batteries of twenty-pounder Parrott guns veered off to the left on the Jamestown Road, making their way to Warren's Neck, a strip of land between two creeks which flowed into the Roanoke River west of Fort Gray. From here Terry intended to charge the fort. Hoke's and Ransom's brigades also took leave of the Jamestown Road after learning that a bridge up ahead had been destroyed. Moving the two units off to the right, they crossed the intervening stream over a mill dam, then took up with the Washington Road one mile below its junction with the Jamesville Road.

Advancing northward, Hoke defeated the Twelfth New York Calvary in a sharp skirmish at the road junction. About four-hundred yards beyond this point he set up a battle line by stationing his brigade on both sides of the Washington Road. Ransom's troops settled in to the right of Hoke's, with their right flank to the south, below town on the Mill Road.[21]

By now activities within the Union camp were proceeding at a frantic pace. Against the background of a long drum roll were the sounds of artillery shells screaming overhead aimed at advancing Confederates south of town. Excited Union soldiers scrambled for their haversacks and rifles, then rushed to strengthen rapidly filling trenches. In the streets panic had overtaken many civilians, particularly women, who in tears beseeched Yankee chaplain A. S. Billingsley for prayers in their behalf. Some of these citizens and others, including children and wounded, were evacuated on a small steamer around eleven o'clock that night. This required two trips, and on one return voyage two hundred men of the One hundred and first Pennsylvania were aboard as reinforcements for Wessells.

Under cover of dark that night, General Hoke ordered Colonel Mercer to shift his entire brigade to the left of Washington Road. In support of this move, advance artillery emplacements were laid down within effective firing range of Fort Wessells. By early dawn hours, action also got underway at Fort Gray. Under protection of his artillery, Colonel Terry sent his forces forward, but due to extremely effective enemy fire, his advance lasted only briefly. Fortunately, the two hundred-pounder Parrott in Battery Worth proved ineffective. Terry's artillery could claim some significant successes by sinking the *Bombshell* as it was attempting to deliver messages to the fort.

Despite all heavy activity during daylight hours on April 18, there were very few position changes between the opposing sides, but this would change within hours. Almost in desperation the Confederates waited for the *Albemarle's* arrival. While the Sixteenth Connecticut Volunteer's band was playing patriotic tunes after supper, General Hoke decided to act decisively. At 5:00 Ransom's brigade with fourteen pieces of artillery advanced to the federal line, taking a nearby position east of Fort Williams. This move was intended to confuse the federals regarding Hoke's intended objective, Fort Wessells . Ransom's operations were stubbornly challenged by enemy artillery fire, but onward they pushed against heavy showers of grape and falling iron bolts. For its part, Confederate artillery in this sector from 6:00 until 10:00 P.M. delivered an intense, deadly fire into its enemy , facilitating Ransom's push forward to within eight hundred yards of Fort Williams. This move was to be only a demonstration, and Ransom's infantry had been ordered to contain its firepower. Assuredly, excitement and danger were not lacking within ranks during this advance. Suddenly, a missile fired from a federal gunboat soared over Plymouth and struck at about 150 yards ahead of the Eighth North Carolina; then, with a forward bounce, it exploded among the men of company

H, killing or wounding fifteen. Out of respect General Ransom ordered the fallen soldiers buried at night to insure proper internment.[22]

While Ransom's demonstration was in progress, Hoke was advancing toward his objective, but encountering extremely heavy volleys of musketry and artillery fire from Fort Wessells. After surrounding the redoubt, Confederate infantry repeatedly attempted to capture the works. In one of these charges Colonel Mercer was killed, and immediately replaced by Colonel W. G. Lewis. At this time, the federals began throwing improvised hand grenades, actually six-pound cannon balls with attached special ignition fuses; because of these, the Confederates temporarily called off their assault. With additional artillery having been brought up, Hoke set up a crossfire, concentrating on a small enclosure in a corner of the fort. Federals went for cover when shells began striking the building's roof and chimney. There followed a huge explosion, sending metal fragments throughout the redoubt. One of these shell particles struck and killed the fort's commander, Captain Nelson Chapin, of the Eighty-fifth New York. The wrecked installation suffered even further destruction when hit by two shells from a federal gunboat. Convinced any further resistance was pointless, the garrison surrendered at 11:00 P.M. Hoke had won an important tactical victory; from this vantage point, he could concentrate his artillery on his opponent's right flank. If the present assault upon Plymouth was to be concluded successfully, the *Albemarle's* participation was imperative. But as yet the vessel had not arrived.

Actually the ironclad was nearby. At 10:00 P.M. on Monday, April 18, Commander Cooke was three miles above Plymouth, but because of river obstruction, further passage seemed impossible. The maiden voyage of the *Albemarle*— accompanied by a flatboat equipped with forges and sledge hammers to make final repairs — had not been without disappointment and trials. On Sunday night according to historian Michael Ballard, "bolts fastening the main coupling of the center shaft were wrenched loose."[23] There followed a six-hour delay, and later the rudderhead was damaged, causing four more hours of lost time, furthermore, because of the current's swiftness, navigation was extremely difficult, particularly around the numerous river bends. The crew was compelled to steer their craft backwards, with heavy chains dangling from the bow section to steady their course.

After a brief reconnaissance by the crew, the *Albemarle* at 2:30 A.M. on April 19 weighed anchor and continued its course downriver, assisted by extremely high waters caused by recent rain, as it passed Fort Gray and Battery Worth, both installations opened fire, but with only minimal effect. Cooke did not respond to these federal harassments, since his first objective was to clear all enemy craft from the river. About one and one-half miles below town, he met his first test. Coming toward him were the two Union gunboats *Miami* and *Southfield*, lashed together by chains. Aboard the former, Commander Flusser hoped to entangle the Confederate ram between the two gunboats and pour fire into the entrapped vessel. Sensing the dangers confronting him, Cooke steered the *Albemarle* sharply southward, then turned, ramming the *Southfield* at full speed. Torn open, the *Southfield* quickly filled with water and began to sink. But now Cooke faced an alarming situation. The *Albemarle's* prow was engaged in the *Southfield's* frame, and as she sank, pulling the iron-clad's bow downwards below the open port-holes, it seemed for a few moments that the vessels were destined to go down together. However, when the *Southfield* settled on the river bottom, rolling over on her side, the ram was released, and the *Albemarle* righted itself. Quickly the *Miami's* crew separated their craft from the ill-fated *Southfield* while firing into the *Albemarle* during its brief awkward plight. Actually, federal guns were unable to inflict any harm upon the southern ram. When Union commander Flusser ordered his nine-inch rifled gun to be fired using a percussion shell at extremely close range from its target, his gunner was hesitant. Flusser pulled the lanyard himself, and was killed instantly by a flying fragment piercing his heart. Lieutenant Charles A. French took command and ordered the *Miami, Whitehead,* and *Ceres* downstream, headed for Albemarle Sound.[24]

After probing federal lines during the early morning hours of April 19 following the *Albemarle's* victory, General Hoke decided to alter his battle plans. Bringing in some of his troops at Fort Gray and placing them closer to the main enemy line, he also installed heavy guns at Fort Wessells. Subsequent heavy artillery and infantry skirmishes convinced the attacking commander that his best move should be aimed a the Union left flank. There his forces would not encounter a large Parrott gun, and because of the *Albemarle's* performance, no enemy gunboats would run interference. Ordering increased pressure from his own brigade and Kemper's on the federal center and right, Hoke that afternoon called for General Ransom to move eastward across Conaby Creek, follow the Columbia Road north, then recross the Conaby, continuing on the same road as it made a sharp turn westward into Plymouth.

The brigade moved without serious incident over the roundabout route until it arrived at the Columbia crossing of the Conaby. Quickly Ransom ordered his artillery to silence a strong federal outpost. In his haste to cross the creek ahead of his men and before a pontoon bridge was laid across the stream, General Ransom experienced some rather tense moments. With his horse becoming stuck in deep mud at the creek's edge, the general was compelled to dismount in a most unconventional manner by sliding over the animal's head and pulling himself across to the other side of the stream. Not being a swimmer, he could have lost his life here. Instead, once across the stream, he organized a charge that drove the remaining enemy from what had been a well-fortified position. For reasons unknown to him, General Ransom's own mounts had not caught up with him for this campaign. His present horse was on loan to him by Captain W. H. Day's father of Halifax County, and the general dispatched a squad of men to rescue the unfortunate animal with instructions to return it to its owner.[25]

Thanks to a quickly constructed pontoon bridge, Ransom managed to move his entire brigade across the creek by midnight. Under a full moon, the general deployed his troops for the coming battle — from right to left the Fifty-sixth, Twenty-fifth, Eight, Thirty-fifth, and Twenty-fourth. At the most critical point of the line opposite the Union outpost of Fort Comfort, Ransom placed his old regiment, the Thirty-fifth.[26] His last activity that evening was to call his colonels together to give them final orders for the next day, but he did not ask for their advice, since it was he who had planned and intended to execute the bloody work ahead.[27] According to a historian of the time, a courier that evening overheard General Ransom speaking "words of kindness and caution," and he said that he would not have one life lost unnecessarily for the "glory of beating the Yankees in the morning."[28]

At last, just before daybreak a rocket flew, advising Hoke that Ransom's attack was imminent.[29] On horseback with sword held high above his head, Ransom rode along his line, and then in his commanding voice he ordered, "Attention brigade. Fix bayonets. Trail arms. Forward march." The charge was on.[30]

The Fifty-sixth and Twenty-fifth regiments were forced to grapple with problems. A drove of stampeding cattle required flanking, and then the men became mired in a waist-deep marsh. Once these obstacles were overcome, the way was clear for the two regiments to advance into streets of east Plymouth. The Eight and Twenty-fourth regiments were responsible for capturing federal redoubts to the left of Columbia Road. The *Albemarle* offered timely assistance to the brigade by firing shot and shell into Conaby and Comfort outposts. In the meantime, Colonel Lewis's command and Kemper's brigade continued to mount increased pressure on the Union right and center; under these circumstances, General Wessells was compelled to spread his firepower, rather than concentrating on a given sector. As planned, the Thirty-fifth North Carolina charged and captured Fort Comfort, crossing the deep ditch surrounding the installation, then scrambling up an embankment, and finally engaging in a severe contest with several companies of the One hundred and first Pennsylvania and several members of the Second Massachusetts. Following this capture, General Ransom referred to the redoubt as Fort Jones in honor of the Thirty-fifths commander. All that remained was the fall of Conaby redoubt; then Ransom's forces could overcome Pennsylvania and Connecticut infantry occupying Union left flank trenches. Confederate artillery concentrating on this area was stopped, and the Eight charged, overcoming the surrounding ditch and then attempting to scale the outpost's walls. From inside, desperate federals threw out hand grenades and delivered a stream of musket fire through openings of the log enclosure. Several Confederates fell fatally wounded, rolling down the embankment, shot in the head. In their turn, members of the Eighth aimed their guns through the palisades and bore down heavily on their enemies while other regimental members crashed through a rear gate of the works. This action brought out an immediate surrender by those survivors inside.[31]

Having captured the two federal outposts on Columbia Road, General Ransom was free to employ his entire brigade against the town of Plymouth. General Wessells dispatched reinforcements from the Eighty-fifth New York on his right, but they proved ineffective. In town, house-to-house and street-to-street fighting was employed. Confronted with continuous fire from yards, fences, and windows, the brigade slowly moved forward, eliminating their enemies with vigorous return fire. After making its way through town, part of the Fifty-sixth North Carolina advanced as far as Battery Worth, and with two cannons, which had been captured, compelled the installation's surrender. This left only one major federal position still remaining; Fort Williams. As the main Union fortification of the town, it was well defended by guns and strongly reinforced; a history of the time describes it as surrounded by "a ditch thirty feet deep and thirty feet wide, with a stockade in the center of pine poles ten and twelve inches in diameter, joined together by iron cables, and the entrance protected by a massive iron door."[32] By this time, Hoke's forces on the west side of town were joined with Ransom's on the east side, surrounding the formidable outpost. General Ransom, after a careful reconnaissance, concluded that the fort, because of its defensive strength could not be captured by infantry without extremely high casualties. He then signaled for the *Albemarle* to come up and take position.[33] In the meantime, however, the Eight regiment attempted to charge the fort by advancing to the edge of the surrounding ditch but found crossing the ditch impossible. As the regiment's history records, this assault was reckless and unnecessary. It was made under the flush of victory, not by order of the commanding general."[34]

At the bottom of the main street that led from the river to the fort's entrance, the *Albemarle* positioned itself and prepared to fire. The first shot fell short, killing and wounding several men of the Thirty-fifth, who had assumed a position across the street in readiness for an assault upon command. Quickly the regiment was pulled back closer to the river, and again the *Albemarle* opened fire on Fort Williams.[35] After three or four shells exploded within the compound, General Ransom dispatched a member of his staff to demand unconditional surrender. General Wessells responded by requesting to confer with the officer in command. During the conference that followed, Wessells was miffed when Hoke implied that he would give no quarter if the federals continued to resist.[36] The Confederates then renewed their attack in a more spirited fashion with musketry and exploding shells causing heavy Union losses. A much subdued Union general surrendered his command. From a practical standpoint, the siege of Plymouth was concluded, except for sporadic firing in isolated pockets where Union soldiers had not received word of the commander's surrender. To the west of town, Fort Gray hoisted a white flag around 2:00 P.M. Following, the capitulation of Fort Williams, those Union soldiers refusing to surrender were summarily shot, as were several captured southern deserters, on orders of General Hoke. Some Union black troops and former Confederates now fighting as federals fled in panic for nearby swamps, hoping to escape what they believed was certain retribution from their captors. Organized details pursued these fugitives, and the resulting sounds of musketry emanating from the swamp area created rumors of a massacre.[37]

Casualty figures for both sides are confusing and contradictory. General Wessells summed up all of his losses in one figure, 2,834 killed, wounded, missing and captured; he believed Union dead and wounded did not exceed 150, but his chaplain considered the figure of 225 more accurate. Besides Commander Flusser and a seaman being killed by ordnance mishap, one hundred Union sailors drowned, eleven were wounded, and eight were captured. Hoke's final report contained no statistics concerning Confederate casualties, but probably most reputable statistical estimates would have around 125 killed and between 400 and 700 wounded.[38] Ransom's brigade alone suffered 87 killed and at least 500 wounded.[39] As for prisons, Hoke disposed of these expeditiously by sending Wessells and his immediate staff to Richmond's Libby Prison; enlisted men and regimental officers were marched under escort to Tarboro, where they traveled by train to Georgia and were confined in the notorious Andersonville Prison. Wessells was ultimately exchanged on July 3, 1864. He returned to New York where he carried out nominal duties for the duration of hostilities.

Praise for the Plymouth victory was quick and spontaneous. Hoke received congratulations and news of promotion to major general in a telegram from President Davis. Shortly thereafter, Colonel Dearing was promoted to brigadier general, and Lieutenant Colonel Gaston Lewis, who succeeded Colonel Mercer, was also raised to a rank of brigadier general. Matt W. Ransom whom Will Burgwyn would later call "the hero of the third and last day's battle by which the town's surrender was brought about," was not promoted.[40] For this careless lack of recognition, as many of Ransom's friends considered it, the state made partial restitution when the General Assembly included his name with Hoke's and Commander Cooke's in a "joint resolution of thanks to the officers and men of their respective commands for this brilliant victory." In its turn, the Confederate congress offered similar formal tributes.[41]

If General Ransom harbored any feeling that he had been slighted by not being promptly acknowledged in his vital role at Plymouth, he never revealed such sentiments publicly. As a matter of fact, there is nothing to indicate he did so privately. Quite simply, General Hoke had allowed Matt Ransom the freedom to make his own decisions at Plymouth, and Ransom had used that freedom wisely and well.[42] At first opportunity Matt telegraphed Pattie, "I am safe, my brigade greatly distinguished itself." A follow-up letter contained sincere thanks for having come through the recent ordeal safely and without injury; such good fortune he attributed to the deity. He wrote of having paid a visit to the *Albemarle*, where Captain Cooke had requested to send some presents to Mrs. Ransom. Once again, he offered generous praises in behalf of his brigade and closed, "Kiss the dear boys. God bless and preserve us and bring us together in joy and love."[43]

General Hoke lost little time before putting his forces in motion for their next objective, Washington, North Carolina. Alerted to this, federal commander General O. J. Palmer evacuated his troops during the night of April 26, setting fire to the town as he withdrew.[44] Pressing on to New Bern, Hoke and Ransom were obviously determined to repeat their performance of just a few days previously at Plymouth. Immediately, siege operations were invoked, capturing several outer works surrounding the city. During these initial operations which offered great encouragement to the attacking Confederates, Hoke suddenly received orders from President Davis to cease all North Carolina activities and immediately return with his command to Petersburg.[45] The sense of urgency indicated in these orders of May 6 reflected in large measure the anxiety of Confederate leaders over the most recent Union conduct on several fronts.

At that moment, two imposing federal armies were converging upon the vital area of Richmond and Petersburg. Once again, North Carolina, at great expense to her own interests, found herself compelled to defend this particular front against a determined enemy.

On May 4, the Army of the James, with upward of 40,000 troops under General Benjamin F. Butler, had captured City Point, Virginia, and was now in a position to threaten both Petersburg and Richmond.[46] Further north the Army of the Potomac, with at least 118,000 effectives — under formal command of General George C. Meade, but following strategy dictated by Grant — was locked in combat with Lee's forces of about 62,000.[47] From May 5 to May 7 both armies engaged in a series of bloody confrontations destined to be known as the Battle of the Wilderness. In official dispatches to Washington, Grant estimated his losses from his crossing of the Rapidan River to May 11 as eleven general officers killed, wounded, or missing, and "probably twenty thousand men."[48] As measured by previous conduct and standards, the Union army had suffered a major catastrophe. To Grant, however, this was not a defeat, but only an incident in his overall plan of forcing the Army of Northern Virginia to fight a continuous campaign of seemingly endless battles.

On the night of May 7 Grant chose to disengage from his enemy, as Lee had anticipated, and moved south and east to Spotsylvania.[49] Here, for ten consecutive days, the Union and Confederate armies experienced an ordeal even more bloody than the Battle of the Wilderness. Of great tactical importance was the fact that the northern supreme commander was now choosing the battle sites, not the southern supreme commander. Though none realized it at the time, the Wilderness campaign had another very important and telling result. The fierce fighting by General Lee's forces would constitute this army's final great counterattack.[50] At this point there seemed sufficient evidence Lee's army was fighting just to survive.[51]

Without question, Lee knew he was confronted with an opponent whose style and methods of conducting war were far different from those of his predecessors. "Grant is not a retreating man," Lee informed his aides: moreover, he observed, now "the Army of the Potomac has a head."[52]

Not until May 3 had Lee been able to determine the seriousness of Butler's intentions. The determination, when it came, had led to his warning to the Confederate War Department to prepare for another campaign against Richmond.[53] In response to this threat and Davis's subsequent order, the return trip of Hoke's command to Virginia was swift. Once these forces arrived, events seemed to proceed at an even faster pace.

Reaching Kinston at 8:00 A.M. on May 8, Ransom's brigade proceeded by way of Goldsboro to Weldon, and from here northward the trip was by rail as far as Jarratt's Station. Because of recent federal cavalry activities and the severing of the rail line, the march was resumed along the tract to Stoney Creek, a distance of about twenty miles. As Ransom and his men made their way in darkness of night, they heard the weird hootings of nearby great swamp owls. This brought responses here and there along the line: "That is a bad sign, boys; hard times in old Virginia, and worse a'coming."[54]

When the brigade arrived at Stoney Creek on May 10, trains were waiting. The voyage ended several hours later at Petersburg, where the brigade was quickly hurried to Swift Creek on the Richmond Pike and assigned to General Bushrod Johnson's division.[55] In this area the day before, Union major Generals Quincy A. Gillmore and William F. Smith had attempted to carry out their respective assignments. Having reached the railroad at Chester Station, Gillmore's forces had torn up a minor section of tracks, while Smith in marching on Whithall Junction had met with determined Confederate skirmishes. The two generals finally combined their forces in what was intended as an attack upon Johnson, who, after stubborn resistance, eluded his opponents by taking up a position behind Swift Creek.

In spite of a heavy likelihood that federal troops in great force lay across this path ahead, General Hoke on the morning of May 11 moved out from Swift Creek with the brigades of Ransom, Johnson, and Johnson Hagood, and headed for Drewry's Bluff.[56] As he had expected, as he moved north Hoke encountered a sizable federal force at Chesterfield Courthouse; these troops, however, withdrew to the river side of the pike. At Half-Way House, the Confederate general offered battle, but his offer was refused. As a result, the way now became clear for Hoke to move his forces into Drewry's Bluff. This fort, which was known by a variety of names including the Union appellation of Fort Darling, stood approximately seven miles below Richmond, south of and flanking the James River. It was manned by heavy artillerists, and during the critical period from May 5 to May 10, several thousand War Department clerks and munitions workers stood by waiting call for emergency duty. During this brief interval, only two brigades (around 3,000 combat soldiers) were involved in Richmond's defense; protecting Petersburg, there were no more than 2,000 men. Robert Ransom, Jr., who was in charge of these limited forces, found himself not only threatened by Butler's presence south of Richmond, but for a moment seriously challenged by General Philip Sheridan at the outer works north of the Confederate capital. With his two brigades and a light battery, Matt Ransom arrived at the vital area where effective southern artillery had just repulsed a federal attack. Fortunately, Sheridan did not renew his assault, which freed Matt and his troops to resume their position at Drewry's Bluff.[57]

To meet the latest threat developing against Richmond, Confederate authorities turned to their most available and, as he was generally considered, most competent senior officer. General P. G. T. Beauregard was detached from his assignment at Charleston and given command of Confederate forces in North Carolina and in Virginia below the James. The charismatic general arrived at Petersburg on May 10 to assume his new command.[58] Known to be bombastic on occasion, he was nevertheless well regarded for his capability.[59] Following his arrival at Petersburg and the days which immediately followed, he would, with Braxton Bragg's assistance, assemble a Confederate army of nearly 20,000 troops.[60]

Each passing day witnessed a continuing buildup in Confederate strength south of the James, making it harder for Major General Benjamin F. Butler to fulfill Grant's overall strategic plan, which called for an attack upon Richmond. Grant wanted Butler to cover the south side of Richmond, extending his left flank to touch the James. If that objective could be met, Grant planned to position Meade's army where its first flank connected with Butler's left, effectively crossing the river.[61] Rather than launching offensive operations, the Army of the James had thus far behaved defensively. This was illustrated on May 6 when Butler's two corps moved westward and, after reaching the base of Bermuda Hundred Peninsula, were given orders by local commanders to establish a line of entrenchments three miles in length with the right flank on the James and the left resting on the Appomattox. Next day, when Generals Smith and Gillmore were outfought and outmaneuvered by General Bushrod Johnson, the two federal commanders recommended to Butler that Petersburg should be taken from the east. To accomplish this, it was necessary in their judgments, to return to Bermuda Hundreds and there board steamboats, or construct a pontoon bridge across the Appomattox. This proposal General Butler quickly and angrily denied. On May 12 Butler again put his forces in motion, but this time headed north in the direction of Drewry's Bluff. Six days previously he could have made this move against far less resistance than now awaited him.

Helping to push this onslaught was Ransom's brigade, comprised of abut 1,800 officers and men posted on the extreme right of the Confederate line, defending Drewry's Bluff and facing Petersburg.[62] On the afternoon of the twelfth, the brigade advanced down the pike southward, occupying breastworks at a point where the fortified line crossed the road. Here the line terminated but changed its course, running off virtually at a right angle toward the river.[63] Almost immediately after taking up their positions, Ransom and his men met the first federal assault upon Drewry's Bluff. (Before this outbreak occurred, Generals Hoke and Ransom were conferring in a farmhouse located in the assault's path and narrowly escaped capture.[64]) Advancing federals were greeted with sharp musketry fire, particularly from the Forty-sixth Regiment, which held a position on top of a steep bank of earth while below them in a ditch their fellow soldiers swiftly reloaded and handed up fresh rifles.[65] As the Confederates repelled the frontal attack, a federal line was extended around the brigade's right flank, a movement facilitated by a thick cover of woods. When the line was fully completed, Ransom's right and rear positions became extremely vulnerable. At last, after the brigade's front was stabilized and a final Union assault had been repulsed, Ransom ordered the Forty-ninth and Twenty-fifth regiments into action on his endangered right flank. Charging over their works while delivering a rapid destructive volley, the two units completely overcame their opponent's line. In the process, however, the brave and much respected Captain Cicero Durham was killed leading the Twenty-fifth.

The next two days featured renewed, overwhelming federal attacks. On the thirteenth another attempt was made to flank Ransom's right and rear positions, but the brigade managed to holdout successfully until darkness, at which time it retired to a main line of defense. Next day, May 14, General Ransom experienced another cruel combat wound.[66] Consistent with his habit of giving only minor thought to his own safety, he was up front rallying a line of sharpshooters when a minnie ball struck his left arm. This time, both bones of the forearm were shattered. Matt was in a state of extreme pain and shock, and the appearance of his wound seemed to indicate immediate amputation. As a historian of the period records it, Matt arrived at Chimborazo Hospital in a semiconscious condition and "submitted himself to the surgeons with the injunction to save his arm even at the risk of his life."[67] Fortunately for Ransom, it was his friend and old regimental surgeon Dr. Charles J. O'Hagan who decided the fate of the injured arm, and it was he who performed the required surgery. He removed the splintered ends of the bones clearing the way for the remaining parts to knit together on their own. Eventually the arm healed just as the surgeon had anticipated. It was shorter than before, but Matt still had the use of both the arm and the hand.[68]

Worried and anxious, but drawing some comfort from Doctor O'Hagan's excellent reputation, William Hood waited for news of his wounded general.[69] Whatever the outcome, the faithful courier was ready to perform any required duty. With federal troops holding stretches of the railroad, returning to Verona this time would be a very risky affair. The worst possibility, of course, was General Ransom's capture — and what a prize his thoroughbred Ion would be to some Yankee cavalryman.

Chapter IX

Back at Verona

The news that General Ransom had been wounded appeared in the Petersburg newspapers on May 16, and on this date his prospects of returning home by rail seemed very remote.[1] Bridges had been destroyed over Nottoway River and Stoney Creek and at Jarratt's Depot. Apparently, federal forces still remained and occupied five or six miles of rail in the vicinity of Chester and Half-Way House. No mail had arrived over this route for the past eleven days.[2]

This grim situation, which involved communications between Richmond and Petersburg as well as southern approaches to these centers, soon received some brief relief. On May 16 Beauregard furiously attacked Butler's advance units at Drewry's Bluff. By late afternoon federal forces were in retreat and subsequently took up defensive shelters behind their entrenchment line on Bermuda Neck. In this campaign, Butler lost 4,100 men; Beauregard's losses were also heavy. By now Grant's campaign strategy in Virginia was seriously behind schedule. By Grant's own appraisal, Butler's army was "completely shut off from further operations directly against Richmond as if it had been a bottle strongly corked."[3] Now Beauregard could dispatch 6,000 troops of his command to General Lee, then fighting a furious battle at Spotsylvania Courthouse. With these troops and 2,500 others reporting from the Shenandoah Valley to add to his strength, Lee could continue running interference with Union strategy; however, he could no longer hope to implement any strategy of his own.[4]

With federal troops effectively neutralized in the area for a time, road and rail communications were quickly restored between Richmond and Petersburg, including points south to Weldon. These efforts greatly facilitated the return of Matt Ransom and William Hood to North Carolina.

Thus the Ransom family was restored, at least for a time. Pattie and Matt had many subjects for conversation, for every day brought news items of both local and widespread interest. For example, in the General Assembly currently meeting at Raleigh, strong sentiments for peace prevailed, with some members insisting on the soundness of convening a state convention to deal with the matter. There were no indications, however, of a willingness to abandon the Confederate cause, nor was there any apparent mood to accept what might be regarded as objectionable peace terms. Yet there were hopes that somehow, acceptable terms might be negotiated.[5] Finally emerging from these divided counsels was a formal resolution passed by both houses at Governor Vance's prompting and recommendation. This resolution called for the Confederate government, at an opportune moment following significant results on the field, to officially propose peace on the basis of independence and national sovereignty. At the same time, there was incorporated in the resolution a reaffirmation of "pledges of the resources and powers of this state to the prosecution of the war until the independence and nationality of the Confederate States is established."[6]

The Ransoms, like other citizens of the state, were aware of Wilmington's increasing importance in sustaining the Confederacy's existence. During the coming months, it would become the most important southern city after Richmond. It was protected by Fort Fisher, situated at the entrance of Cape Fear, and this grand installation had proved itself invincible thus far to repeated federal attacks. To cut off the fort, along with its neighboring treacherous inlets, shoals, and islands, the Union had to spread its blockading vessels in an arch of fifty miles. Under these circumstances the federals were simply unable to prevent blockade runners from supplying the Confederacy.[7] Once goods of contraband arrived safely in port, they were conveyed northward on the Wilmington and Weldon Railroad, with the last leg of the journey completed on the Weldon Petersburg line. If any part of this direct connection between Richmond and Wilmington were to come under federal seizure, the impace would be tragic, if not fatal, for the southern rebellion.

In the North during the spring of 1864 a movement developed which received the support of such eminent public figures as General McClellan, G. H. Pendleton, and Governor Horatio Seymour of New York, calling a convention of all the states "to bring about a settlement based upon the Constitution as it was."[8] This proposal was received with great interest and was the cause for much discussion throughout the South. President Davis responded by commissioning a group of distinguished southern citizens to engage in any preliminary steps relating to the matter. However, Lincoln disapproved of this formula, and it came to naught. Another northern public gesture, this time humanitarian in essence, involved attempts to bring about a massive exchange of prisoners as proposed by the Confederate government. Each side was credited with holding at least 30,000 prisoners. Governor Andrew Curtin of Pennsylvania, in his third appeal to the Lincoln administration on the matter, received a reproachful inquiry from Secretary of War Edwin M. Stanton: "Do you come here and ask me to exchange 30,000 skeletons for 30,000 well-fed men?"[9] General Grant apparently spoke for the administration when he summed up his views on prisoner exchange: "If we commence a system of exchange which liberates all prisoners taken, we will have to fight on until the whole south is exterminated. If we hold those caught, they amount to no more than dead men."[10]

With the time growing closer when Lincoln would stand for reelection, many southerners were hoping northern voters would register resounding disapproval of their leader. There seemed ample reason to believe they would do so. The bloody conflict was now in its fourth year, and long casualty lists affected every city and remote hamlet throughout the North. Spring and summer had come, and victory seemed as elusive as ever. While Grant had penned Lee behind Richmond and Petersburg trenches, and Sherman had pushed General Johnston to the very suburbs of Atlanta, the cities were seemingly beyond capturing. In the new aggressive Union strategy, Grant and Sherman together lost more than 90,000 men in a period of less than four months. In the middle of July, Lincoln called for another 500,000 men, and it seemed as if the war would never end.[11] This point received special emphasis that same month when Confederate general Jubal Early and his forces approached Washington, D.C., from the north by way of Silver Spring, Maryland, and for a brief time, the capital seemed in serious danger. Timely arrival of federal reinforcements compelled Early to withdraw below the Potomac, where he continued a menacing posture.

During that exciting moment when General Early's troops lay in waiting on the outskirts of Washington for their next offensive move, President Lincoln rode out Seventh Street Road to Fort Stevens. Arriving there, he climbed a parapet and stood upon it. He had never seen a battle in the current war and wished to see one. It was not really an unreasonable wish; thousands of Union servicemen had already given their lives for a cause he had championed, a cause for which he must take responsibility before his maker. The firing began, and in the midst of flying bullets saturating the air and Union soldiers falling on their faces, a man fell dead no more than five feet from the president. Though strongly urged by the Union commander to get out of the line of fire, Lincoln continued to stand immobile. His height of six feet, four inches, made him a perfect target as well as a very important one. Finally a Union captain, no longer able to restrain himself, yelled, "Get down, you fool!" Lincoln instantly responded, and once under protection of cover, he looked at the captain and said, "I'm glad you know how to talk to a civilian."[12] Years later this captain, Oliver Wendell Holmes, would become a legendary judicial figure as a member of the United States Supreme Court.

Any possible military threat Jubal Early posed was a brief duration. Whatever benefits the Shenandoah Valley offered the Confederacy, either as an access route to the North or a food supply source, Grant was determined to eliminate. His formula involved sending federal armies to "eat out Virginia clear and clean as far as they go, so that crows flying over it for the balance of the season will have to carry their provisions with them."[13] The man selected to carry out this mission was General Philip Sheridan, another total war apostle who shared Sherman's approach to conducting war. To Sheridan appeals from pleading old men, women, and children were completely unpersuasive. On his orders, hay, straw, and barns stored with crops became victims of the torch; any and all livestock was driven from its domain. Anything of benefit to man or beast was to be cleared from the valley. In Sheridan's wake, these unfortunate rural residents were subject to bands of marauding guerrillas operating in the area. These elements consisted of outlaws, deserters, and desperadoes, despised by Confederate and Union troops alike.

In an attempt to provide some relief from these appalling conditions in the valley, Lee dispatched General Early. Described as impetuous, Early was a fighter. However, in taking on Sheridan, his chances for success were narrow. His forces hardly numbered more than 15,000, while his opponent could put in the field some 45,000. His weaponry was obsolete compared to the newest federal automatic firepower. The two contenders met at Winchester, Virginia, resulting in a Union victory. In pursuit of his foe up the valley, Sheridan continued his usual policy of laying waste to the region. In his campaign, Early did receive some relief and support from Confederate partisan John Mosby, who constantly attacked Union rear guard troops; this activity required Sheridan to assign heavy forces to contend against the distraction.

By mid–October Sheridan's forces were camped at Cedar Creek, about twenty miles south of Winchester. While the Union commander was absent in Washington, General Early ordered an attack which came close to routing the entire federal army. As if by a miracle, Sheridan arrived back on the field just in time. In heroic fashion, he managed to rally his troops to score another great Union victory, and the Shenandoah was forever lost to the South.[14]

To confront Lincoln in the coming presidential election, the Democrats turned to a peace platform, which they hoped would win mass approval. However, they soon learned that their candidate, General McClellan, supported continuation of the war until the Union emerged victorious.[15] Thus the Democrats were running on a peace platform with a war candidate. That the two were incompatible was apparent to a number of citizens, including Lincoln, whose political fortunes would surely be enhanced by any subsequent victories on the war fronts.

If since his recent return to Verona General Ransom appeared solemn and at times lost in thought, there were valid reasons for his demeanor. Letters from his father, Robert Ransom, Sr., bespoke a man who preferred to step aside and let a new age follow the current struggle. Mr. Ransom harbored a sense of betrayal on the part of both the southern leaders who had steered his section into secession, and the Lincoln government which made such a course inevitable. What a price the country paid for men with small minds! Never for one moment did the elder Ransom waver in his Whig principles; while honoring his local heritage, he loved his country, and these sentiments he impressed upon his immediate family. Even his dreams and aspirations for his two sons — one with a promising military career, and the other with such a bright future in law and politics — seemed in great peril.

Due to serious matters involving his personal welfare, Mr. Ransom, at his son's insistence, would spend his remaining days at Verona. In his own mind Matt Ransom had resolved that upon him would rest the responsibility of providing aid and assistance to members of his family during the uncertain times ahead.

It was during his calls upon his good friend and neighbor at Thornbury that Matt Ransom fully realized the dreadful penalties war often imposes upon civilians. Henry King Burgwyn, Sr., had suffered a paralyzing stroke four months following his oldest son's death at Gettysburg.[16] Now a second son, William H.S. Burgwyn of Ransom's brigade, had recently been seriously injured at Cold Harbor. A third son, a boy in his teens, George Pollok, was scheduled to join V.M.I. cadets for field service training. The paralysis the stroke had imposed upon Mr. Burgwyn was partial, but physical mobility came only with labored effort, and his brilliant and graceful social parlance of former days was apparently over. Worst of all, this remarkable mind, so generously blessed in range and depth, so alive with interests and aptitudes, now seemed to be suffering under handicaps imposed by failing health. Such circumstances often conspire to make life seem futile, but this attitude Mr. Burgwyn rejected. The former great planter and sage took care to point out that his position concerning secession was not determined until after John Brown's raid; only then did he favor separation of the two sections. Once the war ended, Northampton County and North Carolina would desperately need the talents of men such as Henry King Burgwyn, Sr., and Burgwyn's inability to remain involved in public affairs saddened his friend Ransom greatly.

Another distressing matter for Matt was his brother's deteriorating health over recent months, brought on largely by the frustrating burdens of command. Not one to stand aside while witnessing inequities or intolerable situations, Robert Ransom, Jr., by impulse spoke out with emphasis and frankness, often times at personal cost. On June 12, 1864, he penned a strong letter to the Confederate adjutant-general complaining that troops of the Army of Northern Virginia were receiving more food rations than members of his own command performing identical duties. Troops of the former received "a half pound of meat, flower bread (at least in part), rice or pease, sugar, coffee, and vegetables"; members of his own command got "but one-fifth pound of meat, and cornbread. If they receive sugar and coffee (only six pounds of one and three of the other to 100 rations) the meat is stopped."[17] That summer Robert Ransom was assigned to Early's command for the 1864 Shenandoah Valley campaign, but on August 10 the North Carolinian, no longer physically able to carry out his duties, was ordered back to Richmond. Here he would ultimately receive orders to report for duty in the Department of South Carolina, Georgia, and Florida.[18]

Sometimes after a session of conversation in their library, Pattie Ransom and her husband would venture into periods of extended silence, she more often reading, and he, especially of late, absorbed in thought. One evening he held in his hands a recently arrived letter dated July 1, 1864, from General G. E. Pickett. The letter contained a lengthy list of plaudits in behalf of Matt Ransom's combat record. "It is seldom," the general stated, "I venture upon a recommendation, nor do I know that one from me would be of much value, but I cannot part from you without wishing that it were in my power to bring your service to the notice of those who have it within their power to reward merit."[19]

If General Ransom wished to engage in serious reflections concerning war, he could call before him an almost endless parade of names and images of men who had given their lives thus far in this costly cause. Some were of modest means and background, while others were of eminent public stature. J. E. B. Stuart would certainly qualify as one of the more eminent figures. Engaged in combat with Sheridan's cavalry at Yellow Tavern about ten miles above Richmond on May 11, 1864, he fell gravely wounded, shot by a dismounted Union cavalryman. He was carried to Richmond, and there, on his death bed, he requested assembled friends to sing "Rock of Ages." He then left his physical pains behind and slipped away at age thirty-one.[20] When informed of Stuart's death, Lee came just short of losing control of his emotions. The slain cavalryman was almost like a son to the general. If, as Lee stated, he had lost his right arm with the death of Jackson, he now, with Stuart's death, had lost "the eyes and ears of his army."[21]

Seated at Stuart's funeral directly behind President Davis, Robert Ransom, Jr., observed the somber ceremony and later reported the scene to his brother in detail. He described how a large crowd of mourners converged on the Church of St. James in Richmond at 5:00 on that evening, May 13, 1864. Before formal ceremonies got under way, Mr. Davis noted there was no saber beside the dead warrior; the Confederate president removed his own and placed it in the casket beside the corpse. Covering the metallic coffin were white springs of laurel. Besides President Davis and his cabinet, other dignitaries included Governor Letcher of Virginia and both houses of Congress. It was a brief and dignified Episcopal service, concluded by a funeral anthem, after which the remains were taken to the local Hollywood Cemetery for burial. Very noticeable and significant was the lack of a formal military escort; every able-bodied Confederate soldier was needed for active duty.[22]

As the weeks passed at Verona, William Hood found himself settling down into a rather set routine of duties that more or less resembled a regular camp situation. A benefit of his several months of duty at Verona was the chance to perceive something of the full character of his brigade commander. In contrast to his singular public dignity and professional bearing, General Ransom in the privacy of his home presented an almost entirely different personality. Here he frolicked with his children, amusing them with pranks; here, too, he showed himself a very sensitive, understanding husband. Yet outside the company of his immediate family and close friends, a rather distant, reserved bearing marked the general's relations with others, and neither small talk nor vulgarity figured in his discourse with associates. While training and instinct cautioned him against hasty speech and conduct, he would on the slightest impulse assume any moral obligation for a vital cause. He always encouraged and rewarded young officers and enlisted men. Earlier in the war Henry King Burgwyn, Jr., still under twenty-one years of age, had applied for a vacant colonelcy. Because of his youth — he was regarded as yet a boy by his brigade commander, Robert Ransom, Jr. — his prospects for promotion seemed very unlikely. In this matter, Matt Ransom disagreed entirely with his brother.[23] Receiving a commission as colonel in another brigade, young Burgwyn went on to prove his bravery and military skills, vindicating many times the confidence and trust of those who had given him initial support. Burgwyn's brother Will would long remember Matt's conduct as an officer; many years later he would write that "he was never known to court martial or put an officer under arrest, never had a private punished or put on extra duty, never asked for a court martial against an officer or private, but the discipline of his command was excellent."[24]

Hood observed many instances of General Ransom's kindness and sympathy toward his soldiers. One very revealing and touching incident had occurred shortly before the general received his most recent wound. In the Petersburg area, Ransom rode upon a detail of men accompanying a prisoner on the way to be executed. The general stopped and made inquiry of the case. He learned the condemned man had been refused a single night furlough to join his nearby visiting family. Believing he could call on his wife and children for a few hours and then return to his command next day without detection, he decided to take a chance. Unfortunately, as Will Burgwyn later narrated the incident, in attempting to rejoin his unit he "missed it on the line of march, was arrested, tried and condemned as a deserter." Convinced the man was truthful in his explanation and was not a deserter, General Ransom ordered the escort to postpone execution until his return. This settled, he wheeled his horse, spurred to full speed, and shouted, "I'll try my man, I'll try my poor fellow!" Shortly afterwards, "he returned from General Lee's headquarters, his horse and himself covered with mud, waving the reprieve above his head." Sadly, this narration does not end on a happy note. Next day this very same soldier fell mortally wounded in combat.[25]

At Verona, Hood enjoyed reading from the Ransoms' extensive library. He also learned much from Matt's discourse. If the general occasionally spoke in an authoritative manner when making references to history, Hood considered this not surprising or offensive behavior. After all, the general was only once removed from the generation that had won colonial independence and then set up one of the most unusual governments known to mankind. His own kinsman, Nathaniel Macon, had sat down in parlance with Washington, Jefferson, and the Randolphs of Virginia. When speaking in public, the general was inclined to use a style of oratory developed in his boyhood attempts to emulate his idol, Daniel Webster of Massachusetts. On no subject did General Ransom demonstrate a greater sense of pride than the subject of his Southern heritage. Yet that pride was completely devoid of narrow provincialism, which had never been allowed to stifle his wide range of interests and his broad outlook on public affairs.

Anticipating that serious, heated sectional issues would arise following the war, Ransom was fond of quoting Thucydides, the great historian who chronicled the wars of ancient Greece. Thucydides told how, with Persian soldiers in overwhelming numbers threatening Athens, the two Greek generals responsible for its defense were not on speaking terms as a result of past rivalry and personal rancor. Just before that critical moment of enemy attack, these two generals approached each other in front of their troops, "impulsively seized each other's hands and exclaimed, 'Let us bury our anger.'"[26] Because of this reconciliation, Athens survived.

Whether wise counsel and productive reconciliation would prevail following present hostilities would be largely determined by the caliber of the leadership then coming forward. These times would necessarily require high qualities of statesmanship as prescribed by Plato in his *Republic*. In Ransom's mind such select leadership once appeared on the American scene in the persons of Washington, Jefferson, and Madison, later joined by Marshall, Jackson, Clay, and Calhoun. These men were all southerners, prompting Ransom to conclude that during the century preceding the war, "the southern people accomplished more for human liberty than all other peoples in the world during all time."[27] Certainly, the general could have turned to William Hood and said, "Son you have every reason to be proud of your southern heritage."

If Hood, under his qualified mentor's guidance, studied the United States Constitution written in Philadelphia in 1787, he had an opportunity to recognize that many principles and objectives in this singular format of government bore striking resemblance to Plato's thesis. For example, those who rule should be qualified to rule; to make certain of this, the president of the United States was to be chosen by a select body known as an electoral college. Also removed from general popular control was the selection of United States senators, who received their positions under authority of their respective state legislatures with an age qualification of thirty-five years, and who served a lengthy term of six years. Apparently, the Senate was intended as a body of wise men who could act as a force against the more impulsive House of Representatives, whose members were elected by qualified voters in the various states. Since in Plato's view, power corrupts power, the system of government was to be a republic, with states sharing a wide latitude of sovereignty with the national government. Very much in compliance with Montesquieu's views as stated in his *Spirit of the Laws*, the newly established government existed under a system of checks and balances.

For years, both legal professionals and laymen have been avidly interested in the judicial career of John Marshall. It was he more than any other individual who modeled the national judicial process, and indeed, the very system of government which emerged under the Constitution of 1787. Nowhere in the Constitution is the Supreme Court given clear authority to declare unconstitutional the acts of Congress and state legislatures. That the high court ultimately assumed such authority involves the dominating and persuasive role of this remarkable jurist. Justice Marshall's decisions reflect a clear, concise mastery of the English language. A serious student, by careful study of these legal opinions along with classical literature and the scriptures, invariably develops a great capacity for written and oral delivery. According to Ransom, a man who lacked competence in communicating with others suffered a real handicap.

The high degree of excellence which Plato insisted that rulers must attain would have some measure of appeal to a bright, active teenage boy. A candidate under this system was required to carry out a well-disciplined preliminary education up to seventeen or eighteen years of age. There followed three years of physical and military performance; next in sequence were ten years of preparation in advanced mathematics, climaxed by five additional years of philosophical study. Those who survived this strenuous program to age thirty-five were then qualified to take up their responsibilities as heads of state. Left to his own imagination, William Hood would decide how well his friend and commanding general fulfilled those essential requirements of leadership as prescribed by the ancient Greek philosopher.

Beyond the peaceful confines of Verona, General Ransom, by means of the media and written exchanges between his brother and close service associates, followed in detail the action on the various military fronts. After the Battle of Drewry's Bluff and Union general Butler's retreat behind his line of defense at Bermuda Hundreds, Ransom's brigade took up positions in trenches with other Confederate forces facing their bottled-up enemy. Believing Lee's defenses weak, and planning to capture Richmond, Grant on June 3 struck at Cold Harbor; once again he met with a sobering defeat. Undeterred, in compliance with his grand strategy, he then determined to capture Petersburg by speedily moving his army south of the James River, hoping his movements would remain secret from Lee. On June 13 Grant detached General W. F. Smith, who arrived with the Eighteenth Corps at Bermuda Hundreds on the following day. The morning of the fifteenth his attack got under way. Meeting this new offensive was Beauregard's command, which inclusive of cavalry and homeguard consisted of hardly more than 2,000 men. After the Confederate line was broken at one critical point, Petersburg waited for Union capture;

but General Smith, who had angered General Butler that May with his suggestions of retreat and defense, now served Grant in the same way. He chose to assume a defensive posture, making no further advances.[28]

To help contend against the latest federal offensive, Ransom's brigade, then stationed at Chaffin's Bluff, received orders to report immediately to Beauregard, and by an all-night march they reached Petersburg at sunrise on June 16.[29] Arriving none too soon, they ran to take on their positions within the inner works south of the city just in time to repel the first advancing federal troops. For this day's attack on Petersburg, three Union army corps were present: Major General William F. Smith's, Major General Winfield Hancock's, and Major General Burnside's, a total force of around 50,000 men.[30] Because he was so desperate for troops, Beauregard was compelled to utilize the force that was pinning down General Butler at Bermuda Hundreds. All day the 10,000 Confederates desperately fought their foes, and when night closed the unequal contest, Beauregard's men were still holding.[31] After dark General G. K. Warren's corps of 17,000 troops arrived to give additional strength to the next federal drive scheduled for the following day. Indeed, by midnight on June 16, the entire Union army of at least 90,000 had moved south of the James River.

Fighting resumed early on the following morning, and throughout the day the federals made assault after assault without success until just about dark, when a part of the Confederate line was punctured and Battery 14 was captured.[32] Around 11:00 A.M. Ransom's brigade was ordered to give support to General Wise, whose forces had abandoned a salient they had occupied. The intended purpose was to reestablish their line, and in the process the Thirty-fifth's colors were captured, but regimental members for their part captured three enemy flags. Loss to the unit was heavy; going in with twenty-eight officers and nearly five hundred men, it came out with eight officers and fewer than two hundred other survivors. The commander, John G. Jones, was shot early in the encounter. He rose, but after a few steps, he was felled again. Calling for help, he started forward once more when he was struck a third time, never to rise. Captain Philip J. Johnson, engaged on the breastworks in hand-to-hand combat with a federal major, was shot in the hand. Dropping his sword, he was at the mercy of his adversary and one of the captain's men shot the major through the head.[33] During the night Beauregard prudently withdrew and took up new and shorter defenses nearer the city.

On June 18 General Meade, with an army of around 70,000 facing about 20,000 Confederates, made a series of uncoordinated, ill-fated attacks. His senior officers of command included G. K. Warren, A. E. Burnside, D. B. Birney, and J. H. Martindale.[34] Following the last attack at 4:00 P.M. against Confederate works, Grant ordered a cessation of offensive operations. The siege of Petersburg was about to begin.

For the next eight months Ransom's brigade would share the same fate as other Southern military units serving in the Petersburg area. As their military history described it, they "lived in the ground, walked in wet ditches, ate … cold rations in ditches, slept in dirt covered pits."[35] Breastworks of the opposing side were so close in places that it was certain death or injury to expose one's person, making it necessary to relieve posts under protection of night, crawling along ditches to find them.

Since food could not be cooked in this area, it was prepared in cook yards sometimes a mile to the rear, and then brought forward on men's shoulders. During this time, Captain Lawson Harrill of Company I, Fifty-sixth Regiment, described the Confederate soldiers living in underground bomb-proof shelters as scantily clothed, almost barefooted, and half-starved. They would eat anything. Harrill wrote that he was "invited to a squirrel dinner made of wharf rats."[36]

By now it was most difficult for men of the Confederate army to be granted leave of absence from their units. Marriage seemed to be the most acceptable reason for granting furloughs. Colonel R. T. Bennett in approving such a request is said to have recorded the following: "The application of A. B. private for twenty days furlough is approved. The Colonel commanding is of the opinion from personal experience that the time asked for, twenty days, is not more than sufficient to consummate the nuptials and recover from their effects."[37]

Probably one of the brigade's most unusual experiences occurred during dawn hours of July 30 when the federals exploded four tons of black powder beneath a Confederate fort. Access to this installation had been gained by a regiment of former Pennsylvania coal miners, who secretly burrowed a long tunnel originating from their lines. A great crater resulted from the explosion, but because of poor coordination and leadership, the federals failed to capitalize on this unique opportunity to break the Petersburg line. During the initial construction of these Confederate breastworks, Ransom's brigade had contributed its fair share of labor, and at the time of the blast it occupied trenches on the left of the salient. The Twenty-fifth and Forty-ninth were ordered out of their works to give needed assistance in repelling federal troops who poured through the gaping hole. These two regiments joined with William Mahone's division to drive the federals back; while this activity was in progress, the Thirty-fifth, with its thin line of defense, repulsed several enemy assaults. Apart from being involved in a skirmish on August 21 at Davis House, the brigade spent the remaining summer within the inner works protecting Petersburg.[38]

News from other fronts offered little encouragement to southerners. On July 18, 1864, President Davis relieved General Joseph E. Johnston of his post as commander of the Army of Tennessee. Critics of this move contended two blunders were committed: the removal itself, and the replacement of Johnston with John B. Hood, which many considered an even more serious error.

Johnston had engaged in defensive tactics against a numerically superior, better-equipped opposing army. With every advance by Sherman, his lines of communications became progressively more complicated. Furthermore, at any time, a miscalculation or error of judgment on his part could prove fatal to his army. Watching the political front, the southern commander had wished to avoid a major slug-out resulting in a Union victory, which would promote northern enthusiasm for the war and possibly assure Lincoln's reelection.[39] Strategy of this kind rarely wins popular acclaim, but in a military sense, it can be very practical and correct under appropriate circumstances. Sherman regarded Johnston as a highly professional officer and was delighted over the prospects of taking on his successor.[40]

When John B. Hood took over his new post, the forces he inherited from General Johnston numbered 70,000 troops. According to some commentary, Hood fell far short of Johnston in intelligence and discretion. Whether such assessment be right or wrong, one point, as historian Peter J. Parish has noted, was certain — he "would fight and sooner than later."[41]

From July 20 through July 28 Hood launched three separate attacks against his enemy, going down in successive defeats with heavy casualties. Following his second encounter, he retreated within Atlanta's defenses. Sherman responded with siege operations, then proceeded to occupy rail communications with the city. Facing the possibility of becoming trapped within the confines of a bombed-out, ruined city, Hood chose to evacuate his remaining forces. He had recklessly destroyed one of the principal Confederate armies of the South.[42] Anywhere or any place Sherman wished to march would now be a cakewalk.

Atlanta's fall on September 1 had great symbolic meaning. Its capture was a tremendous boost to sagging northern spirits and thus an invaluable contribution to the fortunes of Lincoln and the Republican.[43] During the previous four months Union forces had labored exhaustively and suffered tremendous losses for little result, but at last, Grant's strategy seemed to be having a significant effect.[44] During the recent dramatic scenes at Atlanta, Sheridan continued his methodical destruction, leaving the beautiful southern landscape in ruins. Completing his handiwork, on October 7 he reported to Grant, "The whole country from the Blue Ridge to the North Mountains have [sic] been made untenable for the rebel army."[45]

For the remaining year no military activities of any consequence occurred around Petersburg and Richmond, with the possible exception of the Union capture of Fort Harrison at the end of September. One southern combat soldier, commenting on the results of federal military initiatives since May, expressed himself in a very illustrative way: "Grant attempted to go around us, over us, and under us, but was foiled in every attempt."[46] Assuredly the Union commander had met with some serious disappointments, one of which was his failure in late October to sever the Southside Railroad before winter arrived. To his credit, on the other hand, were the consequences of his continued pressure against the Confederate position, which forced Lee to spread his forces in thinner and thinner lines.[47] The Confederate line now covered a distance of around thirty-five miles, beginning at Williamsburg Road east of Richmond and running to Hatcher's Run southwest of Petersburg. To man these lines, Lee could muster no more than 57,402 effective troops, as opposed to 110,364 well-provisioned federal soldiers. Between May 5 and December of 1864, southerners inflicted a loss of 108,000 killed, wounded, and missing upon their enemy, compared to 40,000 of their own.[48] Yet, despite Confederate efforts, their adversaries seemed to become ever more numerous and determined. Morale throughout southern ranks was extremely low; to those who remained in the trenches, the end of the war appeared to be only a matter of time.[49]

It was mid-morning on October 8, a day Pattie Ransom had been dreading for some weeks. She had known all along that her husband was anxious to rejoin his brigade, in spite of continuing pain from his recent, unhealed wound. Each passing day seemed to bring additional news confirming the Confederacy's inevitable collapse. Before month's end the ram *Albemarle* would meet with enemy destruction, and the North Carolina towns of Plymouth and Washington would again fall to federal occupation. This time, when General Ransom returned to his command at Petersburg, he would be required to use a circuitous route to overcome travel uncertainties brought on by enemy intrusion into the area.

What words does a husband use before his wife when he is about to face the heavy risks of death in combat? Only the standard recitations come forth: reassurances that all will come out well in the end; reminders to take precautions for the family's health; promises to keep in touch through letters — the list goes on. To such utterances the wife may appear to give respectful attention, but her mind is occupied with wider matters. Of this duplicity the husband is generally aware. However, the play's the thing, and the performance carries on. To Pattie Ransom the future offered little hope; all seemed so futile. Yet she would never disclose such feelings to her husband, who was offering his life for a cause about which he had earlier expressed great reservations. Even if this cause proved meaningless in the end, he was determined, if Providence granted, to witness the final act.

There was one pleasant note of relief for Pattie Ransom. In the departure scene on that morning of October 8 there stood the boy William Hood, displaying his usual good manners and attempting to lighten the somber mood. In truth, he was no longer a boy. Now nineteen years of age, he had become a man before his time, and for this the war was largely responsible. Perhaps Pattie derived some comfort from the fact that although her husband had decided to return to active duty early, before his wound had sufficiently healed, this young courier would be standing by to provide whatever possible assistance he might render in behalf of his hero.

From her front porch at Verona, Pattie could watch the two horsemen riding their mounts down the long, straight pathway which intersects with the Weldon Jackson Road. Here they turned left; then in a few minutes they were out of sight. Would they ever return? In the privacy of her bedroom, if Pattie Ransom wept for hours in her agonizing grief, who could fail to understand and appreciate her torturous ordeal?

Chapter X

In Lieu of Victories, Glory

By October 15, 1864, General Ransom had joined his brigade at Petersburg, where they were huddled in trenches to defend the Confederate line from a point on the Appomattox River stretching east to the Jerusalem Road.[1] In a letter of this date to Mrs. Ransom, he stated the enemy during the night had shelled his position "at frequent intervals, and though our loss was very slight, one cannot repose pleasantly under bursting shells." The general referred to his personal quarters as "quite comfortable, and if I can stay in them right safe."[2] Cooking of food was carried on two miles behind the lines, "but we really relish the meals." To relieve Mrs. Ransom's anxiety on a very sensitive matter, the general may have been overly complimentary of the food. On the other hand, his comments may have been sincere, as General I. M. St. John about this time became commissary general. Under this new, resourceful officer, for a brief period, there were actually surpluses of meat, bread, and forage.

In his letter, General Ransom clearly revealed a melancholy mood, interspersed with leading personal observations and instructions to Mrs. Ransom. If he were "only sure that Yankees would not get to our home, I would send you so many things, flowers, etc., but now it seems almost silly, doesn't it? I will only try to get you some beautiful books — knowledge is such a treasure, is it not?" As for future military conduct in the Richmond-Petersburg area, there was a strong opinion "that we meet here in a great battle soon. I am not sure of it. Grant's army is very demoralized, and Petersburg and Richmond will hardly fall this winter." This letter concluded: "Please remember that if the Government desires to impress any of the Negroes, I will furnish the desired numbers here and will not let them interfere with those at home."[3]

On the home front, public morale had undergone drastic changes during the past several months. As the year ended and a new one dawned, the pace of events seemed to accelerate, indicating an impending collapse of the Confederacy. In North Carolina virtually all males of military age were either serving the military or hiding from it.[4] Western and central counties continued to be plagued by bands of roving, lawless elements and deserters. The tragic situation would surely worsen now that the war had taken on a more prolonged character. Through his reelection on November 8, Lincoln had received a mandate for continuing his policies, and Governor Vance was returned to office on a platform advocating continued war efforts until independence was achieved.

Nature itself seemed determined to intensify local misery. As the new year began, drenching rains blanketed central regions of the state, and fences, bridges, mills, and railroad tracks were destroyed and washed away. During this same period, two huge, destructive fires in Charlotte and Salisbury consumed great quantities of essential government stores. Yet, in this dismal setting of catastrophe and destitution, when an urgent appeal was made in behalf of Lee's army, North Carolinians of all backgrounds responded with contributions from their almost barren pantries. Food shortages affected every North Carolina home, from the humblest cabin to the grandest plantation. Refined, respectable families whose past style of living had reflected not the slightest economic deprivation now found themselves reduced to bare subsistence levels. Meat was rarely included on household tables; cornbread, sorghum and peas were the sole staples. Dried apples and peaches were in extreme scarcity, and tea and coffee had virtually disappeared. Clothing, too, was in short supply. Children went shoeless in the winter, and women were compelled to make their own footwear and homespuns. Carpets were cut up and used as blankets; window curtains and sheets provided bandages for hospitals.[5] Only in extremely rare instances did some braggart claim to be unaffected by the privations of war.[6]

If the name of William T. Sherman was intruding on many a conversation in North Carolina, there were ample reasons for its presence. With roughly a third of Atlanta in flames and in the hands of looters, its factories, warehouses, and railroad installations destroyed, the innovative northern general departed from this stricken city on November 15, 1864. Moving in four spread-out columns, Sherman's force of 60,000 lived off the land and kept to a moderate pace, sometimes about fifteen miles or less each day. This army employed its destructive talents over an area about two hundred and fifty miles long and fifty miles wide, from Atlanta to Savannah. Food items, work animals, cattle, railroads, bridges, mills, workshops, and many public buildings were the usual victims. Countless Negroes flocked to the rear and flanks of this advancing force, and joining them were stragglers, looters, thieves, and deserters of both sides.[7]

Nowhere alone the federal army's route was it seriously challenged by opposing forces. Rightfully concerned with being trapped, Confederate forces prudently abandoned Savannah on December 21, heading northward in hopes of joining other remaining southern fighting contingents. On the following day, General Sherman, in a public written gesture, offered the city of Savannah as a Christmas present to Present Lincoln.

The consequences of Sherman's march were instantly recognized by northern citizens, and in the South, many of the most dedicated and determined Confederates found themselves in almost total disbelief. The period of suspense concerning the northern commander's next move was brief. On January 3, 1865, he began moving his overwhelming forces into the Palmetto State.

Steady, progressive occupation by federal troops over vast areas of the Confederacy provided ample evidence to both North and South that one side was approaching certain victory. Already, in anticipation of this event, a number of confusing and compelling issues had begun to surface, some of which revealed the real meaning of the bloody American conflict. To what extent, if any, would the victorious party be willing to recognize the war as a contest between separate, independent governments, one residing in Washington and the other in Richmond? Or was the entire matter to be regarded as a domestic situation involving massive popular uprising, requiring government intervention and repression? The latter interpretation had been Lincoln's position from the start of hostilities. His refusal to recognize the legitimacy of the Richmond government was entirely consistent with his open denial that states could legally withdraw from the Union. Assuredly, this was an opinion generously shared by the northern public.

For the postwar period, Lincoln seemed to be thinking of a simple plan to replace old Confederate state governments with loyal elements, then make any adjustments necessary for achieving a Union partnership. There was always a possibility that Lincoln's moderate approach would be replaced with a more detailed, demanding formula for restoring southern states to the Union. Within Congress, views had already been expressed that "rebel" states should measure up to certain requirements before returning to Union membership. To Thaddeus Stevens of Pennsylvania, a member of the House of Representatives, there was no question "that exercising full belligerent powers, the United States could rule the former southern states as conquered provinces." Over in the Senate, Charles Sumner of Massachusetts as early as 1862 had dramatically referred to those southern states that had left the Union as having committed suicide.[8] An alternative that surfaced was less harsh; it contended the seceded states should revert to territorial status, which would provide opportunities for federal jurisdiction. A major problem with this contention, as well as the "conquered provinces" and "state suicide" approaches, was that all three conceded the right of secession by states — a right which had never existed, according to Lincoln's government and northern public opinion.

Amidst all the arguments concerning a reconstruction policy for the southern states, troubling questions were inspired by Article IV, section four of the Constitution, in which the United States guarantees every state a republican form of government. Around this challenge northern radicals and moderates alike could muster; however, many perceived some serious obstacles within that guarantee. If abandoning the practice of slavery was one of the prerequisities for setting up republican forms of government, how would this affect such border states as Kentucky and Missouri? More importantly, if at some point it was decided that a republican government must include equality — perhaps even voting rights — for Negroes, what would the northern states do? Discrimination by race was a legal fact in at least a dozen state governments of the North.[9] Such confusion in the Union concerning these vital issues was noted by serious minds in North Carolina and throughout the South. These observers realistically concluded that those trusted with power would ultimately impose their own style of rehabilitation upon the defeated region. Would it be Lincoln's or the radical's views that shaped this final judgment? In any event, before any plans could be implemented, the war must be won, and the means to this end was General Sherman.

Now South Carolina, the first state to secede from the Union, would suffer the wrath of the infamous Union general.[10] Under the most trying conditions, imposed by heavy rains, floods, and swollen rivers, Sherman's remarkable army continued its slow but methodical pace into enemy territory. Where bridges and roads had been washed away, they were replaced; if wagons became mired in mud axle-deep, entire regiments specially trained for such situations freed them by brawn, mules, and ropes. As he chartered Sherman's menacing movements, General Joseph E. Johnston was certain that mankind had not seen such an army since Julius Caesar's time.[11] For an unsurpassed sightseeing experience, Sherman's men delighted in setting fire to extensive stands of towering white pines and enormous oaks. Multicolored flames of red, blue, and yellow, accompanied by the odors and the snapping sounds of hot resin provided a unique, even obscene kind of show. And why not? This was South Carolina, hotbed of secession.

In this milieu of gloom and impending disaster, Charleston braced for the worst kinds of Yankee retribution. Panicky, confused citizens fled the city. Many headed for Columbia, the state capital, where they would suffer a fate at least as severe, if not worse. Rather than face overwhelming odds, the relatively small number of Charleston defenders abandoned the city, which easily fell to Union forces on February 17.

Columbia now became the next objective of the ever-moving army. As Sherman approached, only a small Confederate force was standing by, and they prudently rode away. Upon entering the capital, Union soldiers were surprised to find a number of raging small fires. As the wind increased, these consolidated into one blazing inferno, which reduced the city to an almost total state of ruin. General Sherman contended these fires were started by departing Confederate forces. Local citizens and officials were convinced that they were the work of vandals by the vindictive attitudes of Sherman and his men. Concerning this event and the matter of Union molestation of private property, the general later declared that though he had "never ordered it and never wished it, I never shed any tears over the event, because I believe that it hastened what we all fought for, the end of the war."[12]

Sherman had developed his unique brand of warfare earlier while serving duty in Tennessee. His formula for total war was a drastic departure from the concepts of the time. For Sherman, if human rights and dignity were cast aside in the heat of a conflict, such misfortunes were compatible with his contention that war was hell. He regarded the total population of the South as enemies and was intent on conducting war against civilians as well as military elements. Such activity, he believed, would demoralize Confederate troops as they became aware their cause was being lost on the homefront as well as on the battlefields.[13] The main substance of his plan called for pulverizing the South's capacity to supply its population with the essential needs of modern warfare. Therefore, heavy priority was given to destruction of factories, communications, food, and warehouse stores. These methods to Sherman represented efficiency and certain victory.[14] Unfortunately, this approach to war provides wide latitude for barbarian elements to carry out sordid enterprises that civilized nations normally denounce. In the Carolinas the worst form of license involving destruction of private property and loss of human lives came from self-styled foragers who were absent from their commands for days; according to historian John Barrett, they "always returned with a peace offering in the form of the choicest spoils of the land."[15]

To carry out his mission, Sherman had under his command at least 60,000 men, with about 2,500 wagons and 600 ambulances. With this impressive force he could move about virtually unchecked throughout the South. Following John B. Hood's crushing defeat outside of Nashville on December 15 and 16, only remnants of the Army of Tennessee remained, much too small to effectively challenge Sherman, or for that matter, offer any effective support to Lee.

Early in January North Carolina newspapers began preparing their readers for military invasion.[16] The predicted event took place on March 7, 1865, when Sherman moved into the state. Recent federal activities in eastern North Carolina provided the Union general with some degree of comfort and assistance in his venture into another state. January 12 had witnessed the presence of a federal expedition on the east coast with Fort Fisher as an objective. A December attempt to capture this important installation, under the combined efforts of Rear Admiral David D. Porter and General Butler, had failed because of the latter's incompetence. In the January effort, Admiral Porter was again involved, but this time leading the army forces was General A. H. Terry. After a naval bombardment of the fort for two consecutive days, General Terry placed his forces ashore preparatory to an assault on January 15; the Confederates, outnumbered and overpowered, surrendered that night. After Fort Fisher's fall, southern troops evacuated Fort Caswell, which was then blown up, leaving the lower harbor completely controlled by the Union fleet. The federals rested on their laurels for a few days, then marched upon Wilmington without encountering any resistance on February 22.

On March 11 Sherman arrived at Fayetteville, and here he contacted Union general John Schofield, who by now had established himself firmly on the east coast including Wilmington and New Bern. Plans called for joining the two armies at Goldsboro. To prevent this from happening, Lee brought General Joseph E. Johnston back into active duty to assume command over remaining segments of the Army of Tennessee and all other available troops in North and South Carolina, Georgia, and Florida. Lee was very insistent that General Johnston prevent eastern North Carolina from falling to Sherman's forces. An area of utmost importance, it now served as a primary source of food for Confederate troops around Petersburg and Richmond.[17]

By March 8 Sherman's entire army was fully in place in North Carolina. One wing rested about five miles west of Laurinburg, and the other took a position along the Lumber River. Challenging this entire federal army would have been wholly impractical, but since it was a divided force marching in wings, Johnston planned his attacks against these segmented parts. His ultimate objective called for uniting his forces with Lee should he decide to abandon the Confederate capital; then the combined armies could attack Sherman.[18] On March 21 at Bentonville, Johnston by skill and courage almost delivered a convincing defeat to his adversary. Ultimately, however, the southern commander was overwhelmed by numbers and compelled to retreat, taking up shelter at Smithfield. Two days later he telegraphed to Lee the distressing news that Sherman and Schofield had joined forces at Goldsboro, a distance of 120 miles from Petersburg. The distraught, discouraged general also wrote President Davis, "I can do no more than annoy him."[19]

Upon entering North Carolina, Sherman issued orders that insofar as possible, moderation and fairness should prevail in his soldiers' treatment of North Carolinians.[20] The northern commander believed that substantial Union support prevailed throughout the state, and he expected a generous welcome. That he did not receive one was genuinely felt and noted by the invading army. Despite orders to regulate foraging, the old, loose practice continued; with prospects of battle ahead, and an increasing number of hungry refugees accompanying the Union army, foraging was regarded as a necessity. Neither were any effective restraints imposed upon looting.

Entire communities would long remember the harsh and irrational behavior of federal officers. With Wilmington now occupied, Reverend A. A. Watson, rector of that city's St. James Episcopal Church, was told that he must no longer pray for the Confederate president, as prescribed by the Protestant Episcopal Church of the Confederate states; now he must pray for President Lincoln. When the rector refused to comply, General John M. Schofield ordered the church seized. Its pews as well as pulpit were removed, and the building then served as a hosptial.[21] The Methodist Church on Front Street met with the same fate of federal seizure and was then given over to a black congregation.

Bishop Thomas Atkinson, at his home at Wadesboro on March 3, experienced a hair-raising encounter with an uninvited guest. Fortunately forewarned of the intruder, the bishop instructed his family to retreat to a rear room, while he remained in his library as if reading. A soldier barging into the room in a raving, profane fit demanded the theologian's watch, and when refused, shoved a pistol against the victim's head. At this critical moment, the minister's wife ran into the room, and after she pleaded with her husband, he complied with the ruffian's demands. After rifling trunks and drawers and taking clothes as well as jewelry, the scavenger left. Of course others suffered far worse fates. James C. Burnette, one of Anson County's most venerable and wealthy citizens, was shot on his own threshold because he was without valuables, having given over his watch and money to previous hoodlums. J. P. McLean went through harrowing torture; he was hung up three times by the neck while scoundrels shot at him to force him to disclose hidden personal valuables. W. T. Horne, Jesse Hawley, and Alexander McArthur all suffered the same fate. John Waddell was murdered in his own home. The historian Samuel Ashe notes that the usual practice "was not to shoot to kill, but to hang by the neck. Doctor Hicks of Duplin suffered that way, along with hundreds of others." Once the residences were looted and stripped, they were often burned to the ground.[22]

A sobering aspect of Sherman's theory of total war is that if a nation chooses this approach and later finds itself the loser in a military contest, its leaders should expect nothing less than trial and punishment for war crimes. That such atrocities were committed in the South without knowledge of the highest federal civil and military authorities is hardly a claim worth considering.

Lacking victory on the battlefield, southerners learned they could expect no relief through diplomacy. On December 3, 1865, President Lincoln and Secretary of State Seward met with three Confederate commissioners appointed by President Davis aboard ship at Hampton Roads, Virginia. Political motives lay behind Davis's choices of the southern delegation, which consisted of Alexander H. Stephens, R. M. T. Hunter, and J. A. Campbell. Vice-president Stephens, who had become something of a peace advocate and highly critical of Confederate official policies in general, would now have an opportunity to deal directly with Lincoln in establishing a peace formula acceptable to the South. The outcome of this attempt was anticipated by President Davis. That the sides were widely separated is indicated by the wording of their documents. Jefferson Davis wrote that he was willing to engage in such a conference "with a view to secure peace to our two countries." Lincoln, for his part, wrote of his desire to achieve peace for "the people of our one common country."[23] Lincoln's terms for peace were nothing less than reunion, emancipation, and disbanding of Confederate troops. These conditions were interpreted as unconditional surrender, and unacceptable to Davis. Of the two chief antagonists, the war map clearly favored one.

Sherman was now poised to move north, where he would join the imposing forces of Grant. Sheridan had arrived on the local scene, and General Lee decided upon a desperate move which could, if successful, produce high results. The plan called for a surprise breakthrough of federal lines east of Petersburg at Fort Stedman. A mile or two behind this fort was a military railroad which originated at City Point, and over this route Grant moved supplies to maintain his long siege lines and operations. With Grant getting ready to establish a powerful infantry force in the neighborhood of Dinwiddie Court House, Lee's impending retreat from Richmond was becoming dangerously complicated. Breaking the federal line and defeating a portion of Grant's army would be a victory in itself, but just as importantly, such an event would in all likelihood compel the Union army to withdraw their extreme left flank, thereby affording Lee a continuing retreat route. The Confederate attack would be mounted on Major General John B. Gordon's front. While Gordon reacted favorably to the idea, General Matt Ransom had his doubts.[24]

Plans for the attack called for a predawn assault at a point considered to be a weak link of the Union defense line, where opposing trenches were about one hundred fifty yards apart. Three specially selected columns consisting of one hundred men in each unit were to break quickly through the enemy line, then speedily overcome several small forts assumed to be in the area. From these installations the Confederates would unleash concentrated fire upon the federal rear, while at the same time, strong forces would pour through the break, concentrating on the occupants of the trenches. At this point, cavalry was expected to push forward with the intention of destroying area communications. Almost half of the Confederate infantry on the south side would make up this assault force, and Pickett's division of the north side, if it could arrive on time, would be placed into action.

While Gordon's assault plan seems at first glance to have merit, a more careful examination reveals several serious weaknesses or oversights. Engineers with knowledge of the terrain and the federal armament at this location were not sufficiently consulted. Apparently, qualified artillery personnel were also excluded from the select few who had been privy to the pending operation. Overlooked entirely was the possibility of severe federal firepower during attack or retreat. Although not formally trained as a professional soldier, Gordon had performed remarkably well in several battles and had risen in rank from captain to major general. Competent and experienced in infantry, he was lacking in such technical fields as engineering and artillery.[25]

On March 16 Ransom's brigade was briefly relieved of trench duty when it was ordered to the extreme right of the Confederate line at Hatcher's Run, about seven miles west of Petersburg. Here the men stayed for some few days in a number of army-built shelters.[26] Recent arrivals of new recruits afforded the regiments a degree of strength not seen for some months, and the men greatly enjoyed the chance to be out of the trenches and in the open again.

Unfortunately, they had hardly had time to adjust to their new life when the brigade during darkness of night broke camp, formed ranks, and began to march to an unknown destination. Any mystery was soon resolved when around midnight the troops arrived at Petersburg. Shortly afterwards, they were ordered to take positions they had occupied only a few days before, close to a line between the City Point Railroad and the Norfolk Railroad.[27] Ransom's brigade's left flank was held by the Fifty-sixth North Carolina near the City Point Road; then following in order were the Forth-ninth and Twenty-fifth, with Gordon's troops extending beyond to the right of the Thirty-fifth and Twenty-fourth regiments. Personally forming his line of battle, Ransom — besides commanding his own brigade in this assault — was also in charge of William H. Wallace's South Carolina. Although darkness blotted their view, the troops knew that directly in front of them on Hare's Hill stood Fort Stedman, which hardly rose higher than the terrain behind it; this stockade of poles held together with wire stood at an angle of forty-five degrees to the ground.[28] From the brigade's line to the fort, there was a distance of one hundred and fifty to two hundred yards of open space.

By 4:00 A.M. on March 25, only a few preliminaries remained before the attack. Gordon delivered a speech of encouragement to the sharpshooters, and at the same time, debris the Confederates had placed to obstruct Union advances in order to provide a smoother passage for the men. The storming party began silently advancing, led by Lieutenant W. W. Fleming of the Sixth North Carolina. Over the works of the Forty-ninth they crawled through the obstructions in front of them; then suddenly, breaking the silence, came the signal from sharpshooters of the Forty-ninth under First Lieutenant Thomas Roulac. Ransom's brigade was ready, with their general's words ringing in their ears: "I order you to take Fort Stedman, not attack it."[29] Then again came Ransom's voice, giving orders to Captain Lawson Harrill of Company I of the Fifty-sixth; pointing to a tall pine tree in the federal line, the general directed, "Take your company in at that tree."[30] After reaching the federal lines and successfully crossing the ditches, Ransom's brigade captured Fort Stedman.[31] The entire operation was completed in a manner of minutes, and the sleepy, much-surprised occupants of the fort were quickly sent to the rear.

After swooping down the federal lines on their front, the Forty-ninth prepared the way for other troops to follow, but the line on their left to the river was not taken, though to do so might have been simple enough.[32] Guns of the federal fort on the river would soon inflict a heavy toll on Confederate troops. By now early signs of dawn began to appear, and as men of the brigade looked ahead, Fort Stedman and the enemy line several hundred yards on each side of the fort had been captured. The men could not understand why General

Pickett had not arrived and were disappointed by his absence. It was generally believed he would withdraw from Butler's front at Drewry's Bluff and take up the blank space on the brigade's left flank to the river.

So far, all seemed to be falling perfectly into place for General Gordon. The infantry had performed without fault, and now, carefully selected artillerymen were training four captured Fort Stedman guns on the enemy, along with the ordnance of an adjoining battery, No. 10. As yet, however, the guns that Gordon most anxiously waited to hear — artillery pieces presumably in place at the small forts to the rear behind Stedman — had remained silent. If these guns were employed with maximum effect on the federal rear, the Confederates could enjoy complete victory.[33]

At this point, General Gordon's fortunes began to deteriorate at a rapid pace. Now would have been an ideal time for a renewed attack by fresh troops. Pickett's failure to appear was ostensibly because of breakdowns in railroad transportation, but Gordon had been warned not to expect any timely arrival of support that morning. Reports were now starting to come in announcing that local commanders had failed to locate those rear federal forts to which Gordon attached so much importance. After a long period of suspense and uncertainty, Gordon was left with the painful duty of reporting to General Lee at dawn that the Confederates had failed to reach any rear forts and the offense had been halted.[34]

By this time, the federals had come very much to life. In the early morning light they were massing troops, obviously planning on enclosure movement around Fort Stedman. As for Battery No. 9, the Confederates were never able to capture it, in spite of pushing to within five hundred yards. With the benefits of clear daylight, the federals recaptured Batteries 11 and 12; soon it seemed their entire artillery was delivering a deadly bombardment of Confederate positions at Fort Stedman and Battery 10, making them untenable. Soldiers of the period reported that masses of Union infantry "presented a sublime scene in their long lines of blue"; that "Ransom's brigade felt the impact of these troops on their right flank," and later, as reported by a member of the Twenty-fourth, that "they came in front and rear and poured into us a heavy enfilading fire…. We were now powerless to help ourselves, as the Yankees were closing in upon us from every quarter."[35]

Around 8:00 A.M. Lee called for Gordon to begin evacuation of the captured works. In Ransom's brigade, word went out "to fall back by companies" beginning on the left flank.[36] Due to the rapidly changing battle scene and accompanying confusion, before such orders could be transmitted to the right, the entire line segment was in danger of being cut off and isolated by Union troops.

Confined as the Confederates were in a small, makeshift fort and a narrow line of trenches, their continued presence invited disaster; but every man knew that to retreat across open space to his original position was almost certain death or injury. Under these circumstances, the officers' orders to fall back fell upon many deaf ears.[37] Confederate Lieutenant Colonel R. M. Stripbling wrote that Fort Stedman "demonstrated that Lee's army had lost hope of final success, and the men were not willing to risk their lives in a hopeless endeavor."[38] While the more brave and determined chose to follow orders and attempted to retreat, others decided upon surrender; in some instances there was no choice. Troops who had taken shelter near Battery 9, now isolated with no means of retreat, laid down their arms en masse. After finally returning to their trenches, remnants of the once-proud divisions attempted to count their losses. They estimated that 3,500 men had been left behind, some in the federal installations and some in the field. Of these 3,500, some 1,900 had been taken prisoner.[39]

Action of the day was not concluded. Federal commanders of the II and VI corps correctly believed the Confederate line was weak and urged a general assault. At the moment, with General Meade absent from the field, Major General G. Park was in command, and he declined the responsibility of ordering a general assault. However, Meade later returned to the scene and resumed an attack on the Confederate lines facing the II and VI corps. The assault was carried out that afternoon with good results for Union forces; about 650 more prisoners were taken by the VI Corps, with the II Corps taking approximately 184.[40] Operations throughout the entire day cost the Confederates at least 4,400 or possibly 5,000 men, and of this number, Ransom's brigade could account for 700 casualties.[41] Union losses stood at 2,080. Federal authorities attached little significance to the encounter, and while it was in progress President Lincoln and General Grant were viewing a formal troop parade to the rear and back of the combat zone.[42]

Hours passed, morning gave way to afternoon, and William Hood had not returned to his command. General Ransom knew the boy would never freely surrender. Only two other possibilities remained: either he had suffered from bodily injury, or he had met with a fatal wound. Acting under great emotional strain as a father acts for the welfare of his son, General Ransom under a flag-of-truce arrangement with Union General John F. Hartranft claimed and received one hundred and twenty dead and fifteen seriously wounded soldiers.[43]

Finally, in the mid-afternoon, two stretcher-bearers gently lowered the lifeless body of William Hood to the ground. His many friends were allowed only a few brief moments to view their slain comrade, but they would later recall this sad occasion and ponder its intractable mysteries. While Hood's fellow Confederates surely knew that all soldiers are likely candidates for death, many likely wondered why William Hood should be singled out to meet such a tragic end. Never heard to utter a foul word, repeatedly risking his life to save others, and impulsively responding to suffering and discomfort of battle victims on both sides of the war, he was a rare embodiment of the Christian

ethic. "To do justly, and to love mercy and to walk humbly with thy God"—
this aphorism appears on the cornerstone of Gerrard Hall at the University of
North Carolina. Were a marker to stand at Hood's grave, what a befitting epi-
taph! At this moment, however, the handsome youth simply lay upon the
ground. He would never experience the sensation of embracing a young bride.
No young girl would ever become the benefactress of his warm and tender
disposition. Nor would he ever father beautiful children, providing them with
the legacy of a good, healthy home.

When enumerating costs of war, battle casualties and property losses may
be calculated with some degree of accuracy, but at least one cost cannot be
assessed. What price did those surviving William Hood pay for his demise?
Given more years upon the earth, he could have gone in so many directions.
It is certainly not difficult to imagine he might have selected medicine as a
life's vocation; endowed as he was with strong, steady hands and sensitive
fingers, he might have become a surgeon. Then again, he might have preferred
to assume a legal role; in the capacity of a judge, his decisions would have
been forthright, honest, and fair. Not to be ruled out is a strong possibility
that he might have joined the clergy. Administering to the spiritual needs of
parishioners and fulfilling the many clerical responsibilities came within his
natural talents. Yet there he lay, his future stolen from himself and all those
he might have served.

During the hasty graveside ceremony, did General Ransom shed tears?
Did his voice falter or tremble during any exchange while dirt was hurriedly
shoveled into the grave? We have no answers to these questions. Perhaps out
of respect for a very private matter, the regimental records withheld any com-
ment. Public emotional display is often regarded, particularly by southern
men, as unmanly behavior. We do know that this was a most cruel moment
for the general; he was burying a young man who was practically a son. We
also know this: The official regimental and battalion records disclose that
William Hood was laid to rest in the uniform of a Confederate brigadier general belonging to Matt W. Ransom.[44]

Shortly after the last dirt was packed in place atop the grave, a massive
federal artillery barrage was launched, covering the portion of the field that
included the gravesite.

If all traces of Hood's grave and his physical remains were erased that afternoon, the real part of him, according to his faith, was about to take on new
meaning and added dimension. That eternal life would follow earthly death
he completely believed, entertaining not a single doubt. After all, this was the
promise of his Lord.

Chapter XI

Going Home

As the two opposing armies confronted each other at Petersburg in March 1865, one force was obviously prepared to deliver a fatal strike. Grant's army, fully organized, equipped, and clothed, well-fed and capable of rapid movement, gained even greater mobility on March 27 when Sheridan and his cavalry arrived at Petersburg. Leaving two divisions at Bermuda Hundreds and another north of the James, Grant still retained under his active command for his pending Petersburg offensive 90,000 infantry effectives and 15,000 cavalry personnel.[1] Though hardly in need of any reassurance concerning his front, Grant received a message containing just such sentiments two days before the Fort Stedman attack; Sherman and General Shofield united their forces at Goldsboro, North Carolina, just 120 miles from Petersburg.

Surveying his desperate situation at this time, General Lee, by a letter of March 26, privately advised President Davis that the time had come to pull out of Richmond and Petersburg and combine with forces in North Carolina.[2] The only remaining railway communications with General Johnston involved the Southside Railroad to Burkeville, Virginia, and then over the Richmond and Danville to its terminus. Beyond this point, Confederate forces could rely upon the Piedmont Railroad into Greensboro, North Carolina. Acting on his strategy and Sheridan's implementation, Grant was determined to prevent the Confederates from any use of these facilities. Supplies arriving by rail at Petersburg, as well as all transport westward, traveled over the Southside Railroad. If Sheridan were to cut this rail line at any point beyond Lee's extreme right flank, his retreat would become dangerously complicated. Obviously intent on accomplishing this objective, Sheridan was reported to be in motion again on March 25 when he headed for the federal left flank.[3]

In Richmond the physical environment and public mood clearly bespoke the final hours of the Confederacy. The houses were neglected, their windows uncurtained and unattended; mud and dirt were strewn on streets and walks; shops were scantily supplied with merchandise; people were hungry and shabby clothed. But from the executive mansion at least some pretense of former days was attempted. President Davis, with a serious, tired composure, continued his public rides in the company of his aides. Mrs. Davis assumed a maternal role, nursing her newborn infant and comforting the three older children, who understood the drama unfolding around them. In this tragic atmosphere, writes Ishbel Ross in her biography of Mrs. Davis, "no one attempted flattery or offered encouragement to the Confederate First Lady. The end has come."[4]

Realizing her family's continued residence in the city was tenuous, Mrs. Davis by means of sales and auctions had dispensed with many personal items. Times now required she abandon her remaining silks, laces, feathers, flowers, and gloves. Not neglected for auction were furniture, books, silver, and imported glass objects of art. Pressed by a need for cash, she decided to sell fifty barrels of flour at the market price of eleven hundred dollars a barrel. Overruling this, President Davis reminded his wife of the pressing need of this commodity by troops and local citizens.

Mrs. Davis regarded her husband's last message to Congress in March as the beginning of the Confederacy's final chapter of existence. In this she assessed the southern position far more realistically than her husband. He continued to hold delusions that somehow, despite convincing reverses, the southern cause would prevail. Believing Lee's army would continue fighting, the president talked of moving the government to another location and developing a new military strategy. At the moment, however, he was compelled to deal with a more immediate crisis.

Having in mind his family's welfare, President Davis determined that they must immediately depart Richmond without him. In the privacy of their official quarters, the president handed his wife a purse of gold pieces, keeping only one five-dollar coin for himself. He then provided her with a pistol, and after showing her how to load, aim, and fire it, he instructed her to use it only in case of extreme emergency.

In the last week of March, along almost empty streets, the Davis family by carriage made their way to the train station. Ishbel Ross writes that Mrs. Davis was "no longer Queen of the Confederate Court, but a sorrowing trembling woman about to part from the man she adored, not knowing whether she would ever see him again or what fate might await the Confederacy and its President."[5] The answers to these questions were being determined at that very moment by the battle between opposing forces.

As if in a game of chess, Grant made his first calculated move during the early morning hours of March 29 when he ordered G. K. Warren and Andrew A. Humphrey's corps to advance on Lee's right flank. While these operations were in progress, further south Sheridan moved his strong cavalry forces, capturing Dinwiddie Court House. Always alert, Lee launched a counter move, sending out a detachment four miles to his right to meet Sheridan at Five Forks as he advanced from Dinwiddie Court House. Fully assembled, this force consisted of the brigades of Montgomery D. Course, William R. Terry, and George H. Steuart, assigned to Pickett's division. There was also William H. Wallace's South Carolina, as well as Matt Ransom's brigade; added to these elements were two brigades of General Anderson, and six guns of Colonel William J. Pegram.[6] Manning other vital points were Longstreet, who with weak garrisoned lines was responsible for guarding the works north of the James, and Gordon, who was placed in charge of Petersburg.

To fulfill his mission, Pickett would be required to drive Sheridan out of Dinwiddie Court House, which would frustrate federal plans of overcoming Lee's right flank and save the Southside Railroad. Fitz Lee was already at Five Forks, awaiting the arrival of Tom Rosser and W. H. F. Lee. Combined cavalry and infantry represented a total Confederate force of at least 7,000 men of all arms.[7] Pickett, as senior major general, would be in overall command. No one of a superstitious nature could have regarded this command as a good omen. Pickett had won initial fame during the bloody saga of Gettysburg, but his career since then had been marked by failures and incriminating experiences. The North Carolina campaign was one case in point, and failing to thwart Butler's advance in May, 1864, drove him to a sickbed. A most humiliating incident occurred when conscripts assigned to his division chose desertion rather than service under his command.[8]

During the night of March 29, heavy rains began falling; they would continue over the next thirty-six hours. However, on March 30, despite unpleasant and uncooperative weather conditions, there were some limited troop movements and combat action. Ransom's brigade and Wallace's joined other units of Pickett's division in a battle at Burgess's Mill, driving the federals back to their entrenchments. After this encounter, the Confederates made their way down White Oak Road to Five Forks, arriving there about 4:30 P.M. The hour was late, the troops were fatigued, and the cavalry units had not arrived, so Pickett decided not to push on to Dinwiddie Court House that evening. Intending to resume his march next morning, he took the usual precaution of placing his troops in battle position for the night even though there were no indications of a serious enemy presence.

On March 31, despite flooding conditions and high streams, W. H. F. Lee and Tom Rosser arrived with their cavalry units for action soon to follow.[9] As Sheridan advanced toward Five Forks, he encountered Confederates under Fitz Lee supported by Pickett's infantry. During the ensuing severe contest, the federals were driven back upon Dinwiddie Court House. Events of the day seemed to indicate morale was favorable among Confederate troops, and the old army spirit, or at least a large measure of it, still prevailed.

By the time they arrived at about one-half mile from Dinwiddie Court House, darkness again caused Pickett to halt his forces. Knowing enemy cavalry was heavy in the area and supported with infantry, he wished to avoid overexposure of his forces. His chief duties were to protect the southerners' right flank and to hold the Southside Railroad by guarding its approaches. He therefore decided to position his troops where they could most effectively carry out these duties.[10] Consequently, orders were issued calling for an artillery

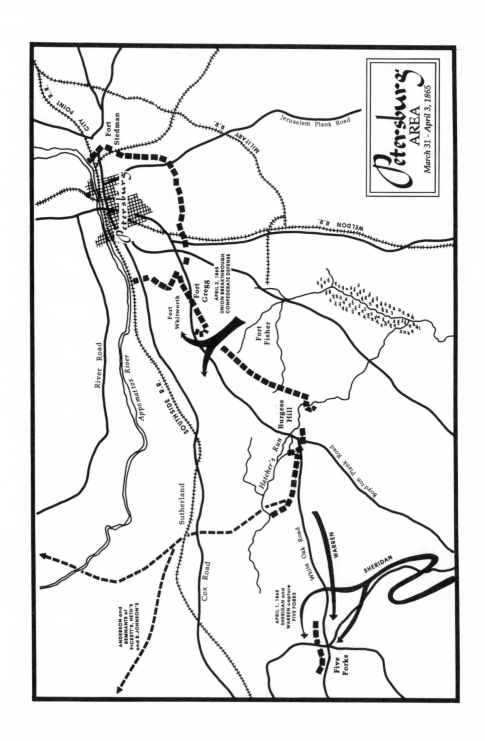

withdrawal to Five Forks at 2:00 A.M., with the main infantry force to follow at 4:00. During the ensuing retreat, federals followed close at hand, but avoided any belligerence at the moment; it was evident, however, that Pickett's left was threatened, and this was a result of events that had transpired on the thirty-first. That morning Lee had ordered General Richard H. Anderson to attack from his works near Burgess's Mill as a diversion intended to support Pickett's move toward Dinwiddie Court House. These activities were also intended to discourage the federals from attempting to break through the lines at the gap between Anderson's right flank and Pickett's left.[11] The struggle that morning had culminated in a loss of about 800 men for the Confederates, who suffered a convincing defeat. Severely reduced in strength and having already loaned two of his brigades to the main advancing force, Anderson was no longer able to provide effective support on Pickett's left. Apparently both Pickett and Fitz Lee were unaware of this — certainly a most fateful oversight.

Federal seizure of the Southside Railroad required a convenient approach by way of Five Forks. Funneling their numerically superior troops here, Union attackers could advance westward on White Oak Road, and above the headwaters of Hatcher's Run turn the Confederate right flank there. So much rested on this vital sector. General Lee's telegram to Pickett reveals these sentiments: "Hold Five Forks at all hazards. Protect road to Ford's Depot and prevent Union forces from striking the Southside Railroad." Relative to Pickett's pullback from Dinwiddie Court House to Five Forks on April 1, Lee chided his subordinate: "Regret exceedingly your forced withdrawal, and hold the advantage you had gained."[12]

Pickett stationed his forces along White Oak Road facing east. On the extreme right was W. H. F. Lee's cavalry. He was flanked on his left by Corse's brigade; then followed Terry's and Steuart's brigades. Next in order were Wallace's and Ransom's brigades. On the later's left flank was a single regiment of Thomas Mumford's division, and on his left was the weak brigade of William P. Robert. Beyond this point to the left was a four-mile gap to Burgess's Mills.[13] Behind these contingents along Ford Road were placed the units of Fitz Lee's cavalry, and as reserves, the two brigades of James Dearing and John McCausland under Tom Rosser were stationed north of Hatcher's Run, allegedly because of the horses' poor condition.[14] No sooner had disposition of troops been completed when a tide of federal skirmishers rolled toward the Confederate line. Pickett's neglect on his left flank has come under criticism by careful reviewers and authorities. Most would agree with Douglas Freeman, who wrote that while "Robert's men were stout fighters ... like most regiments they were lacking in field officers. A stronger brigade should have been in its place."[15]

The evidence of superior Union numbers in the area would be confirmed as events unfolded. To strengthen federal forces, G. K. Warren's corps and Ronald S. MacKenzie's cavalry arrived. The various units which comprised this federal operation consisted of the First, Second, and Third cavalry divisions, roughly 9,000 men; the First, Second, and Third infantry divisions representing Warren's corps, accompanied by five artillery batteries, together totalling 15,787 men; and MacKenzie's cavalry of 1,000 sabers. Total troops numbered 25,787, all under command of General Phil H. Sheridan against a Confederate force of little more than 7,000.[16] The Union commander's strategy called for a feint cavalry attack with hopes of turning the Confederate right flank; at the same time Warren's Fifth Corps was to move up in position to attack the left flank with the ultimate object of crushing the entire force, driving them westward, and isolating them from their position at Petersburg.

At the very outset of his attack, Sheridan received unexpected and certainly unintended assistance from his foes. With Pickett and Fitz Lee feeling comfortable with the deployment of their troops against possible enemy attack, both commanders, without the knowledge of any subordinates, left the field for a social engagement about two miles behind their lines. General Rosser had very recently taken in a fine catch of shad on the Nottoway River and had offered his headquarters as a fish fry for the commanding generals. Between the hours of noon and 1:00 P.M., Fitz Lee mounted up for his luncheon engagement, but before departing, he was briefed by a dispatch from Lieutenant Wythe B. Graham of the Eighth Virginia Cavalry, a unit which was in liaison with Robert's brigade on the extreme left. The dispatch stated that North Carolina troopers had taken refuge in the picket line of the Eighth after being attacked and routed by numerous federal forces east of Five Forks. Their brigade having been split by the attack, some elements had retreated back to General Anderson's lines near Burgess's Mills. This information revealed that Sheridan had at this hour arrived on White Oak Road; having done so, writes Douglas Freeman, he had severed "contact between Pickett's mobile force and the left of the Confederate fortifications."[17] Apparently Pickett had already become isolated, and any reinforcements would be compelled to fight their way through. Fitz Lee, however, drew no such conclusions as he read the report handed to him. He only requested an investigation of the matter, and set off with Pickett to join their waiting host.

The Army of the Potomac and the Army of Northern Virginia were about to meet in their last organized battle, and Matt Ransom's brigade would take part.[18] In deploying his troops at Five Forks, General Ransom stationed the Twenty-fourth on his extreme left; then, going to the right in this order, came the Fifty-sixth, Twenty-fifth, Forty-ninth, and Thirty-fifth.

As planned, around 2:00 P.M. federal cavalry under Wesley Merritt and George A. Custer struck hard on the Confederate right flank. Although severely tested, W. H. F. Lee met the challenge successfully. In the meantime, Warren's corps was pushing ahead through the undefended line to the left of the Confederates. Observing these movements, General Mumford repeatedly sent messengers to Pickett and Fitz Lee that an enemy strike was imminent.[19] Matt Ransom, too, repeatedly attempted to communicate with Pickett.

Around 4:00 P.M., following some delay, Warren began his movement. R. B. Ayre's division struck Ransom's left; the Twenty-fourth repelled several initial attacks, but soon Charles Griffin's and Samuel W. Crawford's federal divisions arrived on the scene.[20] In vain, General Ransom expected the arrival of more Confederate troops to improve the odds against them, now five to one.[21] While advancing federal forces were overwhelming the Twenty-fourth and Twenty-fifth, and the Fifty-sixth was being driven from its flank and rear, Ransom continually regrouped his troops to meet oncoming assaults. He was unaware of more devastating action in the rear, where the divisions of Crawford and Griffin were now overlapping the brigade.[22]

Meanwhile, at the shad bake, the generals continued their delectable meal. There was at least one ominous interruption: two of Rosser's men reported that the enemy was advancing on every road guarded by the division.[23] However, this warning received little attention from the luncheon guests. In the minds of the three southern generals, their positions at Five Forks were well defended and secure. In the present instance they may have believed that the federals were approaching, but evidently they did not believe an attack was under way.[24] Aside from the conjecture that "some acoustical quirk" was involved, no satisfactory reason has been offered as to why Pickett and his associates did not hear the sounds of battle approximately two miles distant.[25]

Around 4:00 Picket requested a courier to carry a message to Five Forks. Rosser responded by offering two men, as it was to custom to send one ahead but in sight of the other. In this fashion the message was dispatched, but moments later a burst of infantry fire was heard south of the stream. In clear view, the startled officers saw the lead courier captured by federal troops while a line of bluecoats moved across the road. This incident abruptly ended the party. Mounting a horse, Pickett sped across Hatcher's Run, continuing his ride southward until he came to a retreating line of cavalrymen on Ford Road; these were part of Fitz Lee's division, and not more than one hundred yards east of them were swarms of federal infantry. Ordering Lee's troops to hold firm, Pickett bent himself forward on his horse. Ducking his head to the animal's side away from the enemy, he successfully braved several hundred yards of angry infantry fire until he arrived at Five Forks. In his attempt to travel the same route, Fitz Lee turned back due to heavy enemy gunfire.

By this time the fighting that had raged as the generals enjoyed their fish fry had ended, and during those very tense moments when Pickett was frantically making his way back to Five Forks, Ransom's, Steuart's, and Wallace's troops battled fiercely with the divisions of General Griffin.[26] There have been claims that some North Carolinians "lost their nerve and took to their heels," but that was not the deportment of others.[27] "We were penned in like rats in a hole," wrote one of Ransom's men later, noting that after they were overpowered, "the few that were left were made prisoners, some being knocked down with the butts of rifles."[28] Then there was Captain J. C. Grier, who emptied his revolver into his enemies and was about to throw the weapon away when he found himself surrounded by Union soldiers, demanding his surrender as they pointed several bayonets at his chest.

Unaware of Crawford's and Griffin's full presence in the brigade's rear, General Ransom decided upon one more charge in hopes of rallying his beleaguered troops while attempting to break through the enveloping lines.[29] Already during the day's action, one horse had been killed under him, and now he ordered Ion to be brought forward. By this time Captain Steerling H. Gee, the brigade adjutant, had been killed, and R. B. Peebles was promoted on the field as the new adjutant.[30]

Bareheaded and mounted on his thoroughbred, which obeyed the slightest command of its rider, Ransom shouted for his brigade to follow him in what would be his last charge in the war.[31] From out of the woods he emerged in front of his troops. Taking steady aim, the opposing federal line opened fire. As if in contempt of the dangers surrounding him, the magnificent jet-black stallion reared on his hind legs, and at that moment a shell fragment tore into his underbelly, disemboweling him. Backwards he fell with his total weight upon the rider. Blood, urine, and bowel waste gushed from the dying animal, while General Ransom, with arm in sling, found himself pinned under his faithful mount. A humble, ugly end was moments away. The man in this pathetic scene had denounced secession as a course of madness; he had warned such a decision would invariably result in wholesale bloodshed; he had repeatedly cautioned his contemporaries on the slight odds of winning such a struggle. Yet, through all of this, he had found it impossible to abandon his state and people during this great moment of history.

The subject of miracles almost always raises doubts and sometimes ridicule, but on this occasion a miracle would occur. When the smoke cleared, Captain P. J. Johnson of the Twenty-fifth and Captain James H. Sherrill of the Forty-ninth saw their stricken commander.[32] Rushing forward in a hail of whining bullets and exploding shells, they threw themselves into their task with the energy that human beings are sometimes granted during extreme emergency. Frantically they pulled and shoved and were at last able to lift the victim. Now extricated and standing, stunned perhaps, and suffering from momentary shock, General Ransom otherwise seemed in good form to his rescuers.[33]

Sheridan knew full well that victory was his. When riding his mount, he encountered a hurdle of confused, demoralized Confederates who were willing to surrender. He excitedly yelled at them, "Go right over there," indicating his own lines. "Get right along, now. Oh, drop your guns, you'll never need them anymore."[34]

Surrender? Surrender, hell! Such option had no appeal to General Ransom and the few remaining members of his command, especially if any means of escape existed. Through a small remaining loophole, Ransom backed his men as they fired their last ammunition directly into enemy ranks.[35] From then on, rifle butts, bayonets, and fists became standard weaponry. Using darkness of night as protection, Ransom directed his dwindling and battered command to the full rear, finally uniting with General Richard H. Anderson's corps on the Southside Railroad. Corse's brigade, which was spared from heavy federal attack, survived in stable condition and was useful as a rallying support during the Confederate retreat. W. H. F. Lee displayed his usual professional competence by repeatedly defeating federal charges; eventually he joined Fitz Lee, who remained with Rosser's men north of Hatcher's Run.

Confederate casualties for that day and prisoners taken by the federal V Corps the next morning, April 2, were 5,244, along with eleven flags and one gun. Prisoners held by federal cavalry are not fully listed. Total losses in Ransom's brigade amounted to seven hundred.[36]

Informed of Sheridan's success at Five Forks at 9:00 that evening, Grant immediately initiated a search for eligible points along Lee's weak lines for possible breakthroughs. The Second Corps was ordered into action south of Hatcher's Run, while at the same time, other corps extending down and around Petersburg delivered a strong cannonade. At 4:00 A.M. the Second Corps cracked the Confederate line in two places — first in the area paralleling Boydron Plank Road, and then near Jerusalem Plank Road where the Federals occupied about eight hundred yards of line — but their advance was halted.[37]

Because of the noise of heavy artillery salvos and fierce fighting, Lee was awakened at dawn and informed of Union penetrations into his lines. Also awakened for the same reasons, A. P. Hill hastily set out with a party of three others in hopes of rallying his scattered, missing troops, and at the same time, locating General Harry Heth's headquarters. Only General Hill and his courier, George Tucker, continued the final leg of their hazardous journey; the other two party members broke away to carry out assignments given en route. Near Boydron Road in a woodland clearing, the two riders observed a cluster of Union stragglers, two of whom had taken protection behind a large tree at a distance of about twenty yards. Both of these two positioned their weapons, one under the other, and prepared to fire.[38] When Hill and Tucker demanded their surrender, two shots rang out; one went wild, and the other ripped off the general's thumb before passing into his heart. Reaching for the riderless horse's reins to make a quick flight, the courier observed Hill on the ground, his arms extended lifeless. By such an end, another legendary southern general closed his life. At least one wish was granted to him, for he had expressed a preference not to survive the fall of Richmond.[39] As ordered by General Lee, Colonel William H. Palmer was assigned the sad duty of informing Mrs. Hill of her husband's death, and providing her and her two infant daughters safe passage across the Appomattox.

At this critical point it was totally impractical for Lee to attempt a continued military presence within his present environs. He could only hope to hold his enemy in check until night with a prospect of allowing his forces to benefit from a head start upon escape roads. Among those telegrams he dispatched on Sunday, April 2, were one to Longstreet, ordering him to report in person at the local scene, and one to President Davis.

St. Paul's Sunday church services were under way with President Davis in attendance when a slight commotion occurred in the rear of the church. A soldier was insisting he carried an important message. The sexton hurried up the aisle, whispered something to President Davis, and handed him a telegram in which Lee stated his intentions of executing a speedy withdrawal from Petersburg, creating the necessity of evacuating Richmond. Abruptly leaving the service, a pale, haggard president called an emergency cabinet meeting and informed members of an immediate removal of the government from Richmond.

Because he was loath to lose his valuables in a departure too hasty for packing and shipping, Davis requested General Lee to postpone for one day an evacuation of his lines. Upon receipt of this request, Lee found it difficult to maintain his usual self-composure; he tore the telegram to pieces, and stomping them into the ground he muttered, "I am sure I gave him sufficient notice."[40] Refusing President Davis's proposal entirely, General Lee insisted on 8:00 P.M. as the final hour for the government's exit from Richmond. In compliance with these instructions, cabinet members were ordered to join President Davis at the train depot around 10:00 that night.

After completing his personal packing and issuing some final instructions, Davis sat down to await word for departure to the train station. Outside his official residence, all indications foretold that the city was headed for doom and destruction. Masses were fleeing in panic jamming and choking outlying bridges; it was almost impossible to negotiate those streets leading to the railroad station. Vandals, black and white, were out to do their mischief, looting ships and the downtown business area. Convicts were free to roam as guards deserted their posts. The lowest elements of society were dipping and sopping up liquor that flowed in the street gutters, thanks to authorities who had ordered the destruction of casks to prevent excessive public drinking.[41]

Under the most trying circumstances brought on by confusion and crisis, Davis finally arrived at the train terminal. At 11:00 that night he and his official party set out on a journey of one hundred and forty miles to Danville, Virginia.

Although reasonable calm prevailed in the city on Saturday, the public mood underwent a drastic change by Sunday evening. By their very nature, certain events contributed to this transition. It became general knowledge that specie held by the Confederate government was being shipped over the last remaining rails. The president's departure and the burning of government records could only be interpreted as signs of official evacuation. Confirmation of Lee's withdrawal from Petersburg erased any remaining stability which might have existed.

It seemed as though few people went to bed Sunday evening. They preferred to walk the streets, exchanging farewells. During the early morning hours came four earth-shaking explosions in quick succession as gunboats were blown up on the James.[42] Windows shattered, chimneys collapsed; the concussions were of such magnitude that many people were thrown to the ground. Fires then spread quickly, and shells stored in arsenals ignited, sending more fiery fragments into the air to injure and kill many citizens. From such rampant incineration many deaths resulted; in one house alone, seventeen people perished. As for the aged, helpless, and infirm, they were left to fend for themselves, and some failed to survive.

After only a few hours, fires left only smoldering remains on Main, Gary, and Canal streets from 8th to 18th streets. The War Department Building went up in flames, while the Customs House, appearing almost forlorn, was spared. Lee's house and that side of Franklin suffered no damage; in the general's front year, guards were posted. Only the broad capitol grounds provided some measure of refuge for victims seeking shelter, and there assembled mothers and children pitifully overburdened with some of their most cherished personal effects.

One observer described what he saw from the summit of a hill as he "looked down upon the grandiose and appalling sight," the most awesome he had ever witnessed. "Richmond was literally a sea of flames" which produced "a canopy of dense black smoke, lighted up now and then by the bursting shells from the numerous arsenals scattered throughout the city."[43]

Abandoning Richmond and Petersburg to their Union captors, General Lee intended to march his forces north of the Appomattox River on a western course for twenty-five miles, then recross that stream, moving in the same direction for ten miles to Amelia Court House, through which passed the Richmond and Danville Railroad. Here, Lee expected to be joined by other forces having made the western trek, including troops from Richmond. These hungry contingent forces were to draw upon rations purportedly awaiting them at this center. Once the newly assembled army was supplied, it would utilize the railroad toward Burkeville about twenty miles distant southwest, and at this point, Lee would undertake his march to North Carolina.

Grant responded accordingly with his own strategy, always capitalizing upon any advantages he might have inherited. Actually, he was required to cover less distance than Lee, being nearer both to Johnson and to Burkeville.[44] Rather than initiating an immediate pursuit, Grant simply ordered Sheridan to move due west, always in a position to block any left turn by Lee's army. Essentially, the armies were competing in a race for time, with the federals seeming to hold the advantage.

Before forty-eight hours elapsed in Lee's retreat operations, he suffered a misfortune from which there was no recovery — a delay. When he arrived at Amelia Court House on April 4, he found that the Richmond troops were not expected until the following day. Perhaps even more serious was the lack of food, for the rations had not been delivered. For the next twenty-four hours canvassing units were sent out to procure food supplies with disappointing results. Not until late afternoon on April 5 was the southern army prepared to resume its march, and by this time, Sheridan's cavalry, supported by 50,000 of Meade's infantry, was already occupying the railroad at Jetersville, a half way point between Amelia Court House and Burkeville. The federals were obviously winning the race.

Discouraged but still determined, Lee decided upon another detour, this time much further westward in an attempt to get beyond the federal flank. Unfortunately for his tormented, besieged troops, the distance between themselves and General Johnston was becoming greater. Then, on April 6, another disaster befell the retreating army in an area of low bottom land near Sayler's Creek. Here, Sheridan's cavalry, Horatio G. Wright's VI Corps, and other elements overpowered the rear guard of the Confederate column, putting 7,500 of them out of action, and Lee's wagon train was heavily mauled and partially destroyed. At the contest's conclusion, Lee found himself surrounded by fleeing Confederate troops of General Richard Anderson's corps. Anderson soon arrived on the scene and met with a cold reception from Lee; he was ordered to the rear to assume command of stragglers, and subsequently relieved of his command. Lee's misgivings were not limited to Anderson. Thanks to his conduct at Five Forks, General Pickett was relieved of his command, and General Bushrod Johnson was similarly unburdened at Sayler's Creek. All three generals were given authorization to "return to their homes."[45]

With the remainder of his army, Lee continued to move westward, and after fighting nonstop for twenty-four hours, he arrived at Farmville.[46] Taking on a few supplies here, he crossed to the north side of the Appomattox, burning the bridge behind so that his weary forces, at least for a time, would be protected from flanking attacks. Many men of the ranks now believed there was no longer any purpose to the march, only moving west to Lynchburg and the mountain country. Desertions were increasing. In some instances, before taking permanent leave, men left their rifles with bayonets stuck in the ground or standing against trees. Others, after abandoning their weapons, continued to accompany the army as vagrants. One disillusioned, hungry North Carolina private in search of food found himself surrounded by federal troops who leveled their guns and demanded his surrender. Raising his arms, dropping his rifle, the skeletal tarheel replied, "Yes you've got me, and a hell of a git you got."[47]

With the march having progressed to a point not far from the headwaters of the Appomattox where it was no longer a formidable stream, once again flank attacks would likely resume. Lee's present army consisted of no more than 8,000 infantry effectives who eagerly looked forward to arriving at Appomattox Station, where freight cars of the Southside Railroad were expected to be standing filled with rations.[48]

Certainly aware of the Confederate's desperate plight, Grant sent a note which arrived in Lee's hands on April 7, calling for the latter's surrender. In his reply, the southern commander inquired what terms Grant might envision. The conditions were quite simple: Lay down all arms and refrain from any further combat action. During the exchange of messages between the two generals, Lee attempted to broaden the scope of their discourse, requesting a more general discussion of how peace might be achieved between North and South. To this, Grant responded that he was not authorized to discuss such topics, only surrender terms.[49]

On April 9 Lee was forced to abandon his last hope of extricating himself from an intolerable situation. On this day Sheridan won the race for Appomattox Station, where he captured the supplies so necessary for Lee's continued efforts. Arriving also were two corps of infantry, which helped to create an insurmountable Union line blocking the road west. Lee was at last without options. His front and flank were held by Sheridan with Meade rapidly moving up in the rear, and there was no possible retreat northward. A grim and saddened General Lee dispatched a message to Grant under a flag of truce, requesting a conference to discuss terms of surrender.

The comfortable, well-furnished brick home of Wilmer Mclean at Appomattox Court House served as the site for Robert E. Lee's surrender of the Army of Northern Virginia to Ulysses S. Grant on April 9, 1865. Lee arrived first that afternoon, flawlessly dressed in a handsome uniform and accompanied by Colonel Charles Marshall. Shortly thereafter, Grant made his entrance on the scene, far more modestly attired in a muddy uniform, wearing a soldier's blouse rather than an officer's, and sporting no saber. In a polite, conciliatory manner, both men completed the somber task before them in the presence of select high-ranking officers. Terms of surrender did not include any federal punitive measures against the disbanded army; officers were allowed to retain their sidearms and horses. Artillerymen and cavalry in the Confederate army owned the horses under their charge, and Lee requested that these men might keep their animals. As a gesture of humanity and as a very practical move toward reconciliation, the federal commander honored this request.

A flurry of activity on the porch instantly drew the attention of the interested onlookers, and from his station, Matt Ransom was provided an excellent view of the scene. As Lee stepped from the doorway, federal officers snapped to attention. The general put on his hat and returned a sharply executed salute. Grant by now was standing on the porch, and both men during a brief exchange stood side by side.[50] Taking his leave, Lee walked down the stairs on to the yard, and in an absent-minded fashion, slapping his gloved hands together several times, he called for his horse, Traveller. Once mounted, accompanied by Colonel Marshall and Sergeant G. W. Tucker, General Lee turned toward the porch where Grant still remained. Without speaking, each lifted his hat in salute to the other. Then Lee spurred his horse and headed

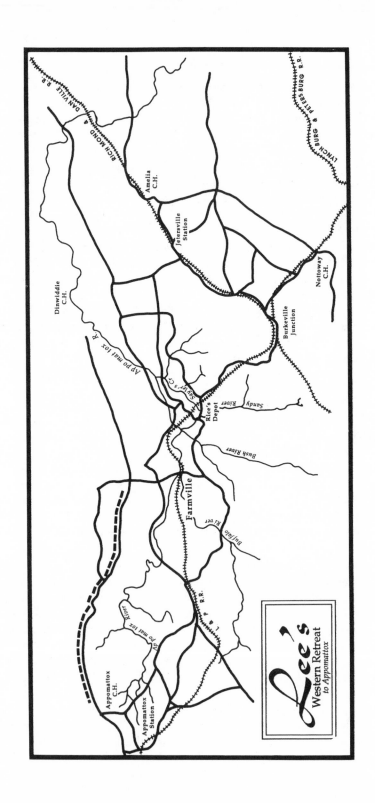

back to his troops to tell them of the surrender.[51] Already word had begun to spread in federal ranks, and muskets and cannon began firing in jubilation. Once again the real valor and compassion of Grant came forward when he immediately issued orders banning all such demonstrations.

Specific plans for conducting surrender activities and related matters now required the attention of appropriate authorities. Once again Grant and Lee met, and among those subjects discussed were the other existing Confederate armies. Since Jefferson Davis and his government had not yet surrendered or been captured, Lee contended he was without authority to make any decisions regarding General Johnston or other troops without consulting the Confederate president. With this, the matter ended; Grant departed for Washington, preferring not to observe the formal surrender ceremonies, and likewise, Lee chose to absent himself on the occasion by returning to his headquarters, where certain final details awaited his attention. A farewell address to his troops was prepared by Lieutenant Colonel Charles Marshall, grandnephew of the distinguished chief justice. Lee, after making a few changes in the original draft, signed the finished document and had copies distributed to corps commanders and ranking members of his staff.

> Headquarters Army of N. Va.
> April 10, 1865
>
> General Orders
> No. 9
>
> After four years of arduous service marked by unsurpassed courage and fortitude, the Army of Northern Virginia has been compelled to yield to overwhelming numbers and resources.
>
> I need not tell the brave survivors of so many hard fought battles, who have remained steadfast to the last, that I have consented to this result from no distrust of them. But feeling that valor and devotion could accomplish nothing that could compensate for the loss that must have attended the continuance of the contest, I determined to avoid the useless sacrifice of those whose past services have endeared them to their countrymen.
>
> By the terms of the agreement, officers and men can return to their homes and remain until exchanged. You will take with you the satisfaction that proceeds from the consciousness of duty faithfully performed, and I earnestly pray that a merciful God will extend to you His blessing and protection.
>
> With an unceasing admiration of your consistency and devotion to your Country, and a grateful remembrance of your kind and generous consideration for myself, I bid you all an affectionate farewell.
>
> R. E. Lee
> General

As officially mandated, a commission of six members consisting of an even number of Confederate and Union officers settled upon the necessary details of surrender.[53] As decided by this group, the final farewell was set for April 12. That morning federal brigadier general Joshua L. Chamberlain, in charge of the surrender proceedings, lined his troops on either side of the Richmond-Lynchburg Road, which extended up a slope behind the courthouse and across the north branch of the Appomattox to the Confederate camps. Now ready for their sad ordeal, these one-proud warriors, without drums or rifles, began their last march in measured cadence. As they came into view, many federals simply stood open-mouthed, staring incredulously at the pathetic picture they presented.[54] Where once there had been formidable regiments, there were now scarcely enough men to form companies.[55] Approaching in the lead was Gordon's corps, followed by Thomas Cobb's Georgia legion, then Robert F. Hoke's North Carolinians. The next unit was of special interest to General Chamberlain because these were the men, writes historian Philip Stern, "who broke the Fifth corps lines on the White Oak Road, and were so desperately driven back on that forlorn night of March 31."[56] In other words, here passed "the proud remnant of Ransom's North Carolinians."[57] General Harry Heth appeared in the procession in front of A. P. Hill's odd corps; then Longstreet and his men came forward, as did the remains of John B. Hood's division and Pickett's command. All day long the ritual continued, with each unit surrendering all arms and flags a short distance east of the courthouse by the main road and two private lanes. At last the proceedings were over, and the whole affair, writes historian William Davis, seemed to have been conducted in "an awed stillness ... as if it were the passing of the dead."[58] All told, including wounded and stragglers, 26,672 men of Lee's army were paroled, and subsequently, in piecemeal fashion, Fitzhugh Lee's 1,559 cavalry surrendered.[59]

For General Ransom the duties of the day had been demanding. From his brigade, which a historian of his time says had "always moved as a machine, well regulated in every part," he surrendered forty-one officers and three hundred ninety-one enlisted men.[60] According to the date of his commission as lieutenant colonel, lacking twenty-nine days, he had served four years as a Confederate soldier.[61] A new era was about to confront the southern people, and for him this was a time for reflection, particularly as to his own future role. He wished to think on this matter, and above all, he wished to rejoin his family.

Chapter XII

After the War

Practical and ideological reasons dictated that Warrenton should be the former brigade's destination in their return march to North Carolina. From this convenient point recent servicemen might continue their homeward journeys to various other points of the state, and since some of them had received their training at Warrenton, returning there might be likened to a homecoming. To General Ransom it was certainly like returning home. Almost four years to the day, he had been inducted into the military here; this was where it all began. On his person the general carried a parole pass issued to him and others following their surrender. Signed by B. R. Johnson, it was dated April 10, 1865.[1] In the haste and confusion marking the brigade's final hours, the headquarters wagon became misrouted, and all of Ransom's personal belongs were temporarily lost, requiring him to draw upon his brother, Robert, Jr., for a change of clothing at Warrenton.[2]

Along the road Ransom was seen giving aid to the exhausted marchers, frequently getting off his horse to give them his place in the saddle, and attempting to buoy their spirits with encouraging words.[3] His men sought every opportunity to talk with him as they retained the deepest respect and loyalty for their former commander. Will Burgwyn later attributed these feelings to the fact that the men "had watched his career as a soldier, which had reflected honor to his state and upon the South, and especially his strikingly brilliant conduct a few days before at Five Forks."[4] In the face of the most weathering enemy fire and severe situations, wrote a historian of the time, "it was only necessary for General Ransom to ride along his lines with an uncovered head and pointing to the direction of the foe.... His soldiers never failed him or he them."[5] To these men of his former ranks who now harbored fears about the future, Ransom replied with confidence that North and South were joined by mutual bonds; both were served by the same great rivers of commerce, tied together by a mass of railroad lines, and dependent upon each other for protection against foreign transgressors. These very points he had advanced in refuting disunion in past years, and if they continued to have relevance, he would stress them again.

The truth was, Ransom had anticipated the plight that would fall upon his people if they tried to solve their sectional differences with the North by force. He had not agreed with the many southerners who, before the war, had contended that the region could withdraw from the Union peaceably because the national government lacked the resolve to forcibly crush such a movement. Both secession and war he had in the past denounced in public forums. Now, having embraced these modes of conduct, southern states were confronted with the results of their unwise decisions. Was it the end of an era, and the beginning of a new one? In Matt Ransom's mind, such was clearly the case. Having strong ties with Jeffersonian democracy and its emphasis upon a rural society, he could not look forward with much pleasure to the fundamental changes that the oncoming urban industrial period would bring. In his judgment, the key to the difficult transition ahead rested with the time-tested Anglo-Saxon practice of patient negotiation and compromise by informed, competent leaders. Only by this means, he believed, would the South be provided an opportunity to influence the new national posture that was destined to emerge.

Not until Matt Ransom had realized that his approach to the sectional struggle was unacceptable to leaders of his own state and to elected officials in the North had he turned to a possible military solution. Like other men of his section he stood with a cause that the popular mind envisioned as a struggle for national independence, the family hearth, personal liberty, and a way of life. Born south of the Potomac, his ancestors had lived in the area for two hundred years. It was the area of his upbringing and education, and all his earthly possessions resided there. Above all, the South was unmistakably his home.[6]

From boyhood to manhood, Ransom had regarded all decisions by civil authorities as final; yet he chose to withdraw his allegiance and loyalty to a government duly installed in Washington, D.C., on March 4, 1861. It was a government he believed dangerously inept and ill-prepared to deal with a national crisis which was in large measure the result of his own conduct. Ransom in his formative years had never anticipated or planned for a military career, yet he eventually earned a reputation as a highly competent commander on the battlefield. Having strong misgivings concerning slavery, he was nevertheless a slaveowner. As indicated, Ransom was highly critical of secession, yet he became a loyal supporter of the Confederacy; and though he was opposed to war, he was among the first volunteers to take up the sword. Such conduct might seem full of contradictions and inconsistencies, but when all of the details are reviewed and placed in their proper setting, an open, fair mind can embrace the logic of Matt Ransom's choices.

During the return march to Warrenton there was no lack of meaningful, even startling, local and national news. On the morning of April 11, Sherman quietly occupied Fayetteville, where he rested his forces for several days. Local arsenals were destroyed, along with the office of the *Fayetteville Observer*, seven cotton factories, and several mills in the vicinity. The wanton destructiveness of Sherman's soldiers left the town in a ruin.[7]

By April 10, Sherman, with an estimated strength of 110,000 men, completed preparations to advance upon Raleigh. Meanwhile, at a discreet, respectable distance from the invader's front, the token forces of Joseph E. Johnston began a retreat in the same westerly direction.[8]

Alarmed over the strong likelihood that Raleigh was about to suffer the same fate of Columbia, South Carolina, former governors William A. Graham and David L. Swain solicited Governor Vance's approval for a meeting with Sherman to sound him out on the possibilities of suspending hostilities following Lee's surrender. Obtaining Vance's reluctant consent, the two ambassadors met with the Union general, but they were compelled to settle for only limited assurances that state and municipal officials would receive protection in the capital.[9] By now, Confederate troops were withdrawn from the city, and state records along with other valuable official accessories had been transferred to Goldsboro.

General Johnston received news of Lee's surrender at 1:00 A.M. on April 11 while encamped at Battle's Bridge, but he chose not to make an immediate announcement on the matter to his troops.[10] According to former governor Graham, the means of achieving peace through the Confederate president were minimal "as long as that unbending man had a platoon of soldiers left to fire rifles."[11] Only reluctantly did Davis allow General Johnston to start the process of negotiations.

Around 7:30 A.M. on April 13, General Sherman and his troops arrived at Raleigh. He immediately established his headquarters at the governor's mansion, and on the following day he received Johnston's request for a meeting. The two Generals met on April 17 and 18 with their respective staffs at a farmhouse belonging to James Bennett a few miles west of Durham Station.

Surprisingly, Sherman laid out the most generous peace terms: Confederates who signed a pledge to refrain from any further war conduct and abandoned their weapons could return home as freemen. State governments were to remain intact, and when their leaders took an oath to support the Constitution, they would receive recognition by the president. Federal courts were to be reestablished. Voting rights of the people would be restored as before the war, and original property rights guaranteed. Actually, these terms of Sherman bore a clear resemblance to what had been Lincoln's generous peace settlement.

Public reaction in the North and in Congress to Sherman's peace offering was swift. His terms were denounced as blasphemous and totally unacceptable. Grant personally carried this news to Raleigh on April 24 when he conveyed to Sherman the message that the only acceptable terms were those tendered to Lee. Once again a conference was required with General Johnston, and this time he was given the conditions set forth by Grant: a cessation of hostilities, with specific terms to be drawn up later. The southern general accepted gladly, surrendering on April 26.[12] With the subsequent surrender of General James G. Martin and his army at Waynesville, peace finally prevailed in North Carolina. Possibly as a portent of times ahead, General John Schofield assumed military command in the state on April 29, issuing proclamations for the cessation of hostilities and the emancipation of slaves, and authorizing plans to establish a police force in every county; the state would be divided into three major areas under jurisdiction of federal army officers.[13]

A fugitive in flight, Jefferson Davis was captured by a detachment of federal cavalry at Irwinsville, about seventy-five miles southeast of Macon, Georgia. The Confederacy was now history. In North Carolina, Governor Vance was taken into federal custody on May 13. Though no formal charges had ever been brought against him, he was confined in the Old Capitol Prison in Washington, D.C.

A most unexpected and shocking event occurred on the evening of April 14 at Ford's Theatre in Washington, D.C.: President Lincoln was assassinated by John Wilkes Booth. According to the perpetrator of this mad act, his motive was to help the South. In truth, he did the South great harm.[14] Historian Claude Bowers notes that "nowhere did the murder fall so like a pall as in the South."[15] The negative image Lincoln had earlier held throughout the southern states had taken on some significant changes and modifications, particularly during that final period of the war when a northern victory seemed assured. To literate citizens of the former Confederacy and to qualified monitors of northern political climes, Lincoln's rational approach to reuniting the two sections was far preferable to those formulas offered by radical elements within the president's own party. Lincoln, before his death, made public his policy of reconstruction under which the former Confederate states could resume their status within the Union. The plan was fair, generous, swift in execution, and generally well received, especially in the South. The president's approach provided all southerners, excluding their leaders, with pardons upon taking an oath to obey all federal laws and support the Constitution. After setting up loyal state governments in which at least 10 percent of the 1860 electorate took the requisite oath to the United States and ratified the Thirteenth Amendment, elections were to be held for members of Congress. Once peace and order prevailed, federal troops were to be withdrawn, and southern people would be on their own to conduct their domestic affairs. Sadly, an assassin's bullet deprived Lincoln of the opportunity to effectively champion his plan, or to do battle with radical Republicans on this vitally important matter. Attention now focused upon the new president and the directions he might follow.

Andrew Johnson was born in Raleigh, North Carolina. At age fourteen, the future president entered a contractual arrangement as an apprentice to a tailor; two years later, he ran away, settling in Greenville, Tennessee. Here, he married, worked at his trade as a tailor, acquired land, and owned a few slaves. His wife taught him to write. In politics he served as a member of the national House of Representatives, as governor of his state, and as a United States senator. After Tennessee was occupied by federal troops in 1862, he was appointed military governor of his state. At the Republican convention in 1864, Johnson, a Democrat, at Lincoln's urging won the nomination for Vice-president to run on a broad Union coalition ticket.

Absent in Johnson's personal manner were those suave qualities generally associated with southern gentlemen of this period; his behavior was inclined to reflect a raw frontier style. One indulgence which might have been excessive was his extreme disdain of the southern aristocracy. Members of this establishment he regarded as pretentious, haughty, insolent, and a threat to middle-class working citizens.[16]

Whether Andrew Johnson would favor a moderate or a punitive official attitude toward the recently seceded states was a question reserved for the future. Certainly his feelings about the Union, as demonstrated in the public record, were no secret. Viewing the Constitution with awe and reverence, he had never departed from its stated principles as he interpreted them. The Union was indissoluble, and the war just concluded had been waged for one single purpose: to preserve national unity. As for the abolitionists and their methods, he openly discredited them, and scoffed at the notion that the war had been fought over slavery.[17] Johnson had denounced the conduct of Jefferson Davis and the seceding states as foolish and irrational. Of Lincoln and his incendiary political campaign, the Tennessee senator was equally critical. He predicted the newly elected president — who had actually lost in the popular vote by almost a million votes — would be turned out of office in four years if the Union prevailed.[18] If by chance Lincoln was disposed to follow generous and rational policies involving southern reconstruction, he would inevitably be confronted by skillful, determined opponents in Congress. Most assuredly such rivals would impose no legal or moral restraints upon themselves as they pursued their own objectives.

Having begun their journey at Appomattox Court House, the remnants of Ransom's former brigade finally made their way into Warrenton. Many families were started at the appearance of their loved ones, and in some cases failed to recognize them. Most likely they were unshaved, with matted, unkempt hair, filthy rags as clothes, and heads crawling with lice. Their return presented a complete contrast to the day they marched away to perform combat roles. Then people had cheered, while bands played spirited martial music. Now the soldiers returned in almost total silence.

At Warrenton General Ransom found warm comfort in the company of his closely knit family. Pattie Ransom, expecting another child soon, was well under the circumstances, and in reasonably good spirits in spite of recently having to contend with the rigors of setting up a new household for the children and herself at Warrenton. This change had been carried out at the general's insistence, as he believed the family's safety was threatened during the post-war period, when Yankee scavengers were expected to continue roaming the countryside. While the family was in Warrenton, treasured household furniture and other valued domestic items from Verona were removed for safer storage at Weldon.

It was a touching reunion when the general embraced his father, who had just recently arrived from Alabama. For Robert Ransom, Sr., only a few months of life remained.[19] Also joining the reunion was Robert Ransom, Jr. Uncomplainingly, he too was contending with a serious health handicap, but like his brother, he was faced with the necessity of providing for a family of young children.

During this period in North Carolina, providing for one's family was no small task, since opportunities hardly existed in either professional or labor fields. Throughout the state were the commonplace sights of abandoned, neglected, or destroyed railroads, factories, public buildings, bridges, roads, churches, barns, and private homes. The torch was not altogether responsible for this disarray of public and private property. Four years of exhaustive war had imposed a severe labor shortage, and a scarcity of construction materials had also contributed to the current demoralizing scenes.

The condition of private and public finance was equally gloomy. Termination of slavery alone liquidated $200,000,000 of personal and state property in the state. During the war, University of North Carolina, banks, colleges, and business groups in North Carolina had been heavy purchasers of state and Confederate bonds. With Confederate bonds now worthless, and with serious doubts hanging over state securities, a number of institutions were sliding into financial ruin. Sharing in this state's economic quagmire were thousands of individuals who had been the state's most affluent, and who had enjoyed the many material benefits and social advantages generally associated with wealth. Now, many members of this class were being driven into bankruptcy, and in some instances total poverty.[20]

Financial loss and physical damage from war can to some degree be measured statistically. On the other hand, how can the important but intangible costs of war be determined? Having sacrificed 19,673 of her sons in combat, and 20,602 more as a result of disease, North Carolina was more than entitled to a period of mourning and reflection. No other state in the Confederacy suffered as many killed and wounded in combat. Of Confederate casualties in the Seven Days' Battle, one-fifth were North Carolinians; at Fredericksburg and Chancellorsville, one-third; and at Gettysburg, one-fourth. The Old North State comprised only one-ninth of the total population of the Confederacy, yet her troops made up one-sixth to one-seventh of the armed forces engaged in combat against the Union.[21]

The degree of despair dominating the public mood in North Carolina after Appomattox is vividly illustrated in a diary entry by Catherine Ann Devereaux Edmonston. She wrote:

> Since we heard of our disaster I seem as tho' in a dream. I go about in a kind of "drowsy dream." I sleep, sleep, sleep endlessly; if I sit in my chair for ten minutes, I doze. I think of it, but I cannot grasp it or its future consequences. I sit benumbed. It is to me like the idea of eternity. I believe it, yes I assent to it, but with a simple mental assent without once comprehending or even feeling it. I sit and hear the young folks ... talk of books, of poetry, and they seem to me to be talking of what was long, long ago. I read books, I liked poetry, when was it? Where are they all gone? I seem to grope after my own ideas, my own identity, and in the vain attempt to grasp it I fall asleep, I am not dejected, am not cast down. Seemingly the loss of New Orleans and of Vicksburg affected me much more. What is it that sustains me? ... I believe it is faith in the country. Faith in the "Cause," an earnest believe that eventually we will yet conquer! We cannot be defeated. That it is which I believe sustains and I pray God I may never lose it.[22]

If such disappointment, grief, and despair existed in Ransom's mind, he never allowed them to surface. Friends and neighbors who called upon him seemed always to pose the same question, though perhaps worded differently each time: "General, what's going to happen to us?" Always he responded with words of hope and optimism. However, these sentiments, accompanied by a warm handshake, seemed always to fall short of the kindness and sympathy he wished to convey. To him the recent "cause" and the old order were gone, never to return. Now that the war had ended, writes C. J. Hendley in an article on Ransom, the general believed southern people must learn "that they had passed through a revolution and that they must accept the new regime."[23] Symbols of the new regime in the North were huge factories with chimneys of belching smoke and fumes, a large natural population being supplemented by throngs of newly arrived immigrants, railroads of impressive mileage, and large, growing cities where impressive personal fortunes were commonplace. These interests as represented in Congress were now free of restrictions or opposition in their efforts to mold a new pattern of government in the postwar period. Defenders of the original republic, which provided a joint partnership between the national government and the states, were no longer present. Thanks to their hasty and unwise decision to embrace secession, not one former Confederate state was represented in Congress.

What intelligent, practical response was required to effectively counter, or at least balance, this new political and economic power? Matt Ransom would certainly rule out any frontal attack. Such attacks, he had found, rarely accomplish their intended objectives. Flanking movements can and often do produce far greater yields. If it were left to him, Ransom would search out those at the helm of power. He would join them, establish a dialogue in hopes of winning their confidence; and if in the process he became indispensable to his newly won colleagues, so much the better. These tactics he had employed with great success in his state legislature. Rightly some might wonder: Did he capitulate or surrender his own principles in this process? Not in the least. Joining the Democratic Party as a Unionist, he mingled and sometimes worked with secessionists, never abandoning his old Whig Party heritage. When developing his political strategy, Matt Ransom never forgot that inside the power center, opportunities for sharing influence and persuasion exist. On the outside of this exclusive circle such opportunities are few, if they exist at all.

Temperament, breeding, and training formed the base of Ransom's rationale of human society and its institutions. Persons of wealth, he believed, had always been the vital force behind any healthy community or national development. Membership of this group should remain open so that qualified entrants willing to lend their time, intelligence, and craft could assume their rightful roles of authority. Darwinian and Masonic perhaps, but as Ransom observed the application of this thesis, he was pleased with its results. And, as often stated by him, he was only impressed with positive results in any human endeavors.

To characterize Matt W. Ransom in the modern vernacular as a man of the people would be completely inappropriate and inaccurate. Such characterization he himself would have regarded with revulsion. Though Thomas Jefferson in his own style of politics portrayed himself as a champion of Yeoman farmers and laboring people, he never asked them to dine at his table; nor did Ransom. The general's personal friends were limited in number, and almost invariably persons of high social and official rank. Before his life's end he would include presidents, secretaries of state and supreme court justices among the parties with whom he enjoyed good rapport. Only on rare occasions did Mrs. Ransom and the general engage in county or township social functions. Theirs was a very private family with no trespassers allowed. Yet this aloofness must not be construed as snobbery. To people of his county who were facing ruin, he gave freely of his little remaining wealth, offering horses, mules, cattle, and seeds to struggling farmers to tide them over a critical period. To those determined to overcome the current economic plight, he was always quick to offer help and encouragement, irrespective of their socioeconomic backgrounds. He was sometimes believed the image of an English country gentleman, but this was not of his doing; he was awarded this status by many friends and admirers. Of course, some few individuals may have felt uncomfortable with the Northampton County planter's aristocratic philosophical outlook and bearing. If these same qualities of personality and character were often debasing to others, they were complimentary to Ransom's generally accepted demeanor.

Would Ransom stand aside for others to assume the challenge of rescuing North Carolina from its paralysis of chaos and confusion? Not likely. From boyhood he had excelled in the leadership role, and there was no apparent reason why he should step out of character this time. At age thirty-nine, aside from a wounded arm in sling, Matt was in reasonably good health. He was still an attractive man, masculine in features and appearance, though some decided physical changes had recently occurred. The formerly jet black hair, now thinning, was becoming streaked with gray, as was his beard. New wrinkles were being etched upon his once-youthful face. His eyes, almost black, were easily his most striking facial feature. They were searching eyes, and depending upon the person on whom they were focused, they could sometimes produce some discomfort. The general was in the prime of his life, and when mounted on a horse, in appearance and demeanor he had no equal.

In the brief time since his return, Ransom had been unable to determine the true state of affairs at Verona as they pertained to future planting operations. With agriculture now beset by so many uncertainties and problems, some planters of the area were compelled to leave ancestral homes in search of new livelihoods. Probably one of the major handicaps for farm operations this coming spring would be a shortage of field hands and laborers. In Northampton County and adjacent areas, former slaves were moving off the plantations. The plight of these unfortunate beings bore heavily upon the minds of Mrs. Ransom and the general. If only, he contended, his workers would hold on for a time, the overdue debts, mortgages, and taxes now threatening Verona might be resolved. In a revived, healthy economy, with hard work and responsible planning, he was certain the future would take on a new meaning that would prove beneficial to all.

Regarding blacks and their recently acquired status as freedmen, General Ransom's views are a matter of record; often they were stated in public forums. Under a reconstructed Union without slavery, he "would impair no right" of the black man. On the contrary, he "would protect him faithfully in every right secured to him by the Constitution." Not only would Ransom protect the black man, he would "educate him, and elevate him to the high position of all the duties and capacities of an American citizen ... never oppress or depress him because he is poor, ignorant and a colored man." A black American should have "every opportunity of improving his physical, mental and moral condition"; Ransom declared he would vehemently "oppose and denounce any man or any party" intending to deny a black person "of these rights and privileges." The next point Ransom stressed with great emphasis. While he "would endeavor most faithfully to do full and complete justice to the colored man, let me once and for all say that I never could consent that the white people of the South, the white people of the country should subordinate their rights, their capacities, their prestige to the colored man. On this subject my convictions are firmly fixed."[24]

There is nothing here that hints at the hypocrisy existing in northern states that maintained exclusionary laws and open discrimination against blacks. Neither is there anything resembling Lincoln's advocacy of deporting blacks to overseas climes. Ransom seemed to be saying to black people, stay here among us, work hard, develop your potential, and benefit from any prosperity which might result from your own endeavors. If he contended that blacks should not be accorded free entitlements in their new lives, he applied the same standards to whites.

Ransom was very concerned that future historians might misunderstand the origins of the war just concluded. "It is incorrect to state," he insisted, "the South went to war over slavery." The South "went to war because of her love for liberty, because of her jealousy of her rights, her liberties and her independence.... The ten millions of southern people who owned no slaves offered their husbands, sons, fathers, brothers upon the alter of their country, a willing sacrifice for independence ... not for slavery."[25]

While it is impossible to know what might have become of slavery had the Civil War never occurred, it is evident that monetarily speaking, the system in its final days proved to be highly questionable, and morally it was indefensible. The British had for over three decades prohibited its practice within the empire, and imperial Russia was on the threshold of eliminating serfdom. In the United States its future was becoming increasingly tenuous, not because of abolitionist efforts, but rather because an increasing number of Southern yeoman farmers and the rising middle class resented the preferential tax laws afforded to slave interests. This was particularly true in North Carolina, where the piedmont area with its growing free-labor market was gaining ascendancy over plantation districts.

How different was the scene at Verona compared to former times! The land was idle, with weeds and grass dominating the rich black soil; the drainage ditches were totally neglected, and no spring gardens had been planted this season. There had been, so recently, black laborers plowing and planting the fields, and clearing land of timber; grooming and attending animals in stables; curing hams and hanging them in smokehouses; repairing farm implements and wagons and shoeing horses. Of dairy and poultry chores, and the countless domestic duties, there was neither sight nor sound. Yet Matt Ransom was determined to bring this idle plantation back to life. In his mind, land was the most precious gift provided to man. Such a prize he would not forfeit without a struggle, and with some degree of impatience he made his plans to get on with the job of earning a livelihood.

During anxious times, people draw upon different sources for support and relief. Harry Adams, generally regarded as one of the great literary intellects of nineteenth-century America, offered two plausible courses for coming to grips with life's mysteries and problems. One could turn to the Virgin for answers, or one could follow a pragmatic, materialistic path (as symbolized by the dynamo). While few, if any, North Carolina rural protestants had ever read Henry Adams, in their own way they pursued the two approaches he offered.

To really understand southerners of this period requires a visit with them in their places of worship. A few miles north and west of Jackson, North

Carolina, stands Pleasant Grove Methodist Church, located at the old Mt. Carmel–Occoneeche and Seaboard-Jackson crossroads. A monograph on this church's history notes that the original church was built in 1836 as a small one-room weatherboard frame building "without ceiling, plaster, paint or even without means of heating." Its name was provided by one of the parishioners, who casually voiced her opinion that the shade trees surrounding the church "made a very pleasant grove for meeting."[26] A Mighty Fortress Is Our God" was a favorite inspirational hymn of the congregation, and behind the pulpit a circut-riding preacher delivered the sermon. Sitting on long, hard wooden benches in worship were the Taylors, Whites, Pritchards, Barretts, Walls, Harts, Stephensons, Hughs, Hargroves, Boones, Webbs and Spiveys. No English parish could claim a more Anglo-Saxon congregation. During early centuries their ancestors had come from Great Britain, on the Isle of Wight, Virginia; they had pushed inland and southward, planting their culture in a strange new world.

Outside the little church, in the period following Appomattox, a quick visual survey was enough to see that the buggies, wagons, and animals pulled up around the building had long outlived their better days. The harnesses were old, have been repaired repeatedly; the horses were a leftover lot, since the better ones had been consigned to the war effort. Inside the church, the owners seemed to reflect a similar state of fatigue, wear, and deprivation. Patched and mended clothing carried no social stigma here, for such garments were the rule rather than the exception. No new bonnets or ribbons adorned the heads of the ladies. The young and middle-aged members were mostly lean; apparently corpulence was uncommon among those whose work began at daybreak and ended after darkness fell. Nevertheless they were a handsome people, possessed of unusual stamina and hardiness, as the war just ended had amply demonstrated. Families were generally large, and during worship services any child who might depart from its usual good behavior could be instantly returned to the fold by a parental glance. These were industrious, largely self-sustaining farmers; very few, if any, had owned slaves. Tending to hold their own ethnic heritage apart from others, they were also disinclined to accept strangers of their own kind until a test period elapsed. Much of their character, of course, was molded by their religion, which stressed that all worldly conditions, including tragedy, existed by God's permission. Responsibility rested upon the individual through his Maker to withstand all trials and tribulations. Death was not to be feared; on the contrary, it was a means to take up a more meaningful eternal life. Those who embraced these principles were prepared to meet life's worst moments.

Out of gloom and despair, hope and optimism can evolve. To help them make this transition, people in the Roanoke Valley turned in numbers to their general. Seated at home alone one day, General Ransom recovered from his pocket several federal bills of currency, which he examined with great interest.

These he had received only the day before from a man just returned from Petersburg, where he had sold a wagonload of Verona-grown pork and poultry.[27] Delighted and grateful as he was to come into possession of good, healthy currency once again, General Ransom could not help feeling amused. It was only a limited cash amount he held in his hand, but at least it was a start.

A grave matter confronting General Ransom was the restoration of his full rights of United States citizenship as accorded by the Constitution. Because he had served in the southern military above the rank of colonel, and owned property allegedly exceeding $20,000 of taxable value, he was excluded from receiving any benefits under the president's general amnesty and pardon program. Those who were excluded had the right to apply for a federal pardon by direct petition to President Johnson. Ransom's written petition for a pardon reveals much about his feelings and his financial circumstances. The request reads as follows:

> Northampton County, N.C
> August 15, 1865
>
> TO: His Excellency, Andrew Johnson, President of the United States of America
>
> SIR:
>
> I have the honor to ask that your Excellency will grant to me a pardon and amnesty for my participation in the late Civil War.
>
> At the commencement of hostilities I was in civil life — entered the military service of North Carolina, was appointed Lt. Colonel of Infantry — was subsequently elected Colonel and afterwards commissioned Brig. General in the Southern Army. I was surrendered with General Lee's Army at Appomattox Court House and pardoned by General Grant.
>
> I do not think that the taxable value of my property will not reach $20,000 — it consists mainly in lands, which are encumbered with a debt exceeding its present value — Before the war, this property was assessed at about $40,000. It has not been abandoned or libelled.
>
> That I acted from a sense of patriotic duty in the War is best attested by the fact that for four years I shared the fortunes of the Southern Army. The issues of the War have been finally determined against us, and I now regard it right to render an unreserved allegiance to the government of the United States, and to do what I can to restore harmony among our people and to promote the happiness and honor of the contry.
>
> With this resolution I have taken and subscribe to the oath of allegiance and amnesty prescribed in your Proclamation — a copy of which is attached, and I trust this will be sufficient assurance that it is my sincere purpose to respect and maintain the government of the United States of America.
>
> I have the honor to be, Sir, very respectfully, your obedient servant.
>
> M. W. Ransom[28]

A little over a year later, there arrived at Jackson, through the United States mail service, an official envelope containing the following document:

Andrew Johnson,
President of the United States of America
Where as M. W. Ransom ... by taking part in the late rebellion against the Government of the United States, has made himself liable to heavy pains and penalties;
And whereas, the circumstances of his case render him a proper object of Executive clemency;
And, therefore, be it known, that — I Andrew Johnson, President of the United States of America, in consideration of the premises, divers other good and sufficient reasons me therunto moving, do hereby grant to the said M. W. Ransom, a full pardon and amnesty for all offenses by him committed, arising from participation direct or implied, in the said rebellion, conditional as follows:

1. This pardon to be of no effect until the said M. W. Ransom shall take the oath as prescribed in the Proclamation of the President dated May 29, 1865.
2. To be void and of no effect if the said M. W. Ransom shall hereafter, at any time, acquire property whatever in slaves, or make use of slave labor.
3. That said M. W. Ransom first pay all costs which may have accrued in any proceedings instituted or pending against his person or property, before the date of acceptance of this warrent.
4. That the said M. W. Ransom shall not by virtue of this warrent, claim any property or the proceeds of any property that has been sold by the order, judgment, or decree of a court under the confiscation laws of the United States.
5. That the said M. W. Ransom shall notify the Secretary of State, in writing, that he has received and accepted the foregoing pardon.

Signed
Thirteenth day of December 1866

Andrew Johnson[29]

Now reinstated as a full citizen with all legal restrictions removed, Matt Ransom, if he so desired, could engage in politics as a candidate for public office. In view of the murky, unsettled state of North Carolina politics at this time, his reluctance to take up such a venture is understandable. Preferring to postpone any political ambitions for the moment, he refused to enter a race against Jonathan Worth running for reelection as governor in 1866.[30]

During the immediate postwar years, Ransom mainly expended his energy in finding a means of regaining his former agricultural yields. By February 1867 his crops included 600 acres of cotton, 400 acres of corn, and 250 acres of wheat.[31] Credit afforded the means by which these crops were put down. Young Matt Ransom, Jr., writing from Oxford, North Carolina, to his father on April 20, 1867, alluded to another problem: "Mother wrote some of the freed people have left you."[32] Then came June, July, and August, with unusual amounts of rainfall, and subsequent months with untimely frosts, destroying all possibilities of good crop yields. Verona's total production of cotton did not exceed fifty bales. Confronted with financial ruin, Ransom moved his family off the plantation and took up residence in a rented house at Garysburg. To earn a livelihood, he opened a law office in Weldon, and by this means he supported his family for several years. In time, however, he and the family would return to Verona, where he would prevail and prosper.

It seems appropriate to end this narrative with a simple analogy. The North Carolina oak in some instances grows to enormous height and bulk, becoming a Goliath of the forests. yet, when exposed to the fury of the elements, such a tree can come crashing down upon the earth, never to assume its majestic postures. On the other hand, the water willow oak, which draws little public acclaim, is possessed of singular qualities including agility and the ability to survive under the most adverse conditions. When exposed to torrential rains and violent winds, the willow will bend and hug the earth for preservation. When the storm subsides, this tree tends to spring upright again as if nothing out of the ordinary had ever happened. So with those who returned to prosperity following the terrible storm that was the American Civil War. Feeling the winds, they bend; they held fast to what was close and dear for protection; but never did they break, nor become uprooted from the ideals and the relationships forming the firm earth that supported them. So it was with many; and so it was for Matthew W. Ransom.

Notes

Chapter I

1. Samuel A'Court Ashe, *History of North Carolina* (Raleigh: Edwards and Broughton, 1925, 2:543. Also, for the general public mood in North Carolina over Lincoln's election, see Joseph Carlyle Sitterson, "The Secession Movement in North Carolina" (Chapel Hill: Department of History and Political Science of the University of North Carolina, the James Sprunt Studies in History and Political Science, Vol. 23, no. 2, 1934), 174.

2. Sitterson, "The Secession Movement," 180.

3. John G. Barrett, *The Civil War in North Carolina* (Chapel Hill: University of North Carolina Press, 1963), 4.

4. Hugh Talmage Lefler and Albert Ray Newsome, *North Carolina: The History of a Southern State* (Chapel Hill: University of North Carolina Press, 1954), 421.

5. Stewart Mitchell, *Horatio of New York* (Cambridge: Harvard University Press, 1938), Also, for an analysis of North Carolina election results for president in 1860, see Lefler and Newsome, *North Carolina*, 420–21.

6. Bruce Catton, *The Coming Fury* (Garden City, N.Y.: Doubleday, 1961), 167–68. This source quotes Congressman Gilmer's letter and Lincoln's response.

7. Lefler and Newsome, *North Carolina*, 414. Lefler and Newsome state that "slavery extension had become largely theoretical." On this matter see Charles W. Ramsdell, "The Natural Limtis of Slavery Extension," *Mississippi Valley Historical Review* 16, no. 2 (September 1929): 161–62.

8. William Catton and Bruce Catton, *Two Roads to Sumter* (New York: McGraw-Hill, 1963), 237–38.

9. *Ibid.*

10. Catton, *The Coming Fury*, 202.

11. Ashe, *History of North Carolina*, 2:567. Also see Sitterson, *The Secession Movement in North Carolina*, 223–27, for statistics concerning votes cast for and against the convention.

12. Lefler and Newsome, *North Carolina*, 415.

13. *North Carolina Standard*, 17 November 1860.

14. Joseph C. Sitterson, *The Secession Movement in North Carolina* (Chapel Hill: University of North Carolina Press, 1939), 199.

15. Catton, *The Coming Fury*, 192.

16. Thomas Bragg, *Diary*, January 3, 1861–May 15, 1862 (Chapel Hill: Copied from original given by Mr. Herbert B. Gilliam for permanent preservation in the Southern Historical Collection, University of North Carolina, 1957), 32–33.

17. Sitterson, *The Secession Movement in North Carolina*, 232.

18. Catton, *The Coming Fury*, 266.

19. Clifford Dowdey, *The Land They Fought For* (Garden City, N.Y.: Doubleday, 1955), 88.

20. *Ibid.*, 88–89. This source reproduces Lincoln's dispatch on April 6 to the South Carolina governor concerning Fort Sumter.

21. Ashe, *History of North Carolina*, 2:578.

22. *Ibid.*, 580–82. Ashe recounts Lincoln's private conversation with Mr. John A. Baldwin.

23. *Ibid.*

24. *Ibid.*, 582. Ashe records the conversation with Mr. John M. Botts.

25. Michael Kraus, *The United States to 1865* (Ann Arbor: University of Michigan Press, 1959), 485–86.

26. Catton, *The Coming Fury*, 327–28. Catton quotes Lincoln's proclamation following the action at Fort Sumter.

27. R.D.W. Connor, *North Carolina Rebuilding an Ancient Commonwealth 1584–1925* (Chicago and New York: American Historical Society, 1929), 143. Connor quotes Governor Ellis's reply to Lincoln's request for troops from the states.

28. *History of North Carolina*, 2:601.

Chapter II

1. R.D.W. Connor, *North Carolina Rebuilding an Ancient Commonwealth 1584–1925* (Chicago and New York: American Historical Society, 1929), 144.

2. *Ibid.*

3. Thomas Bragg, *Diary*, January 3, 1861–May 15, 1862 (Chapel Hill: Copied from original given by Mr. Herbert B. Gilliam for preservation in the Southern Historical Collection, University of North Carolina, 1957), 5–6. Senator Bragg recorded his strong reservations relative to secessionists on 4 January 1861: "These men are rash, impetuous and would precipitate disunion and rush North Carolina out of the Union before she is prepared and while in a helpless condition — no arms, no military organization — there is no need of the hot haste. "Also see Joseph C. Sitterson, *The Secession Movement in North Carolina* (Chapel Hill: University of North Carolina Press, 1939), 201, for Bragg's public statement that North Carolina should call a convention for the purpose of obtaining guarantees from the North; failing in this, North Carolina "should join the South."

4. *North Carolina University Magazine* 10, no. 8 (April 1861), 504. See also *North Carolina Journal of Law* 1, no. 11 (November 1904), 531.

5. Bruce Catton, *The Coming Fury* (Garden City, N.Y.: Doubleday, 1961), 204–15. The description of Montgomery, Alabama, is based upon this source.

6. *North Carolina University Magazine* 10, no. 8 (April 1861), 504–05.

7. Judge R.W. Winston, "Matt W. Ransom," North Carolina Review, *The News and Observer*, 5 February 1911, 2.

8. Matt W. Ransom, formal address before the Dialectic and Philanthropic Societies of the University of North Carolina, 4 June 1856 (North Carolina Historical Section, University of North Carolina Library).

9. Samuel A'Court Ashe, *Biographical History of North Carolina from Colonial Times to the Present* (Greensboro: Charles L. Van Noppen, 1905), 1:422. See also Pocahontas Wright Edmunds, *Tar Heels Track the Century* (Raleigh: Edwards and Broughton, 1966), 72.

10. Charles W. Ramsdell, "The Natural Limits of Slavery Expansion," *Mississippi Historical Review* 16, no. 2 (September 1929), 168.

11. Rosser Howard Taylor, "Slaveholding in North Carolina: An Economic View"

(Chapel Hill: Department of History and Political Science of the University of North Carolina, the James Sprunt Studies in History and Political Science, Vol. 18, 1926), 47. This source contains interesting and revealing observations on the subjects of slavery and ad valorem taxation: "The agitation during the 50's for ad valorem taxation was not a direct attack upon slavery "'per se.' It was primarily an attempt to obtain a more equitable system of taxation. Speculation as to the profitableness of slaveholding based on the testimony of planters, travelers and others seem[s] to warrant the conclusion that in North Carolina slaveholding was not generally profitable." See also William K. Boyd, "North Carolina on the Eve of Secession" (Washington: Reprinted from the Annual Report of the American Historical Association for 1910), 175. Boyd states that Ad valorem taxation in North Carolina may have been the "beginning of a revolt against slavery as a political and economic influence."

12. Joseph C. Sitterson, *The Secession Movement in North Carolina* (Chapel Hill: Univeresity of North Carolina Press, 1939), 214. The author includes a brief outline and discussion of Lincoln's Indianapolis speech on 9 February.

13. Jefferson Davis, *The Rise and Fall of the Confederate Government* (New York and London: Thomas Yoseloff, 1958), 1:227–28.

14. Sitterson, *The Secession Movement in North Carolina*, 245. According to Sitterson, with a "vast majority" of the state's citizens favoring disunion, the only conflict of opinion centered upon whether the event should be accomplished by revolution or secession.

15. Hugh Talmage Lefler, *North Carolina History Told by Contemporaries* (Chapel Hill: University of North Carolina Press, 1965), 285.

16. Winston, "Matt W. Ransom."

17. Lefler, *North Carolina History Told by Contemporaries*, 285.

18. *Ibid.*, 288–89. This source reproduces the ordinance dissolving the union between North Carolina and the Union.

Chapter III

1. Judge R.W. Winston, "Matt Ransom," North Carolina Review, *The News and Observer*, 5 February 1911, 2.

2. Thomas Bragg, *Diary*, January 3, 1861–May 15, 1862 (Chapel Hill: Copied from original given by Mr. Herbert B. Gilliam for permanent preservation in the Southern Historical Collection, University of North Carolina, 1957), 10. Bragg wrote: "Ransom encloses me a letter to his brother advising him to resign his com'n in the army and come to N.C.'s aid if she secedes."

3. William H.S. Burgwyn, "An Address on the Military and Civil Services of Matt W. Ransom" (speech delivered before the Ladies' Memorial Association and Citizens, Senate Chamber, Raleigh, 10 March 1906).

4. Kemp P. Battle, "Ransom Student at University," North Carolina Review, *News and Observer*, 5 February 1911.

5. Unpublished genealogy records compiled by Robert Ransom, Jr., a copy of which is in the possession of Mrs. Martha Ransom Johnston, Littleton, North Carolina.

6. Names of Matt Ransom's sisters were provided by Mrs. Minnie Ransom Norris in a letter dated 18 September 1968, Raleigh, N.C.

7. Warren J. Green, *Recollections and Reflections* (Raleigh: Edwards and Broughton, 1906), 270.

8. Robert Ransom, Jr., unpublished and incomplete autobiography (Southern Historical Collection, University of North Carolina at Chapel Hill).

9. The Ransoms of Virginia and North Carolina were of English stock. Peter Ran-

som after arriving here from England married Ann Seymour; they settled in Elizabeth County, Virginia, which he represented in the House of Burgesses in 1652. From this union James Ransom was born, and he, too served in the House of Burgesses, from 1692 to 1694; other offices James held were justice of the peace in 1680 and vestryman of Kingston Parish, Gloucester County, Virginia. In later years his great grandson of Warren County, North Carolina, who also carried the same first name, married the widow Priscilla Macon. Before and during the American Revolution James earned distinction among his fellow local citizens as a patriot and a member of the Sons of Liberty, who opposed the Tories. Holding office as sheriff, he was also considered a wealthy man of his time. From his marriage to Priscilla was born Seymour Ransom, a half-brother to Priscilla's other son, the famous Nathaniel Macon. Seymour married Birchett Green, and to this couple was born Robert Ransom. Robert took Priscilla Whitaker as his wife, and they with their children resided on Bridle Creek.

10. Josephus Daniels, *Editor in Politics* (Chapel Hill: University of North Carolina Press, 1941), 42–43. This source recounts the visit of Robert, Sr., and Matt to Nathaniel Macon's plantation.

11. *Ibid.*

12. Ransom, Jr., unpublished and incomplete autobiography.

13. Manley Wade Wellman, *The County of Warren North Carolina 1586–1917* (Chapel Hill: University of North Carolina Press, 1959), 74, 81. This was an entertaining and helpful source for a description of the Warrenton Male Academy.

14. *Ibid.*

15. Ransom, Jr., unpublished and incomplete autobiography.

16. Green, *Recollections and Reflections*, 271–72.

17. Lizzie Wilson Montgomery, *Sketches of Old Warrenton* (Raleigh: Edwards and Broughton, 1924), 350–51.

18. Ransom, Jr., unpublished and incomplete autobiography. In the words of Robert, Jr.: "In '42 July — my brother went to Chapel Hill for one half year, but my father was not able to continue him there and he was off for one year until Jan. '44 when he returned to graduate in 1847."

19. Robert W. Madry, "University Has Proud Heritage of 137 Years of Priceless Tradition," *News and Observer*, 14 February 1932.

20. Kemp P. Battle, "Recollections of the University of North Carolina of 1844." According to Universeity library personnel, Battle's unpublished manuscript, offered to the university as a gift, apparently has been misplaced or lost. My reference to the faculty at this time was based upon this source.

21. Battle, "Ransom Student at University."

22. *Ibid.*

23. Samuel A'Court Ashe, *Biographical History of North Carolina from Colonial Times to the Present* (Greensboro: Charles L. Van Noppen, 1905), 1:420.

24. Newspaper clippings on the life of General Matt Ransom, Southern Historical Collection, University of North Carolina at Chapel Hill. On the matter of Ransom and Pettigrew not speaking to each other during their university days, I discovered an interesting item describing how Ransom, following an 1881 speech, was induced in a private conversation to elaborate on his relationship with Pettigrew. His reply was that "they were not on speaking terms." Again "years later, in a free and easy exchange ... We referred to the difference between Pettigrew and himself. He related all the circumstances." It was "suggested to Senator Ransom that probably the college rivalry had much to do with it, which he assented. He then spoke of Pettigrew's genius and character in highest terms and admiration." And then, in "a change of voice, manner and position, he added with

feeling [that] 'if our graduation had been a year off, I would have won, for I was rapidly overhauling him.'"

25. Kemp P. Battle, *History of the University of North Carolina* (Raleigh: Edwards and Broughton, 1907), 1:507. Discussion of Pettigrew's excelling Ransom in math at the university is as follows: "The first honor in the class of 36 members was awarded to James Johnston Pettigrew and Matt Whitaker Ransom 'in the order of their names' the former allowed the Valedictory because a shade better than the latter. In Mathematics Pettigrew's mark was 'excellent' while Ransom's was 'very good.' In other respects they were equal." Also see Ashe, *Biographical History of North Carolina from Colonial Times to the Present*, 1:420, for remarks about Ransom and Pettigrew dividing "first honors of their class."

26. Newspaper clippings on the life of General Matt Ransom, Southern Historical Collection, University of North Carolina at Chapel Hill. Ransom believed he would have eventually eclipsed his rival. Also see *Faculty Journal* 9002, University Archives, University of North Carolina at Chapel Hill, 1:4. Relative to prayers and recitations requiring student attendance at the university during the 1840s, the faculty records read: "The average number of attendances required of each student ... [with regard to] the scholastic and religious exercises of the institution is about 1,400 a year or 5,500 during the complete term of four years. Mr. Ransom is the only member of the graduating class who has never been absent during that period."

27. Nancy Moss Revelle, "Mathew Whitaker Ransom's Political Career" (master's thesis, University of North Carolina at Chapel Hill, 1959), 4.

28. Ashe, *Biographical History of North Carolina*, 1:421.

29. Newspaper clipping from the weekly *Raleigh Register* included among the papers of Mrs. Martha Ransom Johnston, Littleton, North Carolina. The published wedding announcement did not provide the first name of Reverent Stringfellow.

30. Ashe, *Biographical History of North Carolina*, 1:421.

31. Revelle, "Matthew Whitaker Ransom's Political Career," 7.

32. "A Birdseye View of Northampton County." This brochure discusses Northampton County's early settlers, climate, and physiographical features. Also see "Northampton Where Past and Present Merge," *The State*, 29 November 1958, 16–20.

33. *Ibid.*

34. Archie K. Davis, *Boy Colonel of the Confederacy: The Life and Times of Henry King Burgwyn, Jr.* (Chapel Hill: University of North Carolina Press, 1985), 26.

35. Pocahontas Wright Edmunds, *Tar Heels Track the Century* (Raleigh: Edwards and Broughton, 1956), 73.

36. Blackwell P. Robinson, ed., *The North Carolina Guide* (Chapel Hill: University of North Carolina Press), 420. See also "Northampton Where Past and Present Merge." These sources give the completion date of Ransom's home as 1857. See also *The News and Observer*, 12 October 1904, in which the naming of Ransom's plantation is discussed. Following the general's death, one of his sons was quoted by a reporter: "This is where my mother and father loved to live. ... They named it Verona because they were reading Shakespeare's Two Gentlemen here after they were married. It was my mother who named the place."

Chapter IV

1. Josephus Daniels, *Tar Heel Editor* (Chapel Hill: University of North Carolina Press, 1939), 252. Daniels offers a physical description of Raleigh, North Carolina, during this period. Also see Jonathan Daniels, *Prince of Carpetbaggers* (Philadelphia and New York: J.B. Lippincott, 1958), 150.

2. William H.S. Burgwyn, "An Address on the Military and Civil Services of General Matt W. Ransom" (speech delivered in the Senate Chamber at Raleigh before the Ladies' Memorial Association and Citizens, 10 May 1906). Burgwyn quotes a letter to Pattie Ransom from Matt.

3. *Ibid.* Burgwyn describes Matt Ransom's firm belief in strenuous training and discipline of troops.

4. Bell Irvin Wiley, *The Life of Johnny Reb* (Indianapolis and New York: Bobbs-Merrill, 1943), 27.

5. *Ibid.*

6. *Ibid.*, 55.

7. *Ibid.*

8. *Ibid.*, 41.

9. Walter Clark, ed., *Histories of the Several Regiments and Battalions from North Carolina in the Great Civil War, 1861–65* (Goldsboro: Nash Brothers, 1901), 2:599.

10. Robert Ransom, Jr., unpublished and incomplete autobiography (Southern Historical Collection, Univeresity of North Carolina at Chapel Hill).

11. *Ibid.*

12. *Ibid.*

13. W.J. Long or T.W. Mason Papers (Southern Historical Collection, University of North Carolina at Chapel Hill).

14. Samuel A'Courte Ashe, *History of North Carolina* (Raleigh: Edwards and Broughton, 1925), 2:661.

15. Clark, ed., *Histories of the Several Regiments and Battalions*, 1:3–5.

16. Ashe, *History of North Carolina*, 2:636.

17. *Ibid.*, 2:637–38.

18. Burgwyn, "An Address on the Military and Civil Services of General Matt W. Ransom." Burgwyn quotes Ransom's description of his living quarters.

19. *Ibid.*

20. *Ibid.*

21. Ashe, *History of North Carolina*, 2:643. This source enumerates Confederate casualties, both dead and wounded, resulting from the First Battle of Bull Run. Also see Thomas C. Cochran and Wayne Andrews, eds., *Concise Dictionary of American History* (New York: Charles Scribner's Sons, 1962), 119–29, which gives federal statistics, including killed and wounded, for this battle, as well as total troop estimates of both Union and Confederate forces involved.

22. Ashe, *History of North Carolina*, 2:638, refers to the battle as "the greatest," etc. J.G. Randall, *The Civil War and Reconstruction* (New York: D.C. Heath, 1937), 276 notes that the battle proved "indecisive."

23. Wiley, *The Life of Johnny Reb*, 31.

24. See n. 21.

25. Edward Porter Alexander, *Fighting for the Confederacy: The Personal Recollections of General Edward Porter Alexander*, ed. by Gary W. Gallagher (Chapel Hill and London: University of North Carolina Press, 1989), 58. Alexander wrote, "In the panic our advance would have made it likely that Washington City would have been evacuated … the panic would have swept everything."

26. Ashe, *History of North Carolina*, 2:643. Many Southerners "went wild with joy and confidently expected" ultimate success by their forces. See also Douglas Southall Freeman, *Lee's Lieutenants: A Study in Command* (New York: Charles Scribner's Sons, 1943), 1:76. "Independence was won; the war was over."

27. Archie K. Davis, *Boy Colonel of the Confederacy: The Life and Times of Henry King Burgwyn, Jr.* (Chapel Hill and London: University of North Carolina Press, 1985), 80–81.

28. *Ibid.*, 85–86. Davis quotes the letter of Captain Dimmock.

29. *Ibid.* Davis quotes the letter of Zebulon Vance.

30. Matt Ransom, letter to Pattie Ransom, September 4, 1861 (Southern Historical Collection, University of North Carolina at Chapel Hill).

31. E. Merton Coutler, *The Confederate States of America* (Baton Rouge: Louisiana State University Press, the Littlefield Fund for Southern History of the University of Texas, 1950), 187.

32. *Ibid.* Coutler writes that "the United States won the right to institute a blockade," which it "could not logically set up if this commotion was not war."

33. *Ibid.*, 188. Confederate diplomatic agents failed to obtain either Britain's or France's acknowledgment that the Union blockade was illegal. For a detailed review of European and American diplomacy during this period, see Samuel Flagg Bemis, *A Diplomatic History of the United States* (New York: Henry Holt, 1942), 364–378.

34. J.G. de Roulhac Hamilton, *History of North Carolina* (Chicago and New York: Lewis, 1919), 3:7.

35. Peter J. Parish, *The American Civil War* (New York: Holmes and Meier, 1975), 45–46.

36. Bruce Catton, *Terrible Swift Sword* (Garden City: Dougleday, 1963), 167–71.

37. *Ibid.*, 171.

38. Davis, *Boy Colonel of the Confederacy*, 106. Davis discusses the letter from Henry King Burgwyn, Sr., to Governor Clark, 22 February 1862.

39. *Ibid.*

40. John G. Barrett, *The Civil War in North Carolina* (Chapel Hill: University of North Carolina Press, 1963), 108.

41. Clark, ed., *Histories of the Several Regiments and Battalions*, 2:596.

42. J.G. de Roulhac Hamilton, ed., *Papers of Thomas Ruffin* (Raleigh: Edwards and Broughton, 1920), 231.

43. Clark, ed., *Histories of the Several Regiments and Battalions*, 2:594.

44. *Ibid.*, 596.

45. Burgwyn, "An Address on the Military and Civil Services of Matt W. Ransom." Burgwyn relates the conversation between General Holmes and Matt Ransom on the subject of whether the latter should assume command of the Thirty-fifth Regiment.

46. *Ibid.* Burgwyn quotes Matt Ransom's letter of acceptance.

47. Hamilton, ed., *Papers of Thomas Ruffin*, 231–32.

48. Barrett, *The Civil War in North Carolina*, 109.

49. Freeman, *Lee's Lieutenants*, 213.

Chapter V

1. John G. Barrett, *The Civil War in North Carolina* (Chapel Hill: University of North Carolina Press, 1963), 127.

2. Bruce Catton, *Terrible Swift Sword* (Garden City, N.Y.: Doubleday, 1963), 175.

3. Samuel A'Court Ashe, *History of North Carolina* (Raleigh: Edwards and Broughton, 1925), 2:749–50.

4. *Ibid.*, 719. Ashe states that critics of the Confederate conscription law denounced it as "as oppressive, tyrannous and illegal."

5. R. D. W. Connor, *North Carolina Rebuilding an Ancient Commonwealth 1584–1925* (Chicago and New York: American Historical Society, 1919), 2:211.

6. *Ibid.*

7. Hugh Talmage Lefler and Albert Ray Newsome, North Carolina: *The History of a Southern State* (Chapel Hill: University of North Carolina Press, 1963), 366.

8. Ashe, *History of North Carolina*, 717. Ashe discusses the publication of Holden's editorials in the *New York Herald* and quotes the *Philadelphia Inquirer*.

9. *Ibid.*, 739.

10. *Ibid.*, 716.

11. *Ibid.*, 715.

12. Catton, *Terrible Swift Sword*, 177.

13. Joseph B. Mitchell, *Decisive Battles of the Civil War* (New York: Fawcett Premier, 1955), 67.

14. Catton, *Terrible Swift Sword*, 293.

15. *Ibid.*

16. *Ibid.*, 294.

17. *Ibid.*, 302.

18. *Ibid.*, 312.

19. *Ibid.*, 313.

20. *Ibid.*

21. *Ibid.* Also see Ashe, *The History of North Carolina*, 2:720–22. This source provides a clear account of the Battle of Seven Pines.

22. Frontis W. Johnston, ed., *Papers of Zebulon Baird Vance* (Raleigh: North Carolina Department of Archives and History, 1963), 131n.

23. Archie K. Davis, *Boy Colonel of the Confederacy: The Life and Times of Henry King Burgwyn, Jr.* (Chapel Hill: University of North Carolina Press, 1985), 160.

24. *Ibid.*

25. *Ibid.*, 164.

26. Eastern National Park and Monument Assocuation, *Richmond: The Peninsula Campaign* (Acorn, 1985), 32.

27. Peter J. Parish, *The American Civil War* (New York: Holmes and Meier, 1975), 180.

28. Eastern National Park and Monument Association, *Richmond: The Peninsula Campaign*, 33.

29. Ashe, *History of North Carolina*, 2:730.

30. Eastern National Park and Monument Association, *Richmond: The Peninsula Campaign*, 36.

31. Parish, *The American Civil War*, 180.

32. Barrett, *The Civil War in North Carolina*, 128–29.

33. Eastern National Park and Monument Association, *Richmond: The Peninsula Campaign*, 36.

34. *Ibid.*, 40.

35. Walter Clark, ed., *Histories of the Several Regiments and Battalions from North Carolina in the Great War 1861–65* (Goldsboro, N.C.: Nash Brothers, 1901), 1:617.

36. Davis, *Boy Colonel of the Confederacy*, 172.

37. *Ibid.*

38. Richard Wheeler, *Sword Over Richmond* (New York: Harper and Row, 1986), 319.

39. Douglas Southall Freeman, *Lee's Lieutenants: A Study in Command* (New York: Charles Scribner's Sons, 1943), 1:587.

40. Wheeler, *Sword Over Richmond*, 335. Wheeler quotes D.H. Hill's summation of Frayser's Farm.

41. Clifford Dowdey, *The Seven Days* (New York: Fairfax), 305.

42. Barrett, *The Civil War in North Carolina*, 129.

43. Clark, ed., *Hsitories of the Several Regiments and Battalions*, 1:617.

44. *Ibid.* Malvern Hill offered a "position of great natural strength." See also Ashe,

The History of North Carolina, 2:732. From this elevation visibility was good in "all directions for several hundred yards."

45. Clark, ed., *Histories of the Several Regiments and Battalions*, 1:617.

46. Dowdey, *The Seven Days*, 325.

47. *Ibid.*, 326.

48. Eastern National Park and Monument Association, *Richmond: The Peninsula Campaign*, 45.

49. *Ibid.* According to this source, Armistead was expected to signal a "charge with a yell."

50. *Ibid.*, 46.

51. Clark, ed., *Histories of the Several Regiments and Battalions*, 1:619.

52. Robert N. Scott, comp., *The War of the Rebellion: A Compilation of the Official Records of the Union and Confederate Armies, Prepared Under the Direction of the Secretary of War* (Washington: Government Printing Office, 1884), ser. 1, vol. 11 in 3 pt., 2:794.

53. Eastern National Park and Monument Association, *Richmond: The Peninsula Campaign*, 46. Also see Clark, ed., *Histories of the Several Regiments and Battalions*, 1:619–20.

54. Davis, *Boy Colonel of the Confederacy*, 173. Also see Freeman, *Lee's Lieutenants*, 1:598–603, which offers criticism of Magruder because he "acted on assumption and did not get in touch with his support."

55. Clark, ed., *Histories of the Several Regiments and Battalions*, 1:620.

56. Eastern National Park and Monument Association, *Richmond: The Peninsula Campaign*, 46. This source quotes General Porter's description of the action at Malvern Hill.

57. Scott, comp., *The War of the Rebellion*, ser. 1, vol. 2 in 3 parts, pt. 2:794.

58. *Ibid.*

59. *Ibid.*

60. Eastern National Park and Monument Association, *Richmond: The Peninsula Campaign*, 47.

61. Scott, comp., *The War of the Rebellion*, ser. 1, vol. 11 in 3 pts., pt. 2:794–96. See also William H.S. Burgwyn, "An Address on the Military and Civil Services of Matt W. Ransom" (speech delivered in the Senate Chamber at Raleigh before the Ladies' Memorial Association and Citizens, 10 May 1906), for details of Matt's second wound, being struck in the side, and the severity of his arm injury.

62. Scott, comp., *The War of the Rebellion*, ser. 1, vol. 2 in 3 parts, pt. 2:794.

63. *Ibid.*, 794–95.

64. *Ibid.*, 795.

65. *Ibid.*

66. Burgwyn, "An Address on the Military and Civil Services of General Matt W. Ransom."

67. Scott, comp., *The War of the Rebellion*, ser. 1, vol. 2 in 3 parts, pt. 2:795. Losses suffered by the brigade at Malvern Hill are provided in the official report of Robert Ransom, Jr.

68. Catton, *Terrible Swift Sword*, 339.

Chapter VI

1. National Park Service, U.S. Department of Interior, Richmond. A Park Service pamphlet contains information about Chimborazo Hospital under the direction of McCaw. This hospital treated nearly 76,000 patients during the war.

2. William H.S. Burgwyn, "An Address on the Military and Civil Services of Matt W. Ransom" (speech delivered in the Senate Chamber at Raleigh before the Ladies' Memo-

rial Association and Citizens 10 May 1906). Burgwyn cites a reference to the demise of the infant Martha Ransom in a letter from Matt to his wife. Efforts to determine the exact date of death have been unsuccessful. Some years ago there was a small broken marker in the family cemetery at Verona which could have been a child's gravestone. This has since disappeared, probably discarded by laborers.

3. John G. Barrett and Buck Yearns, eds., *North Carolina Civil War Documentary* (Chapel Hill: University of North Carolina Press, 1980), 77.

4. *Ibid.*, 168.

5. Samuel A'Court Ashe, *History of North Carolina* (Raleigh: Edwards and Broughton, 1925), 2:709.

6. *Ibid.*

7. *Ibid.*, 738.

8. *Ibid.*, 752. The source quotes Vance's speech.

9. Franklyn Ray Shirley, *Zebulon Vance: Tarheel Spokesman* (Charlotte and Santa Barbara: McNally and Lofton, 1962), 21.

10. Barrett and Yearns, eds., *North Carolina Civil War Documentary*, 206.

11. *Ibid.*, 47.

12. Archie K. Davis, *Boy Colonel of the Confederacy: The Life and Times of Henry King Burgwyn, Jr.* (Chapel Hill: University of North Carolina Press, 1985), 176.

13. Hugh Talmage Lefler and Albert Ray Newsome, *North Carolina: The History of a Southern State* (Chapel Hill: University of North Carolina Press, 1963), 430.

14. Barrett and Yearns, eds., *North Carolina Civil War Documentary*, 272.

15. Hal Bridges, *Lee's Maverick General: Daniel Harvey Hill* (New York: McGraw-Hill, 1961), 88. Also see Walter Clark, ed., *Histories of the Several Regiments and Battalions from North Carolina in the Great War 1861–65* (Goldsboro: Nash Brothers, 1901), 600.

16. Bridges, *Lee's Maverick General*, 89.

17. *Ibid.*

18. Samuel A'Court Ashe, *History of North Carolina*, 2:744.

19. Shelby Foote, *The Civil War: A Narrative* (New York: Random House, 1986), 1:662. Foote quotes Lee's letter.

20. Catton, *Terrible Swift Sword* (Garden City: Doubleday, 1963), 436.

21. Foote, *The Civil War*, 664.

22. Clark, ed., *Histories of the Several Regiments and Battalions*, 601.

23. Burgwyn, "An Address on the Military and Civil Services of General Matt W. Ransom."

24. Foote, *The Civil War*, 663.

25. *Ibid.*

26. Catton, *Terrible Swift Sword*, 449.

27. *Ibid.*, 450. Catton notes that Lee was provided "a day or so of grace."

28. Douglas Southall Freeman, *Lee's Lieutenants: A Study in Command* (New York: Charles Scribner's Sons, 1943), 2:203.

29. Catton, *Terrible Swift Sword*, 451.

30. Burgwyn, "An Address on the Military and Civil Services of General Matt W. Ransom."

31. Catton, *Terrible Swift Sword*, 453.

32. *Ibid.*

33. *Ibid.*, 454.

34. Clark, ed., *Histories of the Several Regiments and Battalions*, 2:602.

35. *Ibid.*

36. Burgwyn, "An Address on the Military and Civil Services of General Matt W. Ransom."

37. Clark, ed., *Histories of the Several Rebiments and Battalions*, 2:606.

38. *Ibid.*

39. *Ibid.*

40. Catton, *Terrible Swift Sword*, 455.

41. Robert N. Scott, comp., *The War of the Rebellion: A Compilation of the Official Records of the Union and Confederate Armies, Prepared Under the Direction of the Secretary of War* (Washington: Government Printing Office), ser. 1, vol. 19, pt. 1:916.

42. Clark, ed., *Histories of the Several Regiments and Battalions*, 2:607–08. The dialogue between General Jackson, Colonel Ransom, and Private Hood is offered in this source.

43. *Ibid.*

44. *Ibid.*, 604.

45. Catton, *Terrible Swift Sword*, 455.

46. *Ibid.*, 455–56.

47. *Ibid.*, 456.

48. Freeman, *Lee's Lieutenants*, 224.

49. Scott, comp., *The War of the Rebellion*, ser. 1, vol. 19, pt. 1:916.

50. Burgwyn, "An Address on the Military and Civil Services of General Matt W. Ransom."

51. *Ibid.*

52. In a letter to Pattie dated 19 September 1862 (contained in the private papers of Mrs. Martha Ransom Johnston of Littleton, N.C.), Matt Ransom stated his view that the recent battle was a draw.

53. Catton, *Terrible Swift Sword*, 458.

54. *Ibid.*, 459.

55. Henry Steele Commager, ed. *The Blue and the Gray: The Story of the Civil War as Told by Participants* (Indianapolis and New York: Bobbs-Merrill, 1950), 207.

56. Foote, *The Civil War*, 702.

57. *Ibid.*

58. Clark, ed., *Histories of the Several Regiments and Battalions*, 2:608.

59. *Ibid.*, 607.

60. *Ibid.*, 606–07.

61. *Ibid.*, 605.

62. *Ibid.*, 609.

Chapter VII

1. William H.S. Burgwyn, "An Address on the Civil and Military Services of Matt W. Ransom" (speech delivered in the Senate Chamber at Raleigh before the Ladies' Memorial Association and Citizens, 10 May 1906).

2. Harold M. Hyman, ed., *New Frontiers of the American Reconstruction* (Urbana: University of Illinois Press, 1966), 128. Hyman discusses the views of George Julian, Salmon P. Chase and Charles Sumner concerning emancipated slaves. Also, Samuel A'Court Ashe, *History of North Carolina* (Raleigh: Edwards and Broughton, 1925), 2:801. Ashe quotes Sumner concerning Negroes.

3. Burgwyn, "An Address on the Military and Civil Services of General Matt W. Ransom."

4. Wayne Andrews, ed., *Concise Dictionary of American History* (New York: Charles Scribners' Sons, 1962), 381.

5. Burke Davis, *Gray Fox: Robert E. Lee and the Civil War* (New York and Toronto: Rinehart, 1956), 169.

6. *Ibid.*, 160.

7. Walter Clark, ed., *Histories of the Several Regiments and Battalions from North Carolina in the Great War 1861–65* (Goldsboro: Nash Brothers, 1901), 2:610. This source reports both the light casualty rate of the Thirty-fifth Regiment during the Battle of Fredericksburg, and General Robert Ransom's charitable conduct toward local citizens.

8. Henry Steele Commager, ed., *The Blue and the Gray: The Story of the Civil War as Told by Participants* (Indianapolis and New York: Bobbs-Merrill, 1950), 251. This source quotes President Lincoln's letter to General Hooker.

9. Catherine Drinker Bowen, *Yankee from Olympus* (Boston: Little, Brown, 1945), 182.

10. Hyman, ed., *New Frontiers of the American Reconstruction*, 128–29. Hyman quotes Lincoln and others on the subject of newly emancipated slaves.

11. *Ibid.*

12. John G. Barrett, *The Civil War in North Carolina* (Chapel Hill: University of North Carolina Press, 1963), 136–48. Barrett describes the Union raids in eastern North Carolina during December 1862.

13. Samuel A'Court Ashe, *History of North Carolina*, 2:816.

14. Hal Bridges, *Lee's Maverick General: Daniel Harvey Hill* (New York: McGraw-Hill, 1961). Chapter ten of this volume deals with the often strained personal relationship between Lee and General D.H. Hill.

15. *Ibid.*, 149.

16. Barrett, *The Civil War in North Carolina*, 155.

17. J.G. de Roulhac Hamilton, *History of North Carolina* (Chicago and New York: Lewis, 1919), 3:22.

18. Barrett, *The Civil War in North Carolina*, 156–62.

19. Robert N. Scott, comp., *The War of the Rebellion: A Compilation of the Official Records of the Union and Confederate Armies, Prepared Under the Direction of the Secretary of War* (Washington: Government Printing Office, 1884), ser. 1, vol. 18:961.

20. Barrett, *The Civil War in North Carolina*, 190–91.

21. Bruce Catton, *Never Call Retreat* (Garden City, N.Y.: Doubleday, 1965), 3:157.

22. Andrews, ed., *Concise Dictionary of American History*, 169.

23. *Ibid.*

24. Catton, *Never Call Retreat*, 157.

25. *Ibid.*

26. *Ibid.*

27. Bridges, *Lee's Maverick General*, 193.

28. Catton, *Never Call Retreat*, 158.

29. Barrett, *The Civil War in North Carolina*, 162–66.

30. Papers of Matt W. Ransom (Southern Historical Collection, University of North Carolina at Chapel Hill). Matt Ransom's commission as a brigadier general is dated 15 June 1863.

31. Clark, *Histories of the Several Regiments and Battalions*, 2:612–13.

32. *Ibid.*, 613.

33. Andrews, ed., *Concise Dictionary of American History*, 400.

34. Archie K. Davis, *Boy Colonel of the Confederacy: The Life and Times of Henry King Burgwyn, Jr.* (Chapel Hill: University of North Carolina Press, 1985), 352.

35. Barrett, *The Civil War in North Carolina*, 171.

36. Hamilton, *History of North Carolina*, 3:43.

37. Ashe, *History of North Carolina*, 2:820.

38. *Ibid.*, 833–34.

39. Barrett, *The Civil War in North Carolina*, 164.

40. Burgwyn, "An Address on the Military and Civil Services of General Matt W. Ransom."

41. Clark, ed., *Histories of the Several Regiments and Battalions*, 2:613–14.

42. *Ibid.*

43. The incident of a federal cavalryman being killed in front of Mr. Henry Boone's house was related to the writer by Mr. Rogers J. Boone of Jackson, North Carolina.

44. Burgwyn, "An Address on the Military and Civil Services of General Matt W. Ransom. In the race to Boone's Mill, Burgwyn says, "the thoroughbreds [Matt's men] proved equal to the demands on them."

45. *Ibid.* Also see Scott, comp., *The War of the Rebellion*, 2:985. Both Burgwyn and Scott are very useful in reconstructing the Boon's Mill skirmish.

46. Scott, comp., *The War of the Rebellion*, 2:985. The figures given are from General Ransom's official report on Boon's Mill.

47. Burgwyn, "An Address on the Military and Civil Services of General Matt W. Ransom."

48. Clark, ed., *Histories of the Several Regiments and Battalions*.

Chapter VIII

1. Samuel A'Court Ashe, *History of North Carolina* (Raleigh: Edwards and Broughton, 1925), 2:783.

2. Walter Clark, ed., *Histories of the Several Regiments and Battalions from North Carolina in the Great War 1861–65* (Goldsboro: Nash Brothers, 1901), 2:616.

3. Newspaper clipping included among the papers of Mrs. Martha Ransom Johnston, Littleton, North Carolina. In this account, Robert Ransom, one of Matt Ransom's sons, stated: "General Pickett and his wife, with many Confederate officers, spent much of the winter and spring of '63 and '64 at our home place, Verona."

4. John G. Barrett, *The Civil War in North Carolina* (Chapel Hill: University of North Carolina Press, 1963), 203.

5. *Ibid.*, 204–07.

6. *Ibid.*

7. J.G. de Roulhac Hamilton, *History of North Carolina* (Chicago and New York: Lewis, 1919), 3:23.

8. Barrett, *The Civil War in North Carolina*, 207.

9. *Ibid.*

10. General Ransom's letter of March 8, 1864, is included among the papers of Mrs. Martha Ransom Johnston. The reference to Ransom's capture of stores in Suffolk is found in William H.S. Burgwyn, "An Address on the Military and Civil Services of General Matt W. Ransom" (speech delivered in the Senate Chamber at Raleigh before the Ladies' Memorial Association and Citizens, 10 May 1906).

11. Robert Leckie, *None Died in Vain* (New York: HarperCollins, 1990), 580. According to Leckie, Sherman worried that Grant's "simplicity of character ... would be a fatal flaw."

12. Gene Smith, *Lee and Grant: A Dual Biography* (New York, St. Louis, San Francisco: McGraw-Hill, 1984), 185.

13. Leckie, *None Died in Vain*, 583.

14. Robert N. Scott, comp., *The War of the Rebellion: A Compilation of the Official Records of the Union and Confederate Armies, Prepared Under the Direction of the Secretary of War* (Washington: Government Printing Office, 1897), ser. 1, vol. 51 in 2 parts, pt. 2:857. The source contains General Ransom's orders of 12 April 1864.

15. The Washington Public Library of Plymouth provided the writer with information concerning the town's establishment in 1790 and its incorporation in 1817.

16. Michael Ballard, "A Good Time to Pray," *Civil War Times Illustrated*, April 1986, 16–25, 47. This magazine provided information on federal defense installations at Plymouth, troop unit identities, and naval craft.

17. *Ibid.*, 17–18.

18. *Ibid.*, 18.

19. *Ibid.*, 19–20.

20. *Ibid.*, 20.

21. *Ibid.*

22. *Ibid.*, 21.

23. *Ibid.*, 22.

24. *Ibid.*, 23.

25. The story of Matt Ransom's horse becoming mired in mud is contained in the papers of Mrs. Martha Ransom Johnston.

26. Ballard, "A Good Time to Pray," 24.

27. Burgwyn, "An Address on the Military and Civil Services of General Matt W. Ransom."

28. Walter Clark, ed., *Histories of the Several Regiments and Battalions*, 2:277.

29. Burgwyn, "An Address on the Military and Civil Services of General Matt W. Ransom."

30. *Ibid.*

31. Ballard, "A Good Time to Pray," provided details of this action.

32. Clark, ed., *Histories of the Several Regiments and Battalions*, 2:618.

33. Burgwyn, "An Address on the Military and Civil Services of Matt W. Ransom."

34. Clark, ed., *Histories of the Several Regiments and Battalions*, 1:400–01.

35. Ballard, "A Good Time to Pray," 24–25. Ballard details the vital role of the *Albermarle* in the Battle of Plymouth and the surrender of Fort Williams. On this same matter, see also Clark, ed., *Histories of the Several Regiments and Battalions*, 2:618.

36. Ballard, "A Good Time to Pray," 25.

37. *Ibid.*, 25, 47.

38. *Ibid.*, 47. Also see Clark, ed., *Histories of the Several Regiments and Battalions*, 2:616. Included are casualties concerning Ransom's brigade.

39. Clark, ed., *Histories of the Several Regiments and Battalions*, 2:616.

40. Burgwyn, "An Address on the Military and Civil Services of General Matt W. Ransom."

41. *Ibid.*

42. *Ibid.* Burgwyn states, "General Hoke gave Ransom a free hand at Plymouth and neither had cause to regret it."

43. *Ibid.* Burgwyn quotes Ransom's letter.

44. Clark, ed., *Histories of the Several Regiments and Battalions*.

45. *Ibid.*

46. G.T. Beauregard, *Butler's Attack on Drewry's Bluff: Battles and Leaders of the Civil War* (New York: Century, 1884), 4:207.

47. Bruce Catton, *Never Call Retreat* (Garden City, N.Y.: Doubleday, 1965), 354–55.

48. Clark, ed., *Histories of the Several Regiments and Battalions*, 2:386.

49. Smith, *Lee and Grant*, 200.

50. Bruce Catton, *This Hallowed Ground* (Garden City, N.Y.: Doubleday, 1956), 327.

51. *National Park Historical Handbook* (Washington, D.C., 1951), ser. 13. According to this source, the great army "was fighting for its survival ... with each day's casualties reducing its already thin ranks and food rations becoming more scarce for survivors."

52. Smith, *Lee and Grant*, 198.

53. Catton, *Never Call Retreat*, 346.

54. Clark, ed., *Histories of the Several Regiments and Battalions*, 3:350.

55. *Ibid.*, 2:285.

56. Ashe, *History of North Carolina*, 2:908.

57. Jefferson Davis, *The Rise and Fall of the Confederate Government* (New York and London: Thomas Yoseloff, 1958), 2:508–14. This source providese a detailed discussion of General Robert Ransom's difficult command role in the defense of Richmond during this period.

58. Douglas Southall Freeman, *Lee's Lieutenants: A Study in Command* (New York: Charles Scribner's Sons, 1944), 3:471.

59. Catton, *Never Call Retreat*, 350.

60. *Ibid.*

61. *Ibid.*, 344.

62. Scott, comp., *The War of the Rebellion*, ser. 1, vol. 36 in 3 parts, pt. 3:819.

63. Clark, ed., *Histories of the Several Regiments and Battalions*, 3:351.

64. *Ibid.*

65. *Ibid.*, 351–52.

66. *Ibid.*

67. *Ibid.*

68. Burgwyn, "An Address on the Military and Civil Services of General Matt W. Ransom."

69. Clark, ed., *Histories of the Several Regiments and Battalions*, 2:620. This source states that "Dr. O'Hagan was one of the most skillful Surgeons in the army."

Chapter IX

1. Thomas Roberts, a letter to his niece, Mrs. Matt Ransom, 16 May 1864. A copy of this letter is included in the private papers of Mrs. Martha Ransom Johnston, Littleton, North Carolina. Roberts stated that he had noticed in the Petersburg papers that General Ransom had been wounded.

2. *Ibid.* Mr. Roberts mentioned in his letter, "Yankees have destroyed the bridges over Nottaway River, Stoney Creek and Jarrat's Depot." Also, he said, he had learned the tracks had been torn up around Chester and Half-Way House. Also see Beth Gilbert Crabtree and James W. Patton, eds., *The Journal of a Secesh Lady: The Diary of Catherine Ann Devereux Edmondstone 1860–66* (Raleigh: North Carolina Division of Archives and History, Department of Cultural Relations, 1979), 561. This diary generally confirms the conditions described in Mr. Roberts' letter.

3. Bruce Catton, *Never Call Retreat* (Garden City, N.Y.: Doubleday, 1965), 351.

4. *Ibid.*, 360.

5. Samuel A. Ashe, *History of North Carolina* (Raleigh: Edwards and Broughton, 1925), 2:887.

6. *Ibid.*, 890. Ashe quotes the General Assembly's resolution.

7. Hugh Talmage Lefler and Albert Ray Newsome, *North Carolina: The History of a Southern State* (Chapel Hill: University of North Carolina Press, 1954), 432. Also see John G. Barrett, *The Civil War in North Carolina* (Chapel Hill: University of North Carolina Press, 1963), 63, 130, for more on Wilmington's importance to the Confederacy during the final stages of the war.

8. Ashe, *History of North Carolina*, 2:944–45.

9. *Ibid.*, 972.

10. *Ibid.*, 973–74.

11. Catton, *Never Call Retreat*, 379.

12. Catherine Drinker Bowen, *Yankee from Olympus* (Little, Brown, 1944), 194.

13. Robert Leckie, *None Died in Vain* (New York: HarperCollins, 1990), 610. Leckie quotes Grant in describing his intentions.

14. *Ibid.*, 613.

15. Catton, *Never Call Retreat*, 391.

16. Archie K. Davis, *Boy Colonel of the Confederacy: The Life and Times of Henry King Burgwyn* (Chapel Hill: University of North Carolina Press, 1985), 340.

17. Robert N. Scott, comp. *The War of the Rebellion: A Compilation of the Official Records of the Union and Confederate Armies, Prepared Under the Direction of the Secretary of War* (Washington: Government Printing Office, 1891), ser. 1, vol. 36 in 3 parts, pt. 3:898.

18. Douglas Southall Freeman, *Lee's Lieutenants: A Study in Command* (New York: Charles Scribner's Sons, 1944), 3:575.

19. The letter of General Pickett to Matt Ransom dated July 1, 1864, is included among the papers of Mrs. Martha Ransom Johnston, Littleton, North Carolina.

20. Gene Smith, *Lee and Grant: A Dual Biography* (New York, St. Louis, San Francisco: McGraw-Hill, 1984), 206.

21. Leckie, *None Died in Vain*, 591–92.

22. J.G. de Roulhac Hamilton and Rebecca Cameron, eds. *Papers of Randolph Abott Shotwell* (Raleigh: North Carolina Historical Commission, 1931), 3:84.

23. William H.S. Burgwyn, "An Address on the Military and Civil Services of General Matt W. Ransom" (speech delivered in the Senate Chamber at Raleigh before the Ladies' Memorial Association and Citizens, 10 May 19060.

24. *Ibid.*

25. *Ibid.*

26. Senator Matt W. Ransom, "The South Faithful to Her Duties' (formal speech delivered on the floor of the United States Senate, 1875), 7. A copy of this speech is contained in the University of North Carolina Library.

27. *Raleigh News and Observer*, 11 August 1883, report of a speech delivered by Senator Ransom at Warrenton, North Carolina.

28. Catton, *Never Call Retreat*, 367.

29. Clark, ed., *Histories of the Several Regiments and Battalions*, 2:621.

30. Catton, *Never Call Retreat*, 367.

31. Clark, ed., *Histories of the Several Regiments and Battalions*, 2:621–22.

32. *Ibid.*, 622.

33. *Ibid.*

34. *Ibid.*, 623.

35. *Ibid.*, 624.

36. Lawson Harrill, *Reminiscences 1861–65* (Statesville, N.C.: Brady the Printer, 1901), 30.

37. Kemp Plummer Battle with William James Battle, ed., *Memories of an Old Tar Heel* (Chapel Hill: University of North Carolina Press, 1945), 189.

38. Clark, ed., *Histories of the Several Regiments and Battalions*, 2:624.

39. Bruce Catton, *A Stillness at Appomattox* (Garden City, N.Y.: Doubleday, 1954), 294–95.

40. Peter J. Parish, *The American Civil War* (New York: Holmes and Meier, 1975), 469. Parish mentions Sherman's respect for General Johnston's qualifications as a military commander. Also see Leckie, *None Died in Vain*, 607, for remarks about Sherman being delighted to do combat with General Hood.

41. Parish, *The American Civil War*, 471.
42. Smith, *Lee and Grant*, 230.
43. Parish, *The American Civil War*, 474.
44. *Ibid.*
45. *Ibid.*, 476.
46. Clark, ed., *Histories of the Several Regiments and Battalions*, 2:387.
47. Parish, *The American Civil War*, 475.
48. Clark, ed., *Histories of the Several Regiments and Battalions*, 2:624.
49. *Ibid.*

Chapter X

1. William H.S. Burgwyn, "An Address on the Military and Civil Services of General Matt W. Ransom" (speech delivered in the Senate Chamber at Raleigh before the Ladies' Memorial Association and Citizens, 10 May 1906).
2. Papers of Matt W. Ransom, Southern Historical Collection, University of North Carolina at Chapel Hill. Letter from General Ransom to Mrs. Ransom, 15 October 1864.
3. *Ibid.*
4. John G. Barrett, *The Civil War in North Carolina* (Chapel Hill: University of North Carolina Press, 1963), 243.
5. Hugh Talmage Lefler, *North Carolina History Told by Contemporaries* (Chapel Hill: University of North Carolina Press, 1965), 309.
6. *Ibid.*
7. Peter J. Parish, *The American Civil War* (New York: Holmes and Meier, 1975), 479–80.
8. *Ibid.*, 517.
9. *Ibid.*
10. Robert Leckie, *None Died in Vain* (New York: HarperCollins, 1990), 626. Leckie refers to South Carolina as the state "where it all began."
11. *Ibid.*, 625.
12. John G. Barrett, *The Civil War in North Carolina* (Chapel Hill: University of North Carolina Press, 1963), 295. Barrett quotes Sherman.
13. Bruce Catton, *Never Call Retreat* (Garden City, N.Y.: Doubleday, 1965), 369–70. Catton discusses Sherman's methods of conducting war. Also on the same subject see Barrett, *The Civil War in North Carolina*, 292.
14. *Ibid.*
15. Barrett, *The Civil War in North Carolina*, 294.
16. *Ibid.*, 297.
17. Parish, *The American Civil War*, 567.
18. Barrett, *The Civil War in North Carolina*, 291.
19. Leckie, *None Died in Vain*, 627. Leckie quotes Johnston's letter to Davis.
20. *Ibid.*
21. Samuel A'Court Ashe, *History of North Carolina* (Raleigh: Edwards and Broughton, 1925), 2:957–58.
22. *Ibid.*, 967–68.
23. Wayne Andrews, ed., *Concise Dictionary of American History* (New York: Charles Scribner's Sons, 1962), 419. This source quotes Jefferson Davis's and Abraham Lincoln's statements relative to the peace conference. Also see Catton, *Never Call Retreat*, 420.
24. Burgwyn, "An Address on the Military and Civil Services of General Matt W. Ransom."

25. Douglas Southall Freeman, *Lee's Lieutenants: A Study in Command* (New York: Charles Scribner's Sons, 1944), 3:652.

26. Walter Clark, ed., *Histories of the Several Regiments and Battalions from North Carolina in the Great War 1861–65* (Goldsboro: Nash Brothers, 1901), 2:289.

27. *Ibid.*, 3:299.

28. Freeman, *Lee's Lieutenants*, 3:650.

29. Clark, ed., *Histories of the Several Regiments and Battalions*, from 2:299.

30. Lawson Harrill, *Reminiscences 1861–65* (Statesville, N.C.: Brady the Printer, 1901), 30.

31. Clark, ed., *Histories of the Several Regiments and Battalions*, 3:144.

32. *Ibid.*, 3:144. This source asserts that the line could have been easily taken."

33. Freeman, *Lee's Lieutenants*, 3:649.

34. *Ibid.*

35. Clark, ed., *Histories of the Several Regiments and Battalions*, 2:290.

36. *Ibid.*

37. Freeman, *Lee's Lieutenants*, 3:650. Freeman writes that "officers ordered, threatened, and begged their men to fall back to their old lines in vain."

38. *Ibid.*, 652. Freeman quotes Stripbling.

39. *Ibid.*, 651.

40. *Ibid.*

41. Burgwyn, "An Address on the Military and Civil Services of Matt W. Ransom."

42. Catton, *Never Call Retreat*, 438.

43. Clark, ed., *Histories of the Several Regiments and Battalions*, 3:394.

44. *Ibid.*, 4:576.

Chapter XI

1. Edward Porter Alexander, *Fighting for the Confederacy: The Personal Recollections of General Edward Porter Alexander*, ed. by Gary W. Gallagher (Chapel Hill and London: University of North Carolina Press, 1989), 512–13.

2. Douglas Southall Freeman, *Lee's Lieutenants: A Study in Command* (New York: Charles Scribner's Sons, 1944), 3:655.

3. *Ibid.*, 656.

4. Ishbel Ross, *First Lady of the South* (New York: Harper and Brothers, 1958), 212.

5. *Ibid.*, 214.

6. Walter Clark, ed., *Histories of the Several Regiments and Battalions from North Carolina in the Great War 1861–65* (Raleigh: E.M. Uzzell, 1901), 3:396.

7. Freeman, *Lee's Lieutenants*, 3:658.

8. *Ibid.*

9. *Ibid.*, 659–60.

10. *Ibid.*

11. *Ibid.*, 665.

12. *Ibid.*, 661. Freeman quotes Lee's communications.

13. Clark, ed., *Histories of the Several Regiments and Battalions*, 3:397.

14. Freeman, *Lee's Lieutenants*, 3:664.

15. *Ibid.*, 662.

16. William H.S. Burgwyn, "An Address on the Military and Civil Services of General Matt W. Ransom" (speech delivered in the Senate Chamber at Raleigh before Ladies' Memorial Association and Citizens, 10 May 1906).

17. Freeman, *Lee's Lieutenants*, 3:666.

18. Burgwyn, "An Address on the Military and Civil Services of General Matt W. Ransom."

19. Freeman, *Lee's Lieutenants*, 3:670.

20. Burgwyn, "An Address on the Military and Civil Services of General Matt W. Ransom."

21. Clark, ed., *Histories of the Several Regiments and Battalions*, 3:398.

22. *Ibid.*, 3:146.

23. Freeman, *Lee's Lieutenants*, 3:668.

24. *Ibid.*

25. Bruce Catton, *Never Call Retreat* (Garden City, N.Y.: Doubleday, 1965), 443.

26. Ed Bearss and Chris Calkins, *Battle of Five Forks* (Lynchburg, Va.: H.E. Howard, 1985), 102.

27. *Ibid.*, 95.

28. Clark, ed., *Histories of the Several Regiments and Battalions*,

29. Burgwyn, "An Address on the Military and Civil Services of General Matt W. Ransom."

30. *Ibid.*

31. *Ibid.*

32. Clark, ed., *Histories of the Several Regiments and Battalions*, 2:626.

33. *Ibid.*

34. Gene Smith, *Lee and Grant: A Dual Biography* (New York, St. Louis, San Francisco: McGraw-Hill, 1984), 247.

35. Burgwyn, "An Address on the Military and Civil Services of General Matt W. Ransom."

36. *Ibid.* Burgwyn gives figures for Confederate casualties. The figure for Ransom's brigade is from Clark, ed., *Histories of the Several Regiments and Battalions*, 3:398.

37. Alexander, *Fighting for the Confederacy*, 514.

38. Freeman, *Lee's Lieutenants*, 3:679.

39. *Ibid.*, 677.

40. Shelby Foote, *The Civil War: A Narrative* (New York: Random House, 1986), 884.

41. Hudson Strode, *Jefferson Davis: Tragic Hero* (New York: Harcourt, Brace and World, 1964), 169.

42. Henry Steele Commager, ed., *A Mentor Book New American Library* (New York: The Bobbs-Merrill Company, 1973), 522.

43. *Ibid.*, 524.

44. Catton, *Never Call Retreat*, 449.

45. Freeman, *Lee's Lieutenants*, 3:721.

46. Catton, *Never Call Retreat*, 450.

47. Foote, *The Civil War*, 915.

48. Catton, *Never Call Retreat*, 451.

49. *Ibid.*, 451–52.

50. Senator Matt W. Ransom, "The South Faithful to Her Duties" (formal speech delivered in the United States Senate, 1875), 10. A copy of this speech is contained in the University of North Carolina Library.

51. William C. Davis, *The Campaign to Appomattox* (Jamestown, Va.: Eastern Acorn Press, Eastern National park and Monument Association, 1987), 39.

52. Shelby Foote, *The Civil War*, 955–56. The source reproduces this farewell address.

53. Davis, *The Campaign to Appomattox*, 42.

54. *Ibid.*, 57.

55. *Ibid.*

56. Philip Van Doren Stern, *As End to Valor* (Boston: Houghton Mifflin, 1958), 285–86.

57. *Ibid.*

58. Davis, *The Campaign to Appomattox*, 48.

59. *Ibid.*

60. Clark, ed., *Histories of the Several Regiments and Battalions*, 4:579.

61. *Ibid.*

Chapter XII

1. Papers of Matt W. Ransom, Southern Historical Collection, University of North Carolina at Chapel Hill. Ransom's parole pass is about 7" by 3" in size.

2. William H.S. Burgwyn, "An Address on the Military and Civil Services of General Matt W. Ransom" (speech delivered in the Senate Chamber at Raleigh before the Ladies' Memorial Association and Citizens, 10 May 1906).

3. *Ibid.*

4. *Ibid.*

5. Walter Clark, ed., *Histories of the Several Regiments and Battalions from North Carolina in the Great War 186–65* (Goldsboro: Nash Brothers, 1901), 4:578–79.

6. Robert Lee Flowers, "Matthew Whitaker Ransom: A Senator of the Old Regime," *The South Atlantic Quarterly*, January–October 1905, 4:162. Also see C.J. Hendley, "Senator Ransom," *University Magazine*, o.s., no. 3, January 1905, 25:248.

7. Samuel A'Court Ashe, *History of North Carolina* (Raleigh: Edwards and Broughton, 1925), 2:971. Ashe writes, "The soldiers burned dwellings to please their fancy and created havoc and desolation in sheer wantonness. Nothing of value was left."

8. Glen Tucker, *Zeb Vance* (New York: Bobbs-Merrill, 1965), 393.

9. William S. Powell, *North Carolina Through Four Centuries* (Chapel Hill and London: University of North Carolina Press, 1989), 377.

10. John G. Barrett, *The Civil War in North Carolina* (Chapel Hill: University of North Carolina Press, 1963), 371.

11. Tucker, *Zeb Vance*, 391.

12. William E. Woodward, *Years of Madness* (New York: G.P. Putnam's Sons, 1951), 258.

13. Hugh Talmage Lefler and Albert Ray Newsome, *North Carolina: The History of a Southern State* (Chapel Hill: University of North Carolina Press, 1963), 453.

14. Woodward, *Years of Madness*, 259.

15. Claude G. Bowers, *The Tragic Era* (Boston: Houghton Mifflin, 1957), 4.

16. *Ibid.*, 30–32.

17. *Ibid.*, 32.

18. *Ibid.*

19. Minnie Ransom Norris, in a letter to the author dated 9 November 1968, stated that Robert Ransom, Sr., died in July of 1865 "at the home of Matt Ransom in Northampton County."

20. Lefler and Newsome, *North Carolina*, 448–49.

21. *Ibid.*, 430.

22. Beth Gilbert Crabtree and James E. Patton, eds., *Journal of a Secesh Lady: The Diary of Catherine Ann Devereux Edmondson* (Raleigh: Division of Archives and History, 1979), 695–96.

23. Hendley, "Senator Ransom," 248.

24. Matt W. Ransom, speech made on the floor of the United States Senate (a copy

of which is included in the Southern Historical Collection, University of North Carolina at Chapel Hill), 19–20.

25. Ransom quoted in the *Raleigh News and Observer*, August 11, 1883.

26. For the history of Pleasant Grove Methodist Church the writer is indebted to a splendid monograph on the subject by Mrs. C.G. Matthews of Seaboard, North Carolina. By means of this source and by verbal exchange with her, an attempt was made in the narrative to reconstruct the membership of this period, the mode of worship and the substance of worship.

27. Flowers, "Matthew Whitaker Ransom," 162.

28. General Services Administration, Old Military Records Divison, Washington, D.C. General Ransom's application for a Presidential pardon. August 15, 1865.

29. Papers of Matt W. Ransom, Southern Historical Collection, University of North Carolina at Chapel Hill. Copy of General Ransom's presidential pardon.

30. Ashe, *History of North Carolina*, 2:1045.

31. Papers of Matt W. Ransom. Letter dated February 5, 1867, from Ransom to a business firm in Petersburg, Virginia, stating crops and value for the year.

32. Private papers of Mrs. Martha Ransom Johnston, Littleton, North Carolina.

Bibliography

Alexander, Edward Porter. *Fighting for the Confederacy: The Personal Recollections of General Edward Porter Alexander.* Ed. by Gary W. Gallagher. Chapel Hill: University of North Carolina Press, 1989.

Andrews, Wayne, ed. *Concise Dictionary of American History.* New York: Charles Scribner's Sons, 1962.

Ashe, Samuel A. *Biographical History of North Carolina from Colonial Times to the Present.* Greensboro, N.C.: Charles L. Van Noppen, 1905.

_____. *History of North Carolina.* Raleigh: Edwards and Broughton, 1925.

Ballard, Michael. "A Good Time to Pray." *Civil War Times Illustrated,* April 1986: 16–25, 47.

Barrett, John G. *The Civil War in North Carolina.* Chapel Hill: University of North Carolina Press, 1963.

_____, and Buck Yearns, eds. *North Carolina Civil War Documentary.* Chapel Hill: University of North Carolina Press, 1980.

Battle, Kemp P. *History of the University of North Carolina.* Raleigh: Edwards and Broughton, 1907.

_____. "Ransom Student at University." North Carolina Review, *The Raleigh News and Observer,* 5 February 1911.

_____. "Recollections of the University of North Carolina of 1844." Unpublished manuscript, once in the possession of the University of North Carolina Library, now missing.

_____, with William James Battle, ed. *Memories of an Old Tar Heel.* Chapel Hill: University of North Carolina Press, 1945.

Bearss, Ed, and Chris Calkins. *Battle of Five Forks.* Lynchburg, Va.: H.E. Howard, 1985.

Beauregard, G.T. *Butler's Attack on Drewry's Bluff.* Battles and Leaders of the Civil War. New York: Century, 1884.

Bemis, Samuel Flagg. *A Diplomatic History of the United States.* New York: Henry Holt, 1942.

"A Birdseye View of Northampton County." Brochure.

Bowen, Catherine Drinker. *Yankee from Olympus.* Boston: Little, Brown, 1945.

Bowers, Claude G. *The Tragic Era.* Boston: Houghton Mifflin, 1957.

Boyd, William K. "North Carolina on the Eve of Secession." Washington: Reprinted from the Annual Report of the American Historical Association for 1910.

Bragg, Thomas. *Diary.* Copied from original given by Mr. Herbert B. Gilliam for permanent preservation in the Southern Historical Collection, University of North Carolina at Chapel Hill, 1957.

Bridges, Hal. *Lee's Maverick General: Daniel Harvey Hill.* New York: McGraw-Hill, 1961.

Burgwyn, William H.S. "An Address on the Military and Civil Services of Matt W.

Ransom." Speech delivered before the Ladies' Memorial Association and Citizens, Senate Chamber, Raleigh, N.C., 10 March 1906.

Catton, Bruce. *The Coming Fury.* Vol. 1 in *Centennial History of the Civil War.* Garden City, N.Y.: Doubleday, 1961.

_____. *Never Call Retreat.* Vol. 3 in *Centennial History of the Civil War.* Garden City, N.Y.: Doubleday, 1965.

_____. *Terrible Swift Sword.* Vol. 2 in *Centennial History of the Civil War.* Garden City, N.Y.: Doubleday, 1963.

_____. *This Hallowed Ground: The Story of the Union Side of the Civil War.* Garden City, N.Y.: Doubleday, 1956.

Catton, William, and Bruce Catton. *Two Roads to Sumter.* New York: McGraw-Hill, 1963.

Clark, Walter, ed. *Histories of the Several Regiments and Battalions from North Carolina in the Great Civil War, 1861–1865.* Goldsboro, N.C.: Nash Brothers, 1901.

Commager, Henry Steele, ed. *The Blue and the Gray: The Story of the Civil War as Told by Participants.* Indianapolis and New York: Bobbs-Merrill, 1950.

Connor, R.D.W. *North Carolina Rebuilding an Ancient Commonwealth 1584–1925.* Chicago and New York: American Historical Society, 1929.

Coutler, E. Merton. *The Confederate States of America.* Baton Rouge: Louisiana State University Press, the Littleton Fund for Southern History of the University of Texas, 1950.

Crabtree, Beth Gilbert, and James W. Patton, eds. *The Journal of a Secesh Lady: The Diary of Catherine Ann Devereux Edmondston 1860–66.* Raleigh: North Carolina Division of Archives and History, Department of Cultural Relations, 1979.

Daniels, Jonathan. *Prince of Carpetbaggers.* Philadelphia and New York: J.B. Lippincott, 1958.

Daniels, Josephus. *Editor in Politics.* Chapel Hill: University of North Carolina Press, 1941.

_____. *Tar Heel Editor.* Chapel Hill: University of North Carolina Press, 1939.

Davis, Archie K. *Boy Colonel of the Confederacy: The Life and Times of Henry King Burgwyn, Jr.* Chapel Hill: University of North Carolina Press, 1985.

Davis, Burke. *Gray Fox: Robert E. Lee and the Civil War.* New York and Toronto: Rinehart, 1956.

Davis, Jefferson. *The Rise and Fall of the Confederate Government.* New York and London: Thomas Yoseloff, 1958.

Davis, William C. *The Campaign to Appomattox.* Jamestown, Va.: Eastern Acorn Press, Eastern National Park and Monument Association, 1987.

Dowdey, Clifford. *The Land They Fought For.* Garden City, N.Y.: Doubleday, 1955.

_____. *The Seven Days.* New York: Fairfax.

Eastern National Park and Monument Association. *Richmond: The Peninsula Campaign.* Acorn, 1985.

Edmunds, Pocahontas Wright. *Tar Heels Track the Century.* Raleigh: Edwards and Broughton, 1966.

Faculty Journal 9002, University Archives, University of North Carolina at Chapel Hill, 1:4.

Flowers, Robert Lee. "Matthew Whitaker Ransom: A Senator of the Old Regime." *The South Atlantic Quarterly* 4 (January–October 1905), 162.

Foote, Shelby. *The Civil War: A Narrative.* New York: Random House, 1986.

Freeman, Douglas Southall. *Lee's Lieutenants: A Study in Command.* New York: Charles Scribner's Sons, 1943.

Green, Warren J. *Recollections and Reflections.* Raleigh: Edwards and Broughton, 1906.

Hamilton, J.G. de Roulhac. *History of North Carolina.* Chicago and New York: Lewis, 1919.
_____, ed. *Papers of Thomas Ruffin.* Raleigh: Edwards and Broughton, 1920.
_____, and Rebecca Cameron, eds. *Papers of Randolph Abott Shotwell.* Raleigh: North Carolina Historical Commission, 1931.
Harrill, Lawson. *Reminiscences 1861–65.* Statesville, N.C.: Brady the Printer, 1901.
Hendley, C.J. "Senator Ransom." *University Magazine* 25 (January 1905), 248.
Hyman, Harold M., ed. *New Frontiers of the American Reconstruction.* Urbana: University of Illinois Press, 1966.
Johnston, Frontis W., ed. *Papers of Zebulon Baird Vance.* Raleigh: North Carolina Department of Archives and History, 1963.
Johnston, Mrs. Martha Ransom. Papers. Littleton, N.C.
Kraus, Michael. *The United States to 1865.* Ann Arbor: University of Michigan Press, 1959.
Leckie, Robert. *None Died in Vain.* New York: HarperCollins, 1990.
Lefler, Hugh Talmage, and Albert Ray Newsome. *North Carolina: The History of a Southern State.* Chapel Hill: University of North Carolina Press, 1954.
Long, W.J. Papers. Southern Historical Collection, University of North Carolina at Chapel Hill.
Madry, Robert W. "University Has Proud Heritage of 137 Years of Priceless Tradition." *The Raleigh News and Observer,* 14 February 1932.
Mason, T.W. Papers. Southern Historical Collection, University of North Carolina at Chapel Hill.
Mitchell, Joseph B. *Decisive Battles of the Civil War.* New York: Fawcett Premier, 1955.
Mitchell, Stewart. *Horatio of New York.* Cambridge, Mass.: Harvard University Press, 1938.
Montgomery, Lizzie Wilson. *Sketches of Old Warrenton.* Raleigh: Edwards and Broughton, 1925.
National Park Historical Handbook. Series 13. Washington: 1951.
Norris, Minnie Ransom. Letters to author, 18 September 1968 and 9 November 1968.
North Carolina Journal of Law 1, no. 11 (November 1904), 531.
North Carolina Standard, 17 November 1860.
North Carolina University Magazine 10, no. 8 (April 1861), 504.
"Northampton Where Past and Present Merge." *The State,* 29 October 1958, 16–20.
Parish, Peter J. *The American Civil War.* New York: Holmes and Meier, 1975.
Powell, William S. *North Carolina Through Four Centuries.* Chapel Hill and London: University of North Carolina Press, 1989.
Ramsdell, Charles W. "The Natural Limits of Slavery Extension." *Mississippi Valley Historical Review* 16, no. 2 (September 1929): 161–62.
Ransom, Matthew W. Application for presidential pardon, August 1865. General Services Administration, Old Military Records Division, Washington, D.C.
_____. Papers. Southern Historical Collection, University of North Carolina at Chapel Hill.
Ransom, Robert, Jr., comp. Unpublished genealogy records. A copy is in the papers of Mrs. Martha Ransom Johnston, Littleton, N.C.
_____. Unpublished and incomplete autobiography. Southern Historical Collection, University of North Carolina at Chapel Hill.
Revelle, Nancy Moss. "Matthew Whitaker Ransom's Political Career." Master's thesis, University of North Carolina at Chapel Hill.
Robinson, Blackwell P., ed. *The North Carolina Guide.* Chapel Hill: University of North Carolina Press, 1955.
Ross, Ishbel. *First Lady of the South.* New York: Harper and Brothers, 1958.

Scott, Robert N., comp. *The War of the Rebellion: A Compilation of the Official Records of the Union and Confederate Armies, Prepared Under the Direction of the Secretary of War.* Washington: Government Printing Office, 1884.

Shirley, Franklin Ray. *Zebulon Vance: Tarheel Spokesman.* Charlotte and Santa Barbara: McNally and Lofton, 1962.

Sitterson, Joseph C. *The Secession Movement in North Carolina.* Chapel Hill: University of North Carolina Press, 1939.

_____. "The Secession Movement in North Carolina." Vol. 23, no. 2 of the James Sprunt Studies in History and Political Science. Chapel Hill: Department of History and Political Science of the University of North Carolina, 1934.

Smith, Gene. *Lee and Grant: A Dual Biography.* New York, St. Louis, San Francisco: McGraw-Hill, 1984.

Stern, Philip Van Doren. *An End to Valor.* Boston: Houghton Mifflin, 1958.

Strode, Hudson. *Jefferson Davis: Tragic Hero.* New York: Harcourt, Brace and World, 1964.

Taylor, Rosser Howard. "Slaveholding in North Carolina: An Economic View." Vol. 18 of the James Sprunt Studies in History. Chapel Hill: Department of History of the University of North Carolina, 1926.

Tucker, Glen. *Zeb Vance.* New York: Bobbs-Merrill, 1965.

Wellman, Manley Wade. *The County of Warren North Carolina 1586–1917.* Chapel Hill: University of North Carolina Press, 1959.

Wheeler, Richard. *Sword Over Richmond.* New York: Harper and Row, 1986.

Wiley, Bell Irvin. *The Life of Johnny Reb.* Indianapolis and New York: Bobbs-Merrill, 1943.

Winston, Judge R.W. "Matt W. Ransom." North Carolina Review, *The Raleigh News and Observer,* 5 February 1911, 2.

Woodward, William E. *Years of Madness.* New York: G.P. Putnam's Sons, 1951.

Index